T0376198

Wildflowers
of NOVA SCOTIA

TODD BOLAND

Boulder Publications also publishes these field guides:

Birds of Newfoundland
Edible Plants of Atlantic Canada
Edible Plants of Newfoundland and Labrador
Geology of Newfoundland
Trees and Shrubs of the Maritimes
Trees and Shrubs of Newfoundland and Labrador
Whales and Dolphins of Atlantic Canada and Northeast United States
Wildflowers of Newfoundland and Labrador

And these gardening guides:

Atlantic Gardening
Newfoundland Gardening

Wildflowers
of NOVA SCOTIA

TODD BOLAND

BOULDER
PUBLICATIONS

Library and Archives Canada Cataloguing in Publication
Boland, Todd, author
Wildflowers of Nova Scotia : field guide / Todd Boland.

Includes bibliographical references and index.
ISBN 978-1-927099-48-3 (bound)

1. Wild flowers--Nova Scotia--Identification. I. Title.

QK203.N6B65 2015   582.1309716   C2014-901635-2

Published by Boulder Publications
Portugal Cove-St. Philip's, Newfoundland and Labrador
www.boulderpublications.ca

© 2014 Todd Boland

Editor: Stephanie Porter
Copy editor: Iona Bulgin
Design and layout: John Andrews

Printed in China

 We acknowledge the financial support of the Government of Newfoundland and Labrador through the Department of Tourism, Culture and Recreation.

We acknowledge the financial support for our publishing program by the Government of Canada and the Department of Canadian Heritage through the Canada Book Fund.

CONTENTS

PREFACE

Wildflowers of Nova Scotia will introduce you to more than 700 species of herbaceous wildflowers (plants that die back to the ground in winter) that grow within the province.

I have profiled species that are native to Nova Scotia, as well as many introduced species that have become naturalized (and sometimes invasive) by "jumping the fence" from cultivated areas into wild areas or by unintentional introduction, primarily from Europe.

The only recent printed guide to the flora of Nova Scotia is my previous book *Trees and Shrubs of the Maritimes*, published in 2012. That pictorial guide covers all the woody plants of Nova Scotia but does not describe any of the herbaceous wildflowers. Wildflower resources for the province do exist: Marian Zinck's revised edition of *Flora of Nova Scotia* by A.E. Roland and E.C. Smith covers all the flora of Nova Scotia, but it is a technical book with line drawings—not particularly user-friendly for the budding wildflower enthusiast. The Nova Scotia Wild Flora Society has an online reference guide to several native plants but, unless you have Internet access in the field, that resource has limited usefulness. A downloadable guide to the *Atlantic Coastal Plain Flora of Nova Scotia* (prepared by Megan Crowley and Lindsey Beals) is available, but it covers a specific and localized group of plant species, both woody and herbaceous. It seemed that a dedicated pictorial guide to the wildflowers of Nova Scotia was warranted.

Wildflowers of Nova Scotia is designed to help readers who have limited knowledge of botany identify the common wildflowers of the province, along with some of the rare native species. By grouping plants first by flower colour and then by the overall flower shape, and by using other physical plant features such as flower arrangement and leaf shape and arrangement, this guide offers a step-by-step method of plant identification. It is my hope that this guide will help you recognize many of the province's wildflowers.

Concerns about the environment are at the forefront of everyone's mind these days. One way to better understand nature's interconnected web is by learning to recognize and appreciate its plants in their natural habitats. By helping you identify the wildflowers of Nova Scotia, I hope that this guide will give you a solid foundation for a thoughtful and observant connection to the natural world around you.

ACKNOWLEDGEMENTS

My thanks to all the photographers who graciously allowed me to use their photographs to fill gaps in my image archive. They are listed by name in the photo credits, page 409.

I note with gratitude the contribution of graphic designer John Andrews for both the book's design and his attention to detail in the layout.

Special thanks go to Stephanie Porter and Iona Bulgin for their care with my prose and grammar, which helped this non-English major write with greater definition and focus.

Finally, I would like to thank Gavin Will and Boulder Publications for accepting my book proposal and for having faith that this book would be a successful addition to Boulder's Field Guide series.

INTRODUCTION

Nova Scotia is home to about 1,500 species of native and naturalized plants. This guide focuses on the identification of herbaceous wildflowers—plants that die back to the ground in winter. A few sub-shrubs are included; these superficially appear herbaceous but, in fact, contain wood cells and are truly woody plants. Because they are often called "wildflowers," I have included them in this book. For help in identifying woody trees and shrubs (including sub-shrubs), I refer you to my previous publication, *Trees and Shrubs of the Maritimes*, which is also part of Boulder Publications' Field Guide series.

This present guide is not all-inclusive. Ferns and their relatives are not covered, nor are any grasses or grass relatives, as they are very challenging to identify. Some very rare native plants and locally introduced exotics with limited distributions are not included due to space constraints.

Many of the main flower entries in this guide also include a description of close relatives or lookalike species to help distinguish between them. As a result, over 700 species—native wildflowers and the more common weeds or exotic non-native species—are described. Photographs accompany most of the descriptions to illustrate the flowers, leaves, or other pertinent identification features of a given plant.

The next several pages of this introduction are key to using this guide successfully: these pages explain the system of icons and notations and how to use them in a process of elimination in order to identify a wildflower in the field. But before you get into the "how" of the book, it helps to understand some of the natural factors that influence where different types of wildflowers grow in Nova Scotia.

The Big Picture

Nova Scotia is a relatively small province, only about 55,300 square kilometres; this makes it the second smallest province in Canada after Prince Edward Island. Despite its size, Nova Scotia encompasses a wide variety of habitats and landscapes.

The province is almost surrounded by the Atlantic Ocean—from any point in the province, you will never be more than 67 kilometres from the sea. As a result, the province has an oceanic climate of relatively mild winters and pleasant summers.

Elevation also influences plant life. The effects of elevation are most clearly seen in parts of the Cape Breton Highlands, where the hills can reach more than 500 metres in height (the Highlands' White Hill is the highest point in Nova Scotia, at 535 metres). The exposure at the tops of the Highlands, along with its close proximity to the ocean, results in barren, almost sub-alpine, habitat. Some of the province's wildflowers are confined to such areas.

The nature of the soil is also an important factor. Most plants in Nova Scotia have adapted to acidic soil derived from sandstone or granite, the most common rock types in the province. Others plants are calciphiles, restricted to limestone-derived soil; these are often plants with restricted distributions. Limestone and gypsum outcrops are scattered primarily throughout the northern half of Nova Scotia; the most prominent are in the proximity of Hants, Colchester, and Halifax counties—Windsor to East Milford to Upper Stewiake—and around Bras D'Or Lake, Cape Breton. Several highly restricted plants are found exclusively in these limestone-rich areas.

Perhaps the most interesting, rare, and restricted group of Nova Scotia wildflowers are those referred to as the Atlantic Coastal Plain flora, a unique assemblage of plants found in the southwestern corner of the province (Annapolis and Lunenburg counties and southward). Several of these plants are found only in Nova Scotia and nowhere else in Canada.

A Distinctive Plant Group / Atlantic Coastal Plain Species

Nova Scotia is home to an assemblage of plants that is unique in Canada. These plants are known as the Atlantic Coastal Plain flora. Although Atlantic Coastal Plain plants do occur as far east as Newfoundland and west through parts of coastal New Brunswick (as well as along the Great Lakes of Ontario, Michigan, and Wisconsin), Nova Scotia has the best-developed Atlantic Coastal Plain flora of any Canadian province. The main North American Atlantic Coastal Plain flora regions are the coastal areas from southern Nova Scotia south to eastern Texas.

The Atlantic Coastal Plain was formed at the end of the last glacial period, approximately 10,000 to 14,000 years ago. In that era, the sea level was 60 to 100 metres lower than it is today, and southern Nova Scotia was connected to the eastern seaboard of North America. The range of several Atlantic Coastal Plain species extended as far north as what is now Nova Scotia—and some even to Newfoundland. When the glaciers melted and sea levels rose, the southern Nova Scotia plant populations were cut off from the rest of the eastern seaboard by the newly formed Bay of Fundy. These "outliers" are now at the northern end of each species' distribution range.

Over time, more aggressive species from the interior of Nova Scotia have pushed the Atlantic Coastal Plain species into isolated pockets. Most are found on the gravelly or sandy shores of freshwater lakes and streams and in boggy areas; a few are located in salt marshes. Look for Atlantic Coastal Plain plants in the southwestern Nova Scotia counties of Lunenburg, Annapolis, Yarmouth, Queens, and Shelburne. A small pocket is also found in the southeast Cape Breton Island counties of Richmond and Cape Breton.

Ninety species in Nova Scotia belong to the Atlantic Coastal Plain flora. Many are herbaceous and include such species as Virginia meadow-beauty (*Rhexia virginica*), Plymouth gentian (*Sabatia kennedyana*), and pink coreopsis (*Coreopsis rosea*).

HOW TO USE THIS GUIDE

Wildflowers of Nova Scotia organizes plants by their flowers, starting with flower colour, shape, and inflorescence (arrangement) and then working down to the finer details, including leaf shape and outline.

Examine the Flower / Colour

To use this guide, then, begin by noting the colour of the flower on the plant you wish to identify. For the purposes of this guide, the species have been divided into five main colour groups:

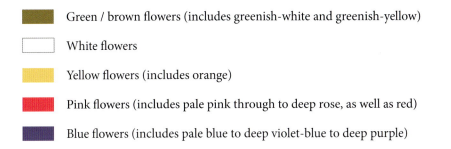

Green / brown flowers (includes greenish-white and greenish-yellow)

White flowers

Yellow flowers (includes orange)

Pink flowers (includes pale pink through to deep rose, as well as red)

Blue flowers (includes pale blue to deep violet-blue to deep purple)

Use the coloured bars at the top of the pages to find the correct section for your flower. The process of describing colour can be subjective—some flowers may be considered pink by one person, for example, and purple by another. If you have a flower that may fall between two categories, please check both colour sections.

Examine the Flower / Shape

Within each colour section, flowers are next organized according to flower shape or outline. Take a close look at the flower itself, noting the number of petals and/or the outline of the flower. Ask yourself these three questions:

1. Is the flower shape unusual (lacking typical flower parts such as sepals and petals)?

Unusual

2. Is the flower shape irregular (having a bilateral symmetry such that you can only cut it in one plane to create halves—most iris or orchids have this shape, for example)?

Irregular

3. Is the flower shape regular (having radial or round symmetry)? If yes, count the number of petals. Are there 3, 4, 5, 6, or 7 or more?

One or more of the above flower shape icons will be in the colour bar at the top of each species page.

Examine the Flower / Inflorescence

Look closely at how the flowers are arranged on the stem—the inflorescence. Is the flower solitary or does it tend to grow in a pair or a cluster? Is it enclosed in a bract (spathe) or does the flower grow from the leaf axils? In this guide, flowers are categorized into one or more of the following types:

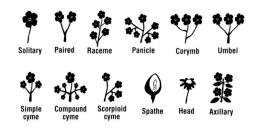

Examine the Leaf

Next, you'll need to note a few key leaf characteristics to narrow down the possibilities:

1. Are the leaves single-bladed (simple), or do multiple small leaflets combine to create a larger leaf (compound)?

2. Are the leaves in a basal rosette at the base of the plant or scattered along the stem? If along the stem, do they extend from either side of the stem in an alternating sequence ("alternate"), are they paired ("opposite"), or do three or more leaves grow from the same point on the stem ("whorled")? Are no leaves apparent?

3. What is the overall shape of the leaf? Leaves in this field guide are categorized as
    i. linear
    ii. elongate or lance-shaped

iii. elliptical

iv. round to egg-shaped

v. deltoid

vi. hand-shaped ("palmately lobed")

vii. oak leaf-shaped ("pinnately lobed")

viii. dissected ("pinnatifid")

ix. in multiple sections ("compound"—see next step)

Linear   Lance   Elliptical   Egg/round   Deltoid   Palmately lobed   Pinnately lobed   Pinnatifid

4. If the leaf is compound, does it have three leaflets (making it "trifoliate" or "ternate"), five leaflets ("palmately compound"), or many leaflets ("pinnately compound")?

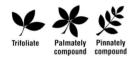

Trifoliate   Palmately compound   Pinnately compound

5. If the leaflets of a trifoliate or ternate leaf are themselves ternate, the leaf is "biternate"; if the leaflets of a biternate leaf are ternate, the leaf is "triternate"; if the leaflets of a pinnately compound leaf are themselves pinnate, the leaf is "bipinnate."

Biternate   Triternate   Bipinnate

6. Is the leaf edge smooth, toothed, or lobed?

Smooth   Toothed   Lobed

Icons on each page illustrate at a glance which of these features each plant has. The plant's status as either a native or an introduced species is also included. The Nova Scotia Wildflowers by Family list (page 374) at the back of the book will also specify whether a plant is introduced or native.

Native   Introduced
Species   Species

It is important to remember that plants do not strictly follow the rules in any of the above categories. For example, a plant may exhibit more than one flower type by producing individual and clustered blooms. Lower leaves may be compound, while upper leaves are single-bladed. In such circumstances, all the relevant icons for flower/leaf forms are included.

Details of each species are summarized in the text, and key identifying characteristics are illustrated in photographs. Your observations about flower colour and flower shape will lead you to the corresponding section of the guide, and the leaf shape and arrangement will help you to narrow down the possibilities. Finally, if you compare the plant you are looking at with the descriptions and photographs on the page, you should be able to identify, or come close to identifying, the flower.

Even with a System, Identifying Plants Can Be Tricky

About 350 species of herbaceous wildflowers which may be encountered in the wilds of Nova Scotia have a dedicated page in this guide. Most entries also describe one or two close relatives. By using the information in each entry, you should be able to identify most species in the field.

No attempt to simplify nature is foolproof—nature is far too complex to fit into a tidy series of icons and colours. It is important, for example, to keep in mind that plants can show considerable variation in their flower colours and leaf shapes. While you are in the field, look around for similar plants, and compare the flowers and leaves on the same plant and on its neighbours. The more you practice and observe, the easier plant identification will become.

A Few Words about Plant Names and Terms

All known living organisms have scientific names. The naming process is known as taxonomy, and it is a science in itself. Taxonomic names are created in Latin, which is considered by scientists to be a "universal" language. Over time, as new information is learned about an organism (especially about its genetic makeup), its scientific name may be changed.

Plants are commonly affected by such name changes. For this reason, each plant in this book is listed by its most-accepted common name; the most current botanical (Latin) name and other common synonyms are also included. Both the common and taxonomic names applied generally follow VASCAN (the Database of Canadian Vascular Plants, data.canadensys.net/vascan/search/). Family names follow the system listed on the Angiosperm Phylogeny website (www.mobot.org/mobot/research/apweb). The listing of the plants within each colour and flower outline group follows Roland and Smith's *Flora of Nova Scotia* (revised by Marian Zinck, 1998).

If you are keenly interested in following botanical name changes, you might want to look at the ongoing Flora of North America project which, when complete, will be a 30-volume online encyclopedia of the entire North American flora (floranorthamerica.org). As a new wildflower enthusiast you may be interested in joining the Nova Scotia Wild Flora Society, a group dedicated to expanding the knowledge of local Nova Scotian flora through regular meetings and field trips (www.nswildflora.ca).

Even though this guide is designed for the novice plant enthusiast—no plant science background is required!—some botanical terms are used. This is because they have precise meanings. Take this guide as your introduction to Botany and refer to the glossary and plant anatomy diagram at the back of the guide for explanations of terms that are new to you. You'll soon become familiar with them.

For those who are more botanically inclined, a list of the wildflowers included in this guide according to their taxonomic family relationships is found on page XX. You can also search for plants by either their (accepted) common name or their Latin name in these indexes.

Not All Plants Like the Same Places

Along the outer edge of each species listing in this guide are habitat tabs, which indicate the major and minor habitat types favoured by the plant described. These habitat indicators provide general guidelines only—you should refer to the habitat description in the text for specific habitat details and locations. In some cases, reference is made to specific counties within Nova Scotia, which are shown on the map on page 8.

Habitat Notes / Forests

Three major forest habitat tabs are used: coniferous forest, mixed forest, and deciduous forest.

Nova Scotia's forests fall within the Acadian forest (which, with the Great Lakes-St. Lawrence forest, forms the larger northern hardwood forest). The Acadian forest marks the transition between the North American boreal forest region to the north, dominated by evergreen conifers, and the central hardwood forest region to the south, dominated by deciduous trees. As a result, the Acadian forest has a mixture of conifers and hardwoods. Cape Breton has considerable areas of boreal forest, dominated by trees such as balsam fir (*Abies balsamea*), black spruce (*Picea mariana*), red spruce (*Picea rubens*), and white spruce (*Picea glauca*), along with deciduous white birch (*Betula papyrifera*) and red maple (*Acer rubrum*).

For the purpose of this guide, if at least 75 per cent of a forest is made up of coniferous trees, then the forest type is considered coniferous. If a forest is 75 per cent deciduous, then it is considered a deciduous forest. Any other combination is considered a mixed forest.

Habitat Notes / Barrens

Barrens are often described as areas stripped of vegetation. In reality, the barrens of Nova Scotia are quite green, but they are dominated by shrubs, particularly ericaceous shrubs (such as blueberry, sheep laurel, and huckleberry), and low, wind-stunted trees, as opposed to the taller trees typical of forests. Within the province, barrens are most often found close to the ocean on headlands that are fully exposed to North Atlantic winds; they are most prevalent along the eastern shore and northern coast of Cape Breton. The high elevation of the Cape Breton Highlands has resulted in barrens near their summits.

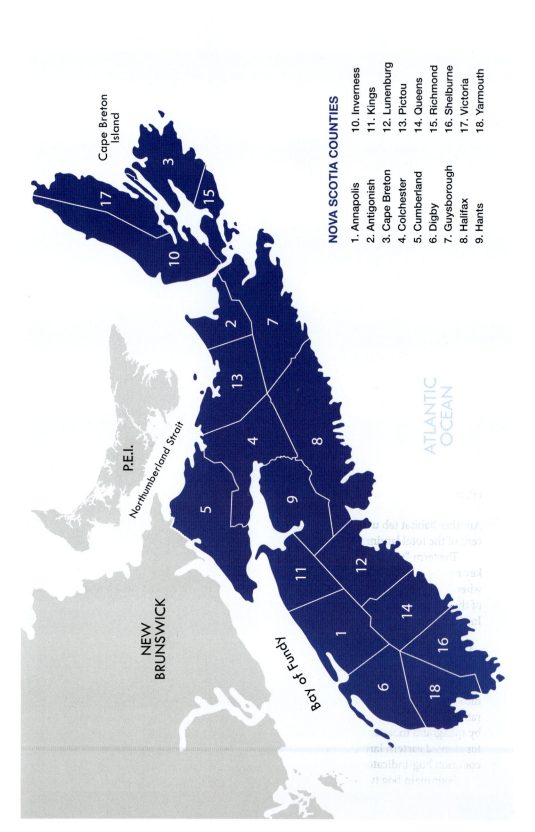

NEW BRUNSWICK

P.E.I.

Northumberland Strait

Cape Breton Island

NEW BRUNSWICK

Bay of Fundy

ATLANTIC OCEAN

NOVA SCOTIA COUNTIES

1. Annapolis
2. Antigonish
3. Cape Breton
4. Colchester
5. Cumberland
6. Digby
7. Guysborough
8. Halifax
9. Hants
10. Inverness
11. Kings
12. Lunenburg
13. Pictou
14. Queens
15. Richmond
16. Shelburne
17. Victoria
18. Yarmouth

Habitat Notes / Coastal

Nova Scotia is almost completely surrounded by the Atlantic Ocean, hence plants associated with the coast are a significant feature of the province's flora. For the purposes of this guide, coastal habitats include sand dune areas as well as gravelly and rocky beaches. Beaches are generally quite narrow, encompassing the land within a few metres of the high-tide line. Dune areas may be significantly wider. Under natural conditions—that is, undisturbed by human activity—sand dune coastlines would feature a series of dunes that mark the transition from outer sand beach to coastal forest vegetation. Today, many areas of sand dunes are severely degraded by human activity.

Not all dunes are created equal. Fore-dunes, closest to the sea, are held loosely in place by specialty grasses. Wind and tides cause them to move and shift over time; they are rarely static. Farther inland, secondary and tertiary dunes appear, the product of uninterrupted plant succession. Secondary dunes are nearly completely covered by vegetation, which is, again, mostly herbaceous with a few woody species. Tertiary dunes are farthest inland and feature more woody species, many of which are wind-stunted versions of the adjacent forest vegetation.

In this guide, salt marshes are also considered coastal habitat. These marshes are often inundated by salt water during the highest tides and, in all cases, are brackish. Salt marshes are most prevalent along the shores of the Bay of Fundy and the Northumberland Strait.

Several herbaceous plant species are typical of coastal habitats and are rarely, if ever, found elsewhere. Some examples are oysterleaf (*Mertensia maritima*), beach-pea (*Lathyrus japonicus*), and sea rocket (*Cakile edentula*).

Habitat Notes / Wetlands

Another habitat tab used in this guide is wetlands, which occupy only about 3 per cent of the total landmass of Nova Scotia.

The term "wetlands" applies to several types of habitats in which water plays a key role. One major wetland group includes the margins of streams, rivers, and lakes, where the ground may be covered by water for at least a few weeks each year. In some of these places, water is present year-round except during the driest summer months. In either case, the soil is always quite moist.

A second major wetland type is peatlands. These areas remain wet year-round, which means that, because of a lack of oxygen in the waterlogged substrate, plant detritus is slow to decompose. It forms a thick layer of organic matter known as peat.

Bogs are the most prevalent category of wetlands in Nova Scotia. Bogs are the most nutrient-poor of the wetland types. Their nutrients come from rain and snow rather than from the mineral soils of surrounding forested areas. Bogs are dominated by sphagnum moss and dwarf ericaceous shrubs. Trees are generally absent, except for stunted eastern larch and black spruce. Pitcher plant (*Sarracenia purpurea*) is a common bog-indicator plant.

Four main bog types occur in Nova Scotia: raised, sloped, flat (including basin and plateau), and blanket. Raised or dome bogs often form in large valleys and cover a relatively large area. Typically, because their central section is raised above their edges, these bogs appear dome-like. In Nova Scotia, raised bogs are restricted mostly to southwestern areas of the province.

Sloped bogs occur in regions with high rainfall, poor drainage, and sloped terrain. They are most prevalent on Cape Breton Island and in Guysborough County. Flat bogs, which form in wet depressions, are relatively small and scattered. Blanket bogs, on the other hand, cover vast areas on both level and sloped terrain, and form mostly in exceptionally wet, cool regions. Generally, they feature many small ponds and exposed bedrock. Blanket bogs are most common in the eastern coastal regions of mainland Nova Scotia and Cape Breton Island.

Fens are another type of wetland. Generally much smaller than bogs, they often occur in poorly drained areas next to larger streams and lakes or as patches inside forests. Because they receive nutrients from surrounding upland areas, they are more nutrient-rich than bogs. As a result, they can support more plant life. Fens often resemble meadows because grasses and sedges dominate. Many wetland orchids make fens their home. Tall white bog orchid (*Platanthera dilatata*) is a good fen-indicator plant.

The terms "swamps" and "marshes" are often used interchangeably. Both are wetlands that are flooded on a regular basis; they are nutrient-rich wetlands and, hence, home to the greatest diversity of wetland plants. Showy lady's-slipper (*Cypripedium reginae*) is a typical marsh plant.

Habitat Notes / Disturbed Areas

In this guide, disturbed areas include roadsides and railway beds; urban areas such as scrublands, vacant lots, and city/town trails; pastures and meadows; and old or recent burn sites. All of these types of habitat have had their natural vegetation removed and underlying soil disturbed. Native wildflowers typical of disturbed habitats include fireweed (*Chamerion angustifolium*), New York aster (*Symphyotrichum novi-belgii*), and pearly everlasting (*Anaphalis margaritacea*).

Disturbed habitat is "new" habitat, and it is also the type of area most often occupied by introduced species, which are often considered weeds. Most frequently of European origin, introduced (or "alien") species are those that have arrived during the last five centuries. Some were brought as ornamentals, but many arrived accidentally, as seeds caught in ship ballast or packing materials. Nearly 20 per cent of all the plant species found in Nova Scotia are not native to the province.

Some introduced plants have increased in population so much that they are now inhabiting natural areas and displacing native species. They are considered "invasive alien plants"—a phenomenon that is a concern worldwide. Plants such as purple loosestrife (*Lythrum salicaria*), coltsfoot (*Tussilago farafara*), and creeping buttercup (*Ranunculus repens*) are prime examples of invasive species in Nova Scotia.

SAMPLE PAGE

Flower shape

Flower arrangement (inflorescence)

Bar colour indicates flower colour**

At-a-glance information about leaf shape, outline, etc.

Family name

Common name

Scientific species name

Other common names

Height the plant may achieve in Nova Scotia

Months in which flowers usually appear

Habitat types the plant is often found in (solid colour)

Habitat types the plant is sometimes found in (outline)

Habitat tabs are not shown if plant does not appear in them

Images show flowers, leaves, plants, and other details that aid in identification

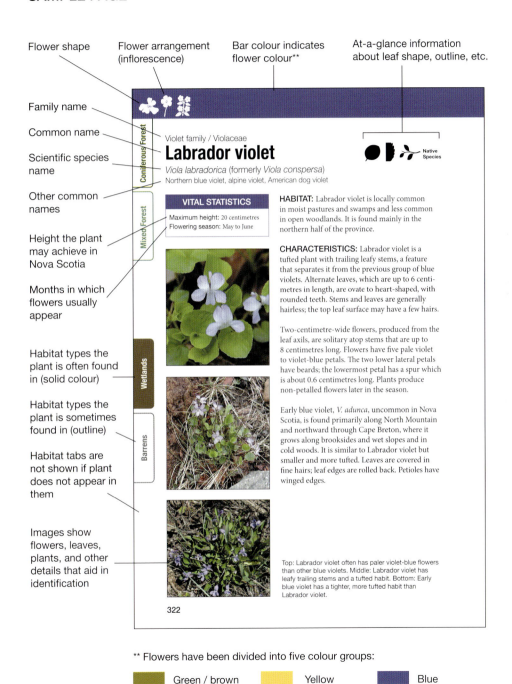

Violet family / Violaceae

Labrador violet

Viola labradorica (formerly *Viola conspersa*)
Northern blue violet, alpine violet, American dog violet

Native Species

Coniferous/Forest

Mixed Forest

Wetlands

Barrens

VITAL STATISTICS

Maximum height: 20 centimetres
Flowering season: May to June

HABITAT: Labrador violet is locally common in moist pastures and swamps and less common in open woodlands. It is found mainly in the northern half of the province.

CHARACTERISTICS: Labrador violet is a tufted plant with trailing leafy stems, a feature that separates it from the previous group of blue violets. Alternate leaves, which are up to 6 centimetres in length, are ovate to heart-shaped, with rounded teeth. Stems and leaves are generally hairless; the top leaf surface may have a few hairs.

Two-centimetre-wide flowers, produced from the leaf axils, are solitary atop stems that are up to 8 centimetres long. Flowers have five pale violet to violet-blue petals. The two lower lateral petals have beards; the lowermost petal has a spur which is about 0.6 centimetres long. Plants produce non-petalled flowers later in the season.

Early blue violet, *V. adunca*, uncommon in Nova Scotia, is found primarily along North Mountain and northward through Cape Breton, where it grows along brooksides and wet slopes and in cold woods. It is similar to Labrador violet but smaller and more tufted. Leaves are covered in fine hairs; leaf edges are rolled back. Petioles have winged edges.

Top: Labrador violet often has paler violet-blue flowers than other blue violets. Middle: Labrador violet has leafy trailing stems and a tufted habit. Bottom: Early blue violet has a tighter, more tufted habit than Labrador violet.

322

** Flowers have been divided into five colour groups:

Green / brown	
White	

Yellow	
Pink	

Blue

ICON LEGEND

Flower Shape

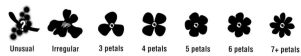

| Unusual | Irregular | 3 petals | 4 petals | 5 petals | 6 petals | 7+ petals |

Flower Arrangement / Inflorescence

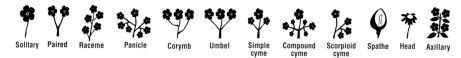

Solitary Paired Raceme Panicle Corymb Umbel Simple cyme Compound cyme Scorpioid cyme Spathe Head Axillary

Simple Leaf Shape

Linear Lance Elliptical Egg/round Deltoid Palmately lobed Pinnately lobed Pinnatifid

Compound Leaf Arrangement

Trifoliate Palmately compound Pinnately compound Biternate Triternate Bipinnate

Leaf Edge Outline

Smooth Toothed Lobed

Leaf Arrangement on Stem

No apparent leaves Opposite Alternate Whorled Basal

Additional Information

Native Species   Introduced Species

12

Plant
PROFILES

Hemp family / Cannabaceae

Hops

Humulus lupulus

Native Species   Introduced Species

VITAL STATISTICS

Maximum height: 10 metres
Flowering season: July and August

HABITAT: Hops is occasionally found in waste places and abandoned homesteads throughout Nova Scotia.

CHARACTERISTICS: Hops, a twisting vine, can reach a height of 10 metres. Opposite leaves are deeply tri-lobed or, less commonly, palmately lobed with toothed edges. Uppermost leaves are often simply heart-shaped. The undersides bear yellow aromatic granules and a hairy midrib. The petiole is nearly as long as the leaf. Stems are covered in short stiff backward-facing hairs. Despite its slightly woody stems, the plant is herbaceous.

Plants are dioecious. Male flowers are produced in small axillary panicles; individual flowers consist of five greenish-white sepals and five stamens. Female flowers are also axillary, with green catkin-like flowers that develop into green to brown globular cone-shaped fruit. This fruit is used in the brewing of beer.

Two varieties of hops occur in Atlantic Canada: native American hops, var. *lupuloides*; and introduced European hops, var. *lupulus*. The difference between the two is subtle.

Top: Details of the female flowers. Middle: Most leaves are palmately lobed. Bottom: Mature female flowers are cone-like.

Disturbed

14

Nettle family / Urticaceae

Stinging nettle

Urtica dioica

HABITAT: Stinging nettle is found in disturbed habitats, usually near settlements or farms, throughout Nova Scotia. It prefers rich, organic soil.

CHARACTERISTICS: Stinging nettle quickly forms a large clump due to prolific rhizomes. Nova Scotia has two subspecies: *dioica* from Europe, and the native *gracilis*. Often exhibiting branched stems, *dioica* is coarsely hairy on both stems and leaves. Its ovate, opposite leaves are sharply serrated with burning, stinging hairs on both surfaces. *Gracilis* typically has smooth un-branched stems and more slender elliptical leaves with stinging hairs only on the lower surface. Both forms have small stipules at the base of the leaves.

Dioica typically has dioecious flowers; *gracilis* is monoecious. Individual flowers of both are indistinguishable from each other: minute and green and produced in wiry, 5- to 15-centimetre-long clusters in the axils of the upper leaves. Close examination reveals four sepals but no petals.

Canada wood nettle, *Laportea canadensis*, is occasional in rich, moist, mixed, and deciduous forests from Kings to Inverness counties. Superficially, it looks like stinging nettle but is less than 100 centimetres tall. Its stems and ovate leaves are also covered in stinging hairs, but they are alternate, not opposite. The minute green monoecious flowers are produced in a terminal rather than an axillary cyme.

VITAL STATISTICS
Maximum height: 150 centimetres
Flowering season: June to July

Top: Stinging nettle's minute flowers are in wiry panicles. Middle: Stinging nettle's opposite leaves are coarsely toothed. Bottom: Canada wood nettle has alternate leaves.

Disturbed

15

Redroot amaranth

Introduced Species

Amaranthus retroflexus

Green pigweed, redroot pigweed, green amaranth

VITAL STATISTICS

Maximum height: 2 metres
Flowering season: August to October

HABITAT: A European species, redroot amaranth is scattered in disturbed sites throughout Nova Scotia.

CHARACTERISTICS: Redroot amaranth is a few-branched annual species reaching to 2 metres in height. The alternate, prominently veined leaves are often 10 centimetres or longer; leaves are long petioled and ovate to elliptical in outline, with smooth but wavy edges. Leaves are hairless except for hairs located along the lower veins and upper stems. The short taproot is often bright red.

Inconspicuous monoecious flowers are produced in dense terminal panicles, with smaller clusters in the upper leaf axils. Close examination of the flowers reveals green to brown papery bracts, three green sepals, and no petals.

White amaranth or tumbleweed, *A. albus*, an introduced annual scattered in Nova Scotia, reaches 100 centimetres in height and is densely branched, appearing almost bush-like. Its branches often arise at right angles to the main stem. Pale green leaves are up to 2.5 centimetres in length, and spatulate with smooth but wavy edges. Small clusters of inconspicuous monoecious flowers are produced among the upper leaf axils. In late fall, plants break at ground level and tumble in the wind, releasing seeds. The species is localized from Hants to Pictou counties.

Top: Redroot amaranth's minute flowers are in dense panicles. Middle: Redroot amaranth panicles are terminal on the stems. Bottom: White amaranth has minute axillary flowers and spatulate leaves.

Native Species

Amaranth family / Amaranthaceae

Glabrous saltbush

Atriplex glabriuscula

Smooth orach, Babington's orach

HABITAT: Glabrous saltbush is encountered along cobble seashores, coastal dunes, and salt marshes throughout Nova Scotia.

CHARACTERISTICS: Glabrous saltbush is an annual species with prostrate ridged stems and a mat-like habit. Leaf shapes are extremely variable. Lower leaves are usually opposite, triangular with two distinct basal lobes, and smooth-edged or with a few irregular teeth. Upper leaves are triangular, lance- to egg-shaped, and alternate or opposite. Leaves are fleshy; they may be green or, often, purple-tinted. Young leaves are often scurfy with silvery powder.

The minute green unisexual flowers (monoecious or dioecious) lack petals and sepals but have a pair of triangular bracteoles (tiny bracts) which enclose the developing fruit. Flowers are produced in small spikes among the upper leaf axils or terminating the stems. Small leafy bracts are scattered throughout the length of the spikes.

Common orach, A. *patula*, is similar to glabrous saltbush but is found in disturbed areas as well as along the coast. Its dense flower spikes lack the small leafy bracts indicative of glabrous saltbush.

The unisexual flowers of *Atriplex* distinguish them from those of the similar, but bisexual, *Chenopodium*.

VITAL STATISTICS
Maximum height: 100 centimetres
Flowering season: July to October

Coastal

Top: Glabrous saltbush's unusual flowers are in small axillary spikes. Middle: Glabrous saltbush has variable leaf shapes. Bottom: Common orach has dense axillary and terminal spikes.

Amaranth family / Amaranthaceae

Common lamb's-quarters

Chenopodium album
White pigweed, white goosefoot

Introduced Species

VITAL STATISTICS

Maximum height: 100 centimetres
Flowering season: July to October

HABITAT: Common lamb's-quarters, a European species, is commonly found in disturbed areas throughout Nova Scotia and is a pest in recently cultivated ground.

CHARACTERISTICS: Common lamb's-quarters is an annual with upright, branching, ridged stems which reach a height of 100 centimetres. Alternate leaves are ovate to diamond-shaped with a few irregular rounded teeth and are slightly fleshy. Young leaves are covered in a silvery powder that often remains on the undersides of mature leaves.

Close examination of the individual minute green flowers reveals five sepals, which enclose the developing seeds, five stamens, and two pistils. Flowers are produced in globular clusters scattered in spikes among the upper leaf axils and branch tips. A silvery powder covering the buds gives them a grey-green appearance.

Oak-leaved goosefoot, *C. glaucum*, is a similar introduced species distinguished by its spreading habit and elliptical, shallowly lobed leaves, which are green above and covered in white farina below. It has a localized distribution in the province.

Chenopodium is similar to *Atriplex* but it has mostly bisexual flowers, the latter unisexual.

Top: Common lamb's-quarters' minute flowers are in globular axillary and terminal clusters. Middle: Common lamb's-quarters leaves have irregularly rounded teeth. Bottom: Oak-leaved goosefoot has shallowly lobed leaves.

Disturbed

18

Virginia glasswort

Salicornia depressa

Common glasswort, pickleweed, sea pickle

Native Species

HABITAT: Virginia glasswort is found on salt marsh mudflats and tidal flats throughout Nova Scotia. The plants are regularly inundated by water during high tides.

CHARACTERISTICS: Virginia glasswort is an evergreen succulent plant with jointed and branched pencil-like stems. Overall, the plant resembles coral. Its green stems turn red in winter. Scale-like leaves, opposite on the stems, clasp the stems so tightly that the plants appear leafless. Inconspicuous flowers are produced on jointed pencil-like spikes that are usually red or purple-tinted.

Sea glasswort, S. *maritima*, is virtually identical to Virginia glasswort in appearance but has a lower stature—reaching 25 centimetres—and is commonly red-tinted even in summer.

Saltwort or tumbleweed, *Salsola kali*, is a multiple branching annual found along sandy shorelines of the province. Plants are superficially similar to glasswort when young but have small spiky linear leaves. Tiny inconspicuous flowers, surrounded by papery, often pink-tinted bractlets, are produced in the upper leaf axils. When seeds are mature, the plant breaks away at ground level and rolls away on the wind, dispersing its seeds.

Sea-blite, *Suaeda maritima*, is a common annual along coastal mudflats. It has fleshy alternate linear leaves on multi-branching stems up to 30 centimetres long. Tiny pale green flowers are solitary or in clusters of two or three among the leaf axils.

Top: Virginia glasswort has green coral-like stems. Middle: Saltwort has spiky linear leaves; flowers are surrounded by papery bractlets. Bottom: Sea-blite has fleshy linear leaves and tiny axillary flowers.

VITAL STATISTICS

Maximum height: 50 centimetres
Flowering season: August to October

Coastal

Buckwheat family / Polygonaceae

Sheep sorrel

Rumex acetosella
Sourweed, field sorrel

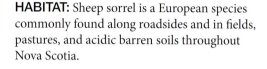

Introduced Species

VITAL STATISTICS

Maximum height: 40 centimetres
Flowering season: June to October

HABITAT: Sheep sorrel is a European species commonly found along roadsides and in fields, pastures, and acidic barren soils throughout Nova Scotia.

CHARACTERISTICS: Sheep sorrel has a mat-like habit and produces abundant underground rhizomes, allowing it to rapidly spread. Leaves are partially evergreen and form overwintering tufts. Lance-shaped with two diverging basal lobes, leaves are hairless, smooth-edged, and dark green, sometimes with a red tint. Throughout summer and early fall, wiry stems arise to 25 centimetres, rarely to 40 centimetres, high. Stem leaves are alternate.

Minute inconspicuous flowers are produced in narrow upright panicles. They are reddish- to yellowish-green with individual nodding flowers. Close examination reveals six sepals but no petals. Plants are monoecious. Seeds are produced within brown papery sepals.

Garden sorrel, *R. acetosa*, has similar, but larger, flowers, on stems reaching 100 centimetres in length. Plants are tap-rooted and produce a clump of long petioled, oblong, lance-shaped to elliptical basal leaves with heart-shaped bases. Erect stems are longitudinally ribbed. Stem leaves are alternate and clasp the stem. Flowers are reddish-green, and the developing heart-shaped papery fruit change from pink to brown. Both species have edible leaves with a zesty sour taste.

Top: Sheep sorrel's red tinted flowers are in narrow upright panicles. Middle: The lance-shaped leaves of sheep sorrel have two diverging basal lobes. Bottom: Garden sorrel looks like a larger version of sheep sorrel.

 **Introduced Species**

Curled dock

Rumex crispus
Curly dock, yellow dock

HABITAT: Curled dock is a European species common along roadsides and in waste places and pastures throughout Nova Scotia. Less commonly, it may be found along coastal beaches.

VITAL STATISTICS

Maximum height: 160 centimetres
Flowering season: June to September

CHARACTERISTICS: Curled dock produces a clump of leaves that arise from a thick taproot. Alternate hairless leaves are lance-shaped with smooth but curly or waved edges. Summer foliage is green, often with a red to brown tint. Basal leaves are evergreen, often strongly tinted red in winter.

Stiff upright stems are ribbed, usually un-branched, and reach 90 to 160 centimetres in length. Flower stems consist of a dense panicle of upright racemes with numerous whorls of small yellowish- to reddish-green flowers. Flowers have three inner and three outer sepals and are either bisexual with three styles and six stamens, or female with just three styles. They have no petals. Seed capsules are dark brown, papery, smooth-edged, and ovate to triangular in outline. Each capsule encloses a single seed.

Blunt-leaved dock, *R. obtusifolius*, a common European weed, often co-occurs with curled dock. It is distinguished by its wider, flatter leaves whose bases are distinctly heart-shaped. Its flowering racemes are narrower and its seed capsule edges have ragged teeth.

Native greater water dock, *R. brittanica*, is distinguished by its preference for wet soils along ponds, swales, and swamps.

Top: Curled dock flowers are in a terminal panicle of narrow racemes. Middle: Blunt-leaved dock has heart-shaped leaf bases. Bottom: Blunt-leaved dock's seed capsule edges have ragged teeth.

Coastal

Disturbed

21

Buckwheat family / Polygonaceae

Seabeach dock

Rumex pallidus

Seaside dock, pale willow dock, white dock

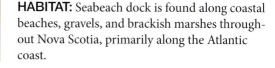

Native Species

VITAL STATISTICS

Maximum height: 100 centimetres
Flowering season: June to September

HABITAT: Seabeach dock is found along coastal beaches, gravels, and brackish marshes throughout Nova Scotia, primarily along the Atlantic coast.

CHARACTERISTICS: Seabeach dock is a clumping hairless plant with wide-spreading stems. Its alternate thick and leathery leaves are linear to lance-shaped, 10 to 20 centimetres long, with smooth or undulating edges. Plants tend to be prostrate along the ground.

Flowers, produced terminally or at the ends of axillary branches, are arranged in a loose panicle of racemes and in whorls of 10 to 20 along the racemes. Individual flowers are 0.6 to 0.8 centimetres wide, with six pale green sepals. The globular seed capsule, or valve, is commonly pale green to white. It has three wings and the tips of the wings barely exceed beyond the valve.

Willow-leaved dock, *R. triangulivalvis* (also known as *R. salicifolius*), also grows in coastal habitats but is found in waste places and disturbed sites with rich soil. Leaves are thin-textured and a paler yellow-green than those of seabeach dock. Flowers are similar to those of seabeach dock, but the valve is brown and the tips of the three wings extend well beyond the developing valve. Willow-leaved dock plants are usually more upright than seabeach dock. It is uncommon and found primarily around Bras D'Or Lake and Hants County.

Top: Seabeach dock often has trailing stems; the narrow leaves have smooth but undulating edges.
Bottom: Willow-leaved dock also has narrow smooth-edged leaves but the plant habit is upright.

Coastal

Spurge family / Euphorbiaceae

Wormseed spurge

 Native Species

Euphorbia vermiculata (formerly *Chamaesyce vermiculata*)

Hairy-stemmed spurge, wormseed sandmat, hairy sandmat, euphorbe vermiculée

HABITAT: Wormseed spurge is widely scattered on gravelly shorelines, along dry sandy roadsides, and in waste places, especially around railway stations.

VITAL STATISTICS

Maximum height: 40 centimetres
Flowering season: July to October

CHARACTERISTICS: Wormseed spurge is a creeping matted plant. The red-tinted stems are covered in long white hairs. The 0.5- to 1.5-centimetre-long finely toothed opposite elliptical to ovate leaves have short petioles. The plant exudes white sap when cut.

The insignificant green flowers are solitary or in small cymes among the upper leaf axils. The pistil, which is the most noticeable portion of the flower, is globular with three forked styles.

Seaside spurge, *E. polygonifolia*, is uncommon, usually confined to sand dunes and shorelines above the high-tide mark. Its waxy blue- or grey-green leaves are lanceolate and smooth-edged. The hairless, often red-tinted stems are not as dark as wormseed spurge stems.

Spotted spurge, *E. maculata*, is found occasionally in the upper Annapolis Valley and the Northumberland Strait where it grows on dry sandy waste areas. Plants are generally larger than those of wormseed spurge and seaside spurge, with 3.5-centimetre-long oblong leaves. Young leaves are covered in fine pubescent hairs that are lost on older leaves. Generally, each leaf has a central purple blotch. Stems are hairy and often tinted red. The flowers, which are 0.3 centimetres in diameter, appear to have four dirty white petals (not true petals) and a central green globular pistil.

Top: Wormseed spurge's red-tinted stems are covered in long white hairs. Middle: Seaside spurge has blue- or grey-tinted lance-shaped foliage. Bottom: Spotted spurge leaves often have a distinct red blotch.

Disturbed

23

Parsley family / Apiaceae

Black snakeroot

Sanicula marilandica
Maryland sanicle

Native Species

VITAL STATISTICS

Maximum height: 120 centimetres
Flowering season: June to August

HABITAT: Black snakeroot grows throughout Nova Scotia along shores and in thickets, meadows, and open woods.

CHARACTERISTICS: Black snakeroot is a clumping plant with mostly solitary stems which are 40 to 120 centimetres tall that arise from a thickened crown. Basal leaves are either palmately five- to seven-lobed or palmately compound, with long petioles. Farther up the stems, the petioles gradually shorten until they are nearly stemless. Individual leaflets are elliptical with toothed edges, alternate, and hairless.

Stems terminate in a panicle of small (1- to 2-centimetre-diameter) rounded umbels which are composed of 15 to 25 minute greenish-white flowers. Individual flowers are either staminate or perfect; the latter has two distinctive long styles. The dry fruit are in clusters of three to eight and are tiny and ovate and densely covered in short hooked bristles.

Yellow snakeroot, *S. odorata*, a rare species found in rich hardwood and alluvial forests from Kings to Inverness counties, is similar to black snakeroot but its plants are shorter, reaching 75 centimetres, with yellow-green flowers.

Top: Black snakeroot produces a terminal panicle of small rounded umbels. Middle: Black snakeroot's upper leaves are palmately compound and nearly stemless. Bottom: Yellow snakeroot has yellow-tinted flowers.

Mare's-tail family / Hippuridaceae

Common mare's-tail

Hippuris vulgaris

Native Species

HABITAT: Common mare's-tail, an aquatic species, grows in shallow, often brackish, coastal pools and along damp shores and, less commonly, along pond/stream shorelines. It is found throughout Nova Scotia but is scattered and localized.

CHARACTERISTICS: Common mare's-tail produces erect unbranched hollow stems that arise from a creeping underwater rhizome. Narrow hairless leaves are produced in whorls of six to 12 and reach up to 3 centimetres in length. Leaves have smooth edges, lack a petiole, and are reduced in size toward the top.

Minute inconspicuous green to purple flowers are produced in the upper leaf axils throughout the summer months.

VITAL STATISTICS

Maximum height: 25 centimetres
Flowering season: June to September

Wetlands

Top: Inconspicuous purple flowers are in the leaf axils.
Bottom: Unbranched stems produce whorls of narrow smooth leaves.

Water-starwort family / Callitrichaceae

Spring water-starwort

Callitriche palustris

Marsh water-starwort, vernal water-starwort, water chickweed

Native Species

VITAL STATISTICS

Maximum height: n/a
Flowering season: May to October

HABITAT: Spring water-starwort is an aquatic plant scattered in slow-moving streams, quiet waters, and wet shores throughout Nova Scotia.

CHARACTERISTICS: Spring water-starwort is an aquatic floating plant that may rarely be terrestrial if water levels drop enough to strand the plant. Usually the delicate stems arch and float along the water's surface. The small pale green leaves, which are generally less than 1 centimetre in length, are opposite or whorled, hairless, and smooth-edged. Leaves are widely spaced but crowded at the stem tips.

The flowers are solitary or in clusters of two or three in the leaf axils. Plants are monoecious, but the minute green flowers are so small as to be inconspicuous.

Large water-starwort, *C. heterophylla*, is less common than spring water-starwort and only subtly different. Large water-starwort tends to have rounder leaves with longer petioles and a deeper green colour, but this difference is not always consistent. The only true difference between the two species is the seed capsules: those of large water-starwort are as wide as they are long and lack thin wings along the margins; those of spring water-starwort are slightly longer than wide, with thin wings along the margins.

Top: Terminal leaves are often crowded. Bottom: Delicate stems usually float on the water's surface.

 **Introduced Species**

Plantain family / Plantaginaceae

Common plantain

Plantago major

Broad-leaved plantain, whiteman's-foot

HABITAT: Common plantain, a European introduction, is commonly found in disturbed areas throughout Nova Scotia.

CHARACTERISTICS: Common plantain forms a low rosette of evergreen round to egg-shaped leaves which are 5 to 20 centimetres in diameter and have three to five distinct ribs and petioles. Leaves are covered in short stiff hairs that impart a rough texture. Leaf edges are smooth but often wavy.

Plants produce several leafless flower stems that arise to 50 centimetres. Flowers are minute and green-brown and arranged in a rattail-like spike.

Narrow-leaved plantain, *P. lanceolata*, another widespread European introduction found in waste places, has upright narrow 10- to 20-centimetre-long lance-shaped basal leaves with distinct ribs, scattered hairs, and smooth edges. Similar to common plantain, narrow-leaved plantain flower stems are leafless, but their minute flowers are clustered into an ovate-shaped, rather than long and narrow, spike.

VITAL STATISTICS

Maximum height: 50 centimetres
Flowering season: June to September

Top: Common plantain has rattail-like flower spikes and a flat rosette of round leaves. Middle: Narrow-leaved plantain has an ovate-shaped spike of flowers. Bottom: Narrow-leaved plantain has a low rosette of lance-shaped leaves.

Disturbed

27

Plantain family / Plantaginaceae
Seaside plantain
Plantago maritime
Sea plantain, goosetongue

VITAL STATISTICS

Maximum height: 30 centimetres
Flowering season: June to September

HABITAT: Seaside plantain is a conspicuous species found along rocky to sandy coastal shorelines, cliffs, and headlands throughout Nova Scotia. More rarely, it may occur along roadsides in coastal communities.

CHARACTERISTICS: A tufted species, seaside plantain has basal upright smooth linear leaves that are succulent, evergreen, and salty when eaten. Younger plants often produce a flat rosette of leaves. Leaves range from deep green to almost brown.

The minute green-brown flowers appear on narrow leafless stems that reach 30 centimetres in height but are more commonly shorter. Flowers usually extend beyond the leaves. They are produced in a dense spike which resembles a rat's tail.

Top: The minute flowers are in rattail-like spikes.
Middle: Older plants often have a tufted appearance.
Bottom: Young plants often have a flat rosette of leaves.

**Introduced
Species**

Common ragweed

Ambrosia artemisiifolia

Annual ragweed, roman wormwood, hogweed, bitterweed

HABITAT: Common ragweed, an introduced European species, is encountered along disturbed roadsides, in meadows and waste places, and on cobble beaches throughout Nova Scotia, most commonly in the Annapolis Valley.

CHARACTERISTICS: Common ragweed, a multiple branching annual species, produces rough-haired stems that reach 100 centimetres in height. Fern-like leaves are pinnately lobed to bipinnately compound, covered in fine hairs, and are opposite or alternate along the stem.

Individual small green flower heads are either male or female and the plants monoecious or dioecious. Female flowers are located in the upper leaf axils; male flowers are in terminal racemes.

Giant ragweed, *A. trifida*, is uncommon and found mostly from Kings County to the Northumberland coast. A European species found in waste places, it grows to 200 centimetres in height and has opposite, mostly tri-lobed leaves which are covered in short stiff hairs and have toothed edges. Small green flower heads are produced in terminal and axillary racemes. Both species cause hay fever.

VITAL STATISTICS

Maximum height: 100 centimetres
Flowering season: August to September

Top: Common ragweed's male flower heads are in narrow racemes. Middle: Finely dissected common ragweed leaves are fern-like. Bottom: Giant ragweed has tri-lobed leaves.

Coastal

Disturbed

Aster family / Asteraceae

Northern pussytoes

Antennaria howellii subsp. *neodioica* (formerly *A. neodioica*)
Howell's pussytoes

Native Species

VITAL STATISTICS

Maximum height: 25 centimetres
Flowering season: June to July

HABITAT: A common species, northern pussytoes is encountered in open woods and on dry meadows and rocky barrens throughout Nova Scotia.

CHARACTERISTICS: Northern pussytoes forms a mat of rosettes. Flowering stems have alternate linear leaves. The basal leaves of trailing stems are 2 to 4 centimetres long and 1 to 2 centimetres wide and are ovate, spatulate to oblanceolate, and smooth-edged. Leaves are densely covered in white hairs, especially on the undersides, which impart a silvery hue to the foliage.

Wiry flower stems arise 10 to 25 centimetres and are topped by a corymb of several 0.5-centimetre-diameter flower heads. Individual flowers have a mass of tiny white or cream disc florets surrounded by cream, pale green, or light brown papery phyllaries.

Parlin's pussytoes, *A. parlinii*, a rare species found in the dry pine forests, old pastures, and rocky embankments of Hants and Kings counties, as well as along the LaHave River, is much larger than northern pussytoes. Its low rosettes of grey-green basal leaves are spatulate to obovate, 3 to 8 centimetres long, and up to 4 centimetres wide. Stem leaves are oblong to lanceolate.

Top: Flowers have brown-tinted papery-textured phyllaries. Bottom: The basal leaves are often spoon-shaped.

30

Aster family / Asteraceae

Beach wormwood

Artemisia stelleriana
Dusty miller

Introduced
Species

HABITAT: Beach wormwood, a native of Japan and Russia, was introduced to Nova Scotia as a garden ornamental. It is occasionally seen along gravelly to sandy beaches and roadsides throughout the province.

CHARACTERISTICS: Beach wormwood forms a matted clump of leafy trailing stems. All parts are densely covered in white felted hairs, making the plant easy to identify. Alternate leaves have an obovate to spatulate outline and are pinnately divided with blunt lobes.

Flower stems are mostly upright and 20 to 70 centimetres in length, with a loose raceme of 0.6- to 0.9-centimetre-diameter flower heads.

VITAL STATISTICS

Maximum height: 70 centimetres
Flowering season: August to September

Top: Flowers are in loose narrow racemes. Bottom: The pinnately lobed leaves are distinctly white and woolly.

Coastal

Disturbed

31

Aster family / Asteraceae

Common wormwood

Artemisia vulgaris
Common mugwort

Introduced
Species

VITAL STATISTICS

Maximum height: 150 centimetres
Flowering season: July to August

HABITAT: Common wormwood, a European introduction, is scattered in disturbed habitats throughout Nova Scotia.

CHARACTERISTICS: Common wormwood has upright branched 50- to 150-centimetre-tall stems which are grooved and slightly woody at their base and often tinted reddish-purple. The ovate-outlined, pinnately lobed leaves are sparsely toothed along their edges. The upper leaf surface is smooth or has scattered white hairs; the lower is densely covered in fine white hairs.

Flowers are produced as a panicle of spikes. Individual flower heads, produced in small clusters along the spikes, are green and covered in grey-white hairs, lending them a distinct grey cast, which is especially noticeable before the flowers open.

Biennial wormwood, *A. biennis*, is a European biennial species found occasionally in waste places. In the first season, plants produce a low rosette of hairless pinnate to bipinnately lobed leaves. In the second season, an unbranched stem with alternate leaves arises to a height of 2 metres. Dense spikes or tight globular clusters of stemless small green flower heads are produced among the upper leaf axils.

Top. Common wormwood produces a panicle of narrow spikes. Middle: Common wormwood leaves are ovate in outline but pinnately lobed. Bottom: Biennial wormwood has unbranched stems and axillary flowers.

Disturbed

32

 **Native Species**

Eastern burnweed

Erechtites hieraciifolia
American burnweed, pilewort

HABITAT: Eastern burnweed is fairly common in moist clearings and waste places, damp open woods, and old burn sites throughout Nova Scotia, except northern Cape Breton Island.

CHARACTERISTICS: Eastern burnweed is a rank-smelling bushy annual species. Stems are grooved and the sparsely hairy alternate leaves are lance-shaped to elliptical, and pinnately lobed with coarsely toothed edges.

Flowers are produced in open panicles, both terminal and from the upper leaf axils. Each flower head is cylindrical and up to 2 centimetres long with a central mass of small pale green disc florets. Ripe seeds have white plumes that are dispersed in the wind like those of dandelions.

VITAL STATISTICS

Maximum height: 70 centimetres
Flowering season: August to September

Top: Individual flower heads are cylindrical with pale green disc florets. Bottom: Flowers are in open panicles.

Mixed Forest

Deciduous Forest

Wetlands

Disturbed

33

Aster family / Asteraceae

Low cudweed

Gnaphalium uliginosum
Marsh cudweed, mud cudweed

Introduced
Species

VITAL STATISTICS

Maximum height: 20 centimetres
Flowering season: July to September

HABITAT: Low cudweed, a common European species, is found in disturbed areas, including gardens, throughout Nova Scotia.

CHARACTERISTICS: An annual species, low cudweed forms a bushy, multiple branched plant which is 10 to 20 centimetres tall. Alternate leaves are linear and smooth-edged; both they and the stems are covered in white woolly hairs that give the plant a silvery appearance. Small clusters of light brown flower heads are produced in the upper leaf axils and at the branch tips.

Rabbit tobacco, *Pseudognaphalium obtusifolium* (formerly *G. obtusifolium*), is scattered in the dry waste places of Kings County and southwestern Nova Scotia. It is an annual that reaches 80 centimetres in height with non-branching stems, alternate lance-linear woolly leaves, and flat-topped corymbs of dirty white bracted flowers in August and September.

Woodland cudweed, once known as *G. sylvaticum*, now known as *Omalotheca sylvatica*, is a native species scattered in disturbed areas and old meadows. Like low cudweed, woodland cudweed is an annual species with linear silvery green woolly leaves. It grows 40 to 60 centimetres tall, is unbranched, has small pale brown flower heads in the upper leaf axils, and has a spike-like tip.

Top: Light brown flower heads are among the upper leaf axils and branch tips of low cudweed. Middle: Rabbit tobacco has flowers in flat-topped corymbs.
Bottom: Woodland cudweed is unbranched and produces a spike-like arrangement of flowers.

Introduced Species

Pineappleweed

Matricaria discoidea (formerly *M. matricarioides*)

Disc mayweed, rayless chamomile

HABITAT: Pineappleweed is an introduced European plant now common in disturbed areas throughout Nova Scotia.

CHARACTERISTICS: An annual species, robust pineappleweed plants are multiple branching and appear bush-like; those growing in less than perfect locations are non-branching and only a few centimetres in height. Plants are hairless. The alternately arranged 5-centimetre-long fern-like dissected foliage is bipinnate to tripinnate, like small carrot leaves. The entire plant has a pineapple-like fragrance when bruised.

Solitary flower heads are formed from the axils of the upper leaves. Each head is about 0.8 centimetres wide, consisting of numerous yellow-green disc florets but no ray florets; hence, the flowers appear petal-less. The base of the flower head has several overlapping green phyllaries that have light brown papery upper edges.

VITAL STATISTICS

Maximum height: 20 centimetres
Flowering season: July to September

Top: The solitary flower heads appear petal-less.
Bottom: The fern-like foliage is finely dissected.

Disturbed

35

Aster family / Asteraceae

Rough cockleburr

Xanthium strumarium
Cockleburr, common cocklebur

VITAL STATISTICS

Maximum height: 60 centimetres
Flowering season: August to September

HABITAT: Rough cockleburr, found along gravelly to sandy beaches above the high-tide line, is occasionally observed in cultivated fields or waste places. In Nova Scotia, it is most often seen in the Northumberland Strait region.

CHARACTERISTICS: Rough cockleburr is a sprawling annual with roughly hairy stems and leaves. The alternate long petioled leaves are up to 12 centimetres wide, maple leaf-shaped, and palmately lobed with sharp teeth.

Monoecious petal-less flowers are produced in compact axillary clusters and terminal spikes. Green seed capsules, which turn light brown with age, are burr-like, ovate with many hooked spines, with two stout teeth at the tip, and often have glandular hairs. They mature when they are 2 centimetres in length.

Top: Small female flowers are in the leaf axila.
Middle: Leaves are maple-like in outline.
Bottom: Burr-like female fruit are covered in hooked spines.

 **Native Species**

Pondweed

Potamogeton species

HABITAT: Pondweed, of which there are 23 species in Nova Scotia, is an aquatic plant that grows in the shallow waters of streams, rivers, ponds, and lakes. Some species prefer flowing water; others prefer still water. Some require acidic water; others are restricted to alkaline water.

CHARACTERISTICS: Due to the large number of similar species of pondweed, they are described here as a group. Some species are entirely submerged, in which case their leaves are thin and translucent. Others have both submerged and floating leaves. The latter are more leathery, with smooth edges. The entire plant is hairless. Depending on the species, leaf shape can vary dramatically from ovate to linear. Leaves, alternate on thin rooting rhizomes, vary from bright green to purple-brown.

Minute flowers are produced on a short spike that rises just above the water's surface. Green to brown, they are composed of four sepals, four anthers, and a short thick style.

VITAL STATISTICS

Maximum height: n/a
Flowering season: July to September

Wetlands

Top: Spike-like flowers are held just above the water's surface. Middle: Stems that reach the surface produce floating leaves. Bottom: Some species of pondweed have purple-brown-tinted leaves.

Arrowgrass family / Juncaginaceae

Seaside arrowgrass

Triglochin maritime

Arrow-grass

Native Species

VITAL STATISTICS

Maximum height: 70 centimetres
Flowering season: June to July

HABITAT: Seaside arrowgrass inhabits saltwater marshes and freshwater calcareous marshes and shores throughout Nova Scotia, often partially submerged.

CHARACTERISTICS: Seaside arrowgrass is a slender upright plant which forms grass-like clumps. The linear fleshy leaves arise directly from the base of non-stoloniferous plants. Leaves are smooth-edged and hairless. The leafless flower stalks produce blooms in a narrow dense spike. Individual flowers are tiny and green with six nondescript tepals. The seed capsules resemble rice grains.

Marsh arrowgrass, *T. palustris*, is essentially con-fined to coastal regions. This species is much like seaside arrowgrass in appearance but is stolonif-erous with narrow seed capsules. Less common than seaside arrowgrass, marsh arrowgrass is found on Cape Breton Island and in the southern counties of Nova Scotia.

Top: The tiny flowers are in narrow spikes.
Middle: Seaside arrowgrass produces grass-like clumps. Bottom: Seed capsules resemble rice grains.

Wetlands

Coastal

Native Species

Sweetflag family / Acoraceae

American sweetflag

Acorus americanus
Sweetflag

HABITAT: American sweetflag is scattered in marshes and along slow-moving streams and pond margins throughout Nova Scotia.

CHARACTERISTICS: American sweetflag is a grass-like aquatic plant with a thick rhizome. Bruised or cut stems and leaves emit a citrus-like fragrance. The hairless toothless leaves are basal and linear, overlapping at their base, and resemble iris leaves.

Flowers are minute and brownish-green and are spirally arranged on a finger-like spadix which is 3 to 7.5 centimetres long. The solitary spadix appears laterally on the sides of leaf-like stems. Close examination of individual flowers reveals six tepals (petals and sepals look alike), six stamens, and a single pistil. The fruiting spadix bears leathery tan-green berries when mature.

VITAL STATISTICS

Maximum height: 80 centimetres
Flowering season: June to August

Wetlands

Top: Flowers are in a finger-like spadix.
Bottom: The linear leaves are similar to those of irises.

Arum family / Araceae

Jack-in-the-pulpit

Arisaema triphyllum

Indian-turnip

Native
Species

VITAL STATISTICS

Maximum height: 100 centimetres

Flowering season: Mid-May
to early July

HABITAT: Jack-in-the-pulpit inhabits shady rich damp woods and swamps throughout the province.

CHARACTERISTICS: Jack-in-the-pulpit has non-branching stems that arise from a turnip-shaped tuber. Each tuber produces one or two trifoliate or, rarely, palmate leaves whose petioles reach 30 to 100 centimetres in length. The hairless leaflets are ovate with smooth edges.

Plants produce a single spathe that arises between two leaves. The spathe is boldly striped in green, white, and purple-brown or just green and white in the variety *viride*. The hood of the spathe arches forward to partially hide the purple spadix within. The variety *stewartsonii* has a ridged hood that makes it more strongly reflexed than that of other varieties. In late summer, the spadix produces a cluster of orange-red berries. All parts of the plant are poisonous if ingested.

Top: The spathe is boldly striped white, green, and purple-brown. Middle: Leaves are usually trifoliate. Bottom: In late summer, the spadix produces a cluster of orange-red berries.

 **Native Species**

Eastern skunk cabbage
Symplocarpus foetidus
Skunk cabbage, swamp cabbage

HABITAT: Eastern skunk cabbage is rare in Nova Scotia but it is found in the swampy woods and wet alder thickets of Digby and Yarmouth counties.

CHARACTERISTICS: Eastern skunk cabbage is unmistakable: its large 30- to 60-centimetre-long heart-shaped leaves are basal, hairless, smooth-edged, and leathery.

This plant is among the earliest wildflowers to bloom in Nova Scotia. In April to May, plants produce nearly stemless 10- to 15-centimetre-high green spathes heavily streaked with purple-brown. The spathes, which arise barely above the mud surface, emit a strong skunk-like odour. Within the spathe is a yellow-green or purple-tinted spadix, which later produces a rough, grey-brown fruit containing a cluster of pea-sized seeds. Plants flower several weeks before the leaves emerge. The flowers actually release heat, which allows them to literally melt through late-lying snow.

Eastern skunk cabbage's contracting roots push the plants deeper into the mud each season: they essentially grow down- rather than upward.

VITAL STATISTICS
Maximum height: 60 centimetres
Flowering season: April to May

Wetlands

Top: The nearly stemless spathes are heavily streaked purple-brown. Bottom: Eastern skunk cabbage produces large clumps of heart-shaped leaves.

Broomrape family / Orobanchaceae

Beechdrops

Epifagus virginiana
Indian-turnip

Native
Species

VITAL STATISTICS

Maximum height: 45 centimetres
Flowering season: August to October

HABITAT: Beechdrops is restricted to beech forests throughout Nova Scotia.

CHARACTERISTICS: Beechdrops parasitizes the roots of American beech, *Fagus americana*. The plant lives for years underground, but, when conditions are optimal, it sends up branched brown to maroon stems that contain many narrow spikes of flowers.

The flowers are in two forms: the lower flowers on each spike are fertile, tiny, and bud-like in shape; the upper 1-centimetre-long tubelike flowers are sterile. The tubes end in four lobes and appear light tan to maroon-brown, but closer examination reveals them to be cream with maroon-purple stripes. The overall brown appearance of the plants causes them to be easily overlooked.

American cankerroot, *Conopholis americana*, is another parasitic relative that is rare in the oak forests of southern Nova Scotia. Overall, this plant is yellow-brown and its shape is similar to that of a cone of an eastern white pine, *Pinus strobus*. American cankerroot has stout fleshy stems which are 10 to 25 centimetres long and covered in brown scales. From April through June a cream-coloured tubular 1.5-centimetre-long flower emerges from the axils of each scale.

Top: Beechdrops' tubelike upper flowers are white with maroon-purple stripes. Middle: Beechdrops' brown stems are leafless and easily overlooked. Bottom: American cancerroot plants are cone-like.

Native Species

Orchid family / Orchidaceae
Frog orchid
Coeloglossum viride
Bracted green orchid, long-bracted green orchid

HABITAT: Frog orchid is rare and localized in Nova Scotia and found mostly on the northern tip of Cape Breton Island. It inhabits open woodlands, turfy shores, and damp meadows, usually in calcareous areas.

CHARACTERISTICS: Frog orchid is a narrow upright plant with up to six lance-shaped to elliptical leaves, which are hairless with smooth edges. The alternately arranged leaves are reduced in size up the stem until they become conspicuous 2-centimetre-long bracts at the base of each flower.

Flowers are produced in a loose cylindrical spike. The 1- to 1.5-centimetre-wide flowers are green. The tongue-like lip is up to 1 centimetre long and often suffused red or brown. The lip ends in three lobes—two larger outer lobes and a smaller middle lobe. The sepals and lateral petals form a hood-like structure above the lip. The nectar spur is short and indistinct.

> ### VITAL STATISTICS
> Maximum height: 35 centimetres
> Flowering season: July to August

Top: Flowers have a tongue-like lip.
Bottom: The narrow upright plants have slender smooth leaves that become reduced in size up the stem.

43

Orchid family / Orchidaceae

Early coralroot

Corallorhiza trifida

Pale coralroot, northern coralroot

Native
Species

VITAL STATISTICS

Maximum height: 20 centimetres
Flowering season: May to June

HABITAT: Early coralroot inhabits moist shady coniferous woodlands from Annapolis County to northern Cape Breton.

CHARACTERISTICS: Early coralroot is a leafless saprophytic species. The smooth yellow to green stem arises 10 to 20 centimetres in height, exceptionally to 30 centimetres.

Flowers are produced in a loose raceme containing three to 15 flowers. Individual flowers are green, sometimes tipped in brown, and are up to 1 centimetre in diameter. The dorsal sepal and lateral petals are angled upward and outward; the lateral sepals are arched downward. The lip is white, variously spotted with purple at its base.

Spotted coralroot, *C. maculata*, which prefers dry old-growth forests, may reach 50 centimetres in height and has reddish-purple stems. Up to 35 brownish-red flowers are produced per stem, and bloom in July. Like early coralroot, the lip of spotted coralroot is also white but more distinctly spotted purple-red. It occurs from Annapolis County to northern Cape Breton and is uncommon to rare elsewhere in the province.

Top: The green flowers of early coralroot have white lips with a few fine spots. Middle: Spotted coralroot has brownish-red flowers whose lips are white with purple-red spots. Bottom: Spotted coralroot has red-tinted leafless stems.

Orchid family / Orchidaceae

Introduced Species

Broad-leaved helleborine

Epipactis helleborine

Eastern helleborine, common helleborine

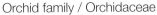

Mixed Forest

Deciduous Forest

HABITAT: Broad-leaved helleborine, a European orchid, has been naturalized in isolated areas across Nova Scotia. It grows in deciduous and mixed forests as well as in open meadows.

VITAL STATISTICS

Maximum height: 80 centimetres
Flowering season: July to August

CHARACTERISTICS: Broad-leaved helleborine is a narrow upright leafy orchid with three to 10 ovate, elliptical, or lance-shaped leaves. Leaves, which have distinct parallel veins and smooth edges, are covered in soft downy hairs. Leaves clasp the stem and are alternate along its length.

Fifteen to 30 flowers are produced in a loose one-sided raceme; each flower is subtended by a narrow leafy bract which is 2 to 6 centimetres in length. Individual flowers are green, often suffused with purple, and are about 2 centimetres in diameter. The lip is commonly white, variously tinted pink, and its inside base is dark purple-brown. Unlike similar orchids in Nova Scotia, this species has no nectar spur.

Top: The lip's inside base is distinctly darkened.
Bottom: Flowers are in loose one-sided racemes.

Disturbed

Orchid family / Orchidaceae

Loesel's twayblade

Liparis loeselii
Bog twayblade

Native
Species

VITAL STATISTICS

Maximum height: 15 centimetres
Flowering season: July

HABITAT: Loesel's twayblade is uncommon in bogs and peaty meadows and along freshwater sandy shorelines throughout Nova Scotia.

CHARACTERISTICS: Loesel's twayblade has greenish-yellow ridged stems. Plants produce two alternate leaves, which are lance-shaped to elliptical, smooth-edged, and shiny and clasp the stems.

Flowers are produced in a loose raceme of two to 25 flowers. Individual flowers are translucent and about 1 centimetre wide and vary from green to yellowish- or whitish-green. The unlobed lip is the most significant part of the flower's appearance: it is keeled like a boat. The sepals and lateral petals are narrow, and the sepals are typically curled under along their length. Flowers are often held horizontally. Overall, flowers have a ragged appearance.

Top: The translucent flowers have a keel-like lip.
Bottom: Each plant produces two alternate leaves.

Wetlands

46

**Native
Species**

Orchid family / Orchidaceae
Broad-leaved twayblade
Listera convallarioides
Broad-lipped twayblade

HABITAT: Broad-leaved twayblade is an uncommon to rare orchid found in cool mossy glades, old-growth woodlands, and swampy shorelines. It is rare from Digby to Antigonish counties but frequent in northern Cape Breton.

CHARACTERISTICS: Broad-leaved twayblade commonly reaches 10 to 20 centimetres in height and, exceptionally, 30 centimetres. Each plant produces a pair of stemless, hairless leaves which are round to elliptical in outline. Smooth-edged leaves are held near the middle of the stem.

Flowers are produced in a loose raceme. Individual flowers are translucent, yellowish-green, and about 1 centimetre wide. Lateral petals and sepals are strongly reflexed. The lip, which is nearly 1 centimetre long, is projected forward and resembles an elongated upside-down heart. It lacks a nectar spur. The flower stem is covered in fine sticky hairs.

VITAL STATISTICS
Maximum height: 30 centimetres
Flowering season: June to August

Top: The lip is projected forward.
Bottom: Each plant produces a pair of leaves.

Orchid family / Orchidaceae
Heart-leaved twayblade
Listera cordata

Native Species

VITAL STATISTICS
Maximum height: 20 centimetres Flowering season: June to August

HABITAT: An uncommon orchid, heart-leaved twayblade inhabits cool, mossy, primarily coniferous woodlands. Scattered throughout Nova Scotia, this flower is more frequent in northern Cape Breton.

CHARACTERISTICS: Despite being the most common *Listera* species in the province, heart-leaved twayblade is often overlooked. Stems reach a length of 10 to 20 centimetres. A pair of 1- to 3-centimetre-long round to heart-shaped stemless leaves is located about halfway along the length of the stem. Leaves are hairless and smooth-edged.

Translucent flowers, produced in a loose to dense raceme, are each about 0.5 centimetres wide and pale green to purplish-brown. The distinct lip is widely forked like a snake's tongue. Flowers have no nectar spur, but the flower stem often has a few sticky hairs.

Southern twayblade, *L. australis*, is extremely rare and has only been found in two locations in Nova Scotia—Kings and Inverness counties. The forked lobes of this species' longer lip hang down or cross rather than being wide-spreading as they are on *L. cordata*. Southern twayblade, which usually grows with cinnamon fern, is an Atlantic Coastal Plain species.

Top: Heart-leaved twayblade's distinct lip is forked like a snake's tongue. Middle: Heart-leaved twayblade produces a pair of round leaves. Bottom: Southern twayblade's forked lip is more elongated than that of heart-leaved twayblade.

Native Species

Orchid family / Orchidaceae

Green adder's-mouth orchid

Malaxis unifolia
Green malaxis

HABITAT: Green adder's-mouth orchid is found in wet habitats throughout Nova Scotia, including bogs, swamps, wet meadows, and moist gravelly slopes. It is easily overlooked due to its small size.

CHARACTERISTICS: Green adder's-mouth orchid is a delicate hairless plant with a single ovate leaf located near the middle of the stem. Rarely, a second leaf clasps the stem.

The crowded flowers appear umbel-like when they first open but later extend to create a spike-like raceme. The earliest flowers are often held horizontally; later ones are more vertical. The flowers, each 0.3 to 0.5 centimetres in diameter, are green. The lip is distinctly three-lobed with two large rounded outer lobes and a smaller, pointed middle lobe. The threadlike petals are strongly recurved. Plants on exposed gravels are very compact, often less than 10 centimetres high, and are yellow-green.

White adder's-mouth orchid, *M. monophyllos* var. *brachypoda*, is rare. It inhabits moist calcareous gravels, swales, and bogs primarily around the shores of the Minas Basin. It also has a stem-clasping single elliptical to ovate leaf, but that leaf is held close to the base of the plant. The 0.3- to 0.5-centimetre-long yellow-green flowers are on a slender raceme. The widely spaced sepals and petals create a starlike effect. The lip, often pointing upward, does not have lobes as green adder's-mouth orchid does; rather, it is rounded at the base, tapering to an elongate central lobe.

VITAL STATISTICS

Maximum height: 30 centimetres
Flowering season: July to August

Top: The crowded flowers of green adder's-mouth orchid appear umbel-like when they open. Middle: Each plant produces a single ovate leaf. Bottom: White adder's-mouth orchid has starlike flowers on narrow racemes.

Orchid family / Orchidaceae

Tall northern green orchid

Native Species

Platanthera aquilonis (formerly *P. hyperborea*)

Northern green bog orchid, leafy northern green orchid

VITAL STATISTICS
Maximum height: 60 centimetres
Flowering season: June to August

HABITAT: Tall northern green orchid is found along roadsides and in open bogs, fens, damp woodlands, open seepages, and peaty barrens. It is more likely to be seen in northern areas of the province.

CHARACTERISTICS: Tall northern green orchid is a narrow erect plant with hollow stems that arise 10 to 60 centimetres from a thickened tuberous root. Leaves are alternate along the stem; the lowermost leaf may reach 20 centimetres in length, and the upper leaves gradually become smaller as they ascend the stem. Leaves are stemless, lance-shaped, hairless, and smooth-edged.

Individual flowers are small, each about 1 to 1.5 centimetres long, yellowish-green, and fragrance-free. Each flower is subtended by a distinct narrow green bract. The lateral petals and dorsal sepal form a hoodlike structure. The lip is elliptical to lance-shaped in outline. The nectar spur is narrow and 0.5 centimetres in length. Flowers are arranged in a dense cylindrical spike.

The similar Lake Huron or fragrant green orchid, *P. huronensis*, was once included with tall northern green orchid as *Platanthera hyperborea*. It often co-occurs with *P. aquilonis* but is distinguished by its whitish-green strongly clove-scented flowers. Robust plants may reach 100 centimetres in height.

Top: The lateral petals and dorsal sepal form a hoodlike structure over the narrow lip. Middle: Flowers are in dense cylindrical spikes. Bottom: Lake Huron green orchid is often more robust than tall northern green orchid.

Native
Species

Orchid family / Orchidaceae

Club-spur orchid

Platanthera clavellata

Green woodland orchid

HABITAT: Club-spur orchid is found among wet meadows, seepages, low woodlands, and peatlands throughout Nova Scotia.

CHARACTERISTICS: Club-spur orchid is often overlooked but surprisingly common. Each plant generally produces a single elliptical hairless smooth-edged basal leaf which is 5 to 15 centimetres in length. Stem leaves are much reduced and alternate.

The flower stem is hollow and may reach 40 centimetres in height, although 10 to 20 centimetres is more common. Individual flowers are about 1 centimetre in length and pale green to yellowish-green. The nectar spur is club-shaped and about 1 centimetre in length. The lateral petals and the dorsal sepal form a hoodlike structure. The lip terminates in three lobes. Flowers are held in a moderately dense terminal spike.

VITAL STATISTICS

Maximum height: 40 centimetres
Flowering season: June to August

Top: The nectar spur is club-shaped. Bottom: Flowers are in moderately dense spikes.

51

Orchid family / Orchidaceae
Tubercled orchid
Platanthera flava
Pale green orchid, southern rein orchid, northern tubercled bog orchid

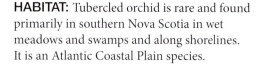

Native
Species

VITAL STATISTICS

Maximum height: 60 centimetres
Flowering season: June to August

HABITAT: Tubercled orchid is rare and found primarily in southern Nova Scotia in wet meadows and swamps and along shorelines. It is an Atlantic Coastal Plain species.

CHARACTERISTICS: Tubercled orchid has two or three smooth alternate lance-shaped to elliptical leaves. The largest leaf may reach 15 centimetres in length.

Ten to 40 0.6-centimetre-wide yellow-green flowers are produced in a loose to dense terminal spike. Lateral petals and a dorsal sepal form an upper hood. Lateral sepals are wide-spreading, often arching backward, while the lip is tongue-like with two small lobes at its base and a distinct bump (tubercle) near the centre. A short 0.5- to 0.8-centimetre-long spur extends behind the lip. Flowers are sweetly fragrant. A narrow leafy bract is located at the base of each flower.

Top: The tongue-like lip has two basal lobes and a distinct bump near the centre. Bottom: Flowers are usually in moderately dense narrow spikes.

Wetlands

Native Species

Orchid family / Orchidaceae

Hooker's orchid

Platanthera hookeri
Green woodland orchid

HABITAT: Hooker's orchid is an uncommon orchid restricted to dry open mixed or coniferous forests. Although it is scattered from Digby County to northern Cape Breton, this flower is nearly absent from the eastern shore.

CHARACTERISTICS: Hooker's orchid produces a pair of ground-hugging round to elliptical leaves, which are up to 15 centimetres long and hairless with smooth edges.

The flower stem arises between the leaves and reaches 30 centimetres in height. Flowers are produced in a loose raceme. Individual flowers are green to yellowish-green and about 2 centimetres wide. These fragrant flowers have a jaw-like appearance. The pointed dorsal sepal and narrow strongly decurved petals form the "upper jaw." The narrow lip is arched forward and upward to form the "lower jaw." Lateral sepals are strongly reflexed; the 1.5- to 2.5-centimetre-long nectar spurs point backward to downward.

VITAL STATISTICS
Maximum height: 40 centimetres
Flowering season: June to August

Top: Flowers have a jaw-like appearance. Bottom: Each plant produces a pair of ground-hugging round leaves.

53

Orchid family / Orchidaceae

Ragged-fringed orchid

Platanthera lacera

Green-fringed orchid

Native Species

Mixed Forest

Deciduous Forest

Wetlands

Disturbed

VITAL STATISTICS

Maximum height: 70 centimetres
Flowering season: July to August

HABITAT: Ragged-fringed orchid appears in acidic moist meadows, clearings, open damp woodlands, and peat bogs throughout Nova Scotia.

CHARACTERISTICS: Ragged-fringed orchid produces a smooth hollow stem that may arise to 70 centimetres, although 30 to 50 centimetres is more common. Plants have two to six alternate elliptical to lance-shaped leaves that become smaller as they ascend the stem. The lowermost leaf may reach 18 centimetres in length. The stemless leaves are hairless with smooth edges.

Plants produce a loose to dense cylindrical spike-like raceme of flowers throughout July and into August. The fragrant flowers are yellowish- to whitish-green and measure 1 to 1.5 centimetres in diameter. Each flower is subtended by a distinct narrow bract. The lip is divided into three deep lobes, each heavily fringed. The downward-curving nectar spur is 1 to 2 centimetres in length.

Top: The flower's lip has three heavily fringed lobes.
Bottom: Flowers are held in cylindrical spike-like racemes.

54

 Native Species

Orchid family / Orchidaceae
Blunt-leaved orchid
Platanthera obtusata
Small northern bog orchid, one-leaved rein orchid

HABITAT: Blunt-leaved orchid is found in cool moist mossy coniferous to mixed woodlands throughout Nova Scotia; it is more likely to be seen in northern and eastern regions.

CHARACTERISTICS: Blunt-leaved orchid generally has a single 5- to 12-centimetre-long leaf near the base of the flower stem. This leaf is hairless and oblanceolate to spatulate in outline, with a smooth edge.

Flower stems are slender and may arise to 30 centimetres, although they are more commonly less than 20 centimetres in length. The stem is terminated by a loose spike of whitish- or yellow-ish-green flowers. Flowers are about 1 centimetre in length. Lateral petals and a dorsal sepal form a hook-like structure. The lip is narrow and 0.4 to 0.8 centimetres in length; the narrow nectar spur reaches similar lengths.

VITAL STATISTICS
Maximum height: 30 centimetres
Flowering season: June to August

Top: The flower's lip is very narrow.
Bottom: Each plant has a single leaf near its base.

Orchid family / Orchidaceae

Lesser round-leaved orchid

Platanthera orbiculata

Small round-leaved orchid

Native
Species

VITAL STATISTICS

Maximum height: 50 centimetres
Flowering season: July

HABITAT: Lesser round-leaved orchid is a rare to uncommon orchid scattered in moist shady mossy woodlands throughout Nova Scotia.

CHARACTERISTICS: Lesser round-leaved orchid produces a pair of round basal leaves which may reach 10 centimetres in diameter. Leaves are relatively shiny, hairless, and smooth-edged.

Flowering stems, which arise between the two leaves, may reach 40 centimetres in height. Greenish-white flowers are produced in a loose raceme. Individual flowers are up to 2 centimetres wide. Sepals are rounded; lateral petals are more pointed and arch upward. The downward-pointing lip is narrow and up to 1.5 centimetres long. The nectar spur is commonly 2 to 2.5 centimetres long.

Large round-leaved orchid, *P. macrophylla*, also rare in Nova Scotia, is found in Hants County and on Cape Breton Island. Its individual parts are slightly larger than the analogous parts of lesser round-leaved orchid; the distinguishing feature is the longer nectar spur, which reaches 3 to 4.5 centimetres in length.

Top: Lesser round-leaved orchid flowers have rounded sepals and narrow lips. Middle: Each plant has a pair of round basal leaves. Bottom: Large round-leaved orchid flowers have very long nectar spurs.

Native Species

Procumbent pearlwort

Sagina procumbens

Bird's-eye pearlwort, matted pearlwort

HABITAT: Procumbent pearlwort inhabits moist, often shady, seepages, cliffs, fresh or brackish shorelines, and damp fields throughout Nova Scotia. Abundant across the province, it can be a weed in damp garden soils.

CHARACTERISTICS: Procumbent pearlwort forms a low bright green evergreen mat. Plants are composed of both multiple rosettes and thin trailing stems up to 15 centimetres in length. Threadlike leaves on the trailing stems are opposite or whorled.

Axillary or terminal flowers are solitary and produced on thin 0.5- to 2-centimetre-long stems. The four or, rarely, five white short-lived petals are each 0.1 to 0.2 centimetres long, half the size of the green rounded sepals. Flowers are only 0.3 to 0.5 centimetres wide. The flowers appear green.

Knotty pearlwort, *S. nodosa*, has similar leaves but a less matted appearance. Stems and leaves are dark green or purple-tinted. Leaf axils often have minute rosettes that root into new plantlets. Flowers are 0.5 to 1 centimetre wide, slightly larger than those of procumbent pearlwort, and have five white petals which are twice the size of the pointed sepals. Knotty pearlwort is more restricted in its distribution: it is scattered from Annapolis to Guysborough counties, inhabiting coastal cliffs and gravelly to sandy shores, often overlying limestone. It flowers from July to September.

Top: The green sepals of procumbent pearlwort are like petals. Middle: Procumbent pearlwort plants produce evergreen mats. Bottom: Knotty pearlwort looks similar to procumbent pearlwort but its flowers have five distinct white petals.

VITAL STATISTICS

Maximum height: 5 centimetres
Flowering season: June to October

Coastal

Disturbed

57

Rockrose family / Cistaceae

Large-pod pinwheel

Lechea intermedia

Narrow-leaved pinwheel, round-fruited pinwheel

Native Species

HABITAT: Large-pod pinwheel is uncommon and widely scattered in Nova Scotia. It grows on acidic dry sandy open areas.

CHARACTERISTICS: Large-pod pinwheel is a slender but tufted plant. It produces several basal shoots that are up to 7 centimetres long and that overwinter to bloom the following season. Elliptical to lanceolate leaves have long hairs along their smooth edges as well as along the lower veins. Leaves on the basal shoots are whorled but are alternate on flowering stems. The stems have soft hairs that hug the stem.

Tiny flowers are produced in narrow panicles. Each flower has five green to reddish-brown sepals; two are narrower and three are broader. These sepals partially enclose the developing seed capsules. Flowers also have five to 15 stamens, three plume-like brownish-red stigmas, and three reddish-brown petals that rarely expand and are concealed by the sepals.

Top: The tiny flowers have five green to reddish-brown sepals and are arranged in narrow panicles.
Bottom: Plants are slender with small narrow leaves.

Barrens

Disturbed

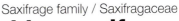

Saxifrage family / Saxifragaceae

Native Species

American golden saxifrage

Chrysosplenium Americana
American watermat, water carpet

HABITAT: American golden saxifrage is encountered in low-lying wet areas throughout the province, with the exception of along the Atlantic coast.

CHARACTERISTICS: American golden saxifrage is a semi-aquatic plant that forms a mat-like growth. Lower stems root as they creep over muddy surfaces. Succulent leaves are mostly opposite, less commonly alternate, and less than 2 centimetres long. They are generally stemless, round, and ovate or fan-shaped with shallowly toothed edges. The entire plant is hairless.

The tiny 0.3-centimetre-wide flowers are solitary at the ends of the upper branches. They are flat and a yellow- or purple-tinted green. The distinguishing features of the flowers are the four green sepals and the eight purple anthers. Each flower has a leaf held below it. The fruit is a tiny two-horned capsule.

VITAL STATISTICS

Maximum height: 15 centimetres
Flowering season: May to July

Top: Flowers are distinguished by four green sepals and eight purple anthers. Bottom: Plants have trailing stems and usually opposite round leaves.

Wetlands

Rose family / Rosaceae

Lady's mantle

Alchemilla species

American watermat, water carpet

Native Species   Introduced Species

VITAL STATISTICS

Maximum height: 50 centimetres
Flowering season: June to July

HABITAT: One native and three introduced species of lady's mantle are found in Nova Scotia. All grow on disturbed sites such as roadsides and old meadows.

CHARACTERISTICS: As the various species of lady's mantle found in Nova Scotia have only subtle differences, they will be described as a group. They are clumping, somewhat mounding, leafy plants with long petioled basal leaves. Flowering stems produce alternately arranged short petioled to sessile leaves with paired stipules. Leaves are toothed, round in outline, and palmately lobed, commonly with nine lobes. Lobe depth is one characteristic used to distinguish among the species. Overall, lady's mantle has a plaited fan-like appearance. Their leaves and stems are covered with silky hairs.

Flowers are tiny, less than 0.5 centimetres wide, and greenish-yellow with four sepals, four green bracts, and no petals. They are produced in panicles at the ends of weak stems.

The species found in Nova Scotia include

- Thin-stemmed lady's mantle, *A. filicaulis*, native along the eastern shore.
- Hairy lady's mantle, *A. monticola*, introduced and localized in Hants, Halifax, and Richmond counties.
- Veined lady's mantle, *A. venosa*, introduced and restricted to Cape Breton Island.
- Intermediate lady's mantle, *A. xanthochloa*, introduced and locally common from Halifax to Digby.

Top: Individual flowers have four green sepals and four narrow green bracts. Bottom: Leaves have a plaited fan-like appearance.

 **Native Species**

Marsh seedbox
Ludwigia palustris
Marsh purslane, water purslane, common water-primrose

HABITAT: Marsh seedbox is an aquatic plant found in shallow and clear but muddy-bottomed pools, lakes, and stream edges. Scattered throughout Nova Scotia, it is most likely to be seen in northern regions of the province.

CHARACTERISTICS: Marsh seedbox has mostly non-branching stems rooted in the muddy bottoms of shallow pools. Stems are upright when under water but sprawl across the water's surface when they extend above the water. The leaves, each up to 4 centimetres long, are opposite, lance-shaped to ovate, and fleshy. They are hairless with smooth edges and often strongly tinted red, especially if growing in full sun.

The solitary flowers are sessile and produced in the upper leaf axils on stems held above the water. Each tiny flower is composed of four green triangular sepals. Petals are extremely small or absent.

VITAL STATISTICS	
Maximum height:	30 centimetres
Flowering season:	Late June to September

Wetlands

Top: Solitary axillary flowers have four green sepals.
Bottom: Red-tinted stems sprawl across the water's surface.

61

Gentian family / Gentianaceae

Branched bartonia

Bartonia paniculata
Twining screwstem, panicled screwstem

Native Species

Wetlands

Barrens

VITAL STATISTICS

Maximum height: 40 centimetres
Flowering season: August to October

HABITAT: Branched bartonia, which occurs on wet acidic, peaty, or sandy soils throughout Nova Scotia, is an Atlantic Coastal Plain species.

CHARACTERISTICS: Branched bartonia is a slender, often overlooked, annual. Plants are usually upright but at times are almost twining in nature. Tiny 0.1- to 0.25-centimetre-long scale-like leaves are yellow-green or purple-tinted, widely spaced, and alternate. They are linear to lanceolate but appear scale-like. The entire plant is hairless.

Flowers are produced in racemes. Individual flowers, which are up to 0.5 centimetres long, have four cream-coloured lance-shaped petals, often with purple tips. Flowers have four yellow or purple anthers and a 0.08- to 0.15-centimetre-long stigma.

Yellow bartonia, *B. virginica*, is found in similar habitats but is uncommon in southern Nova Scotia. It looks similar to branched bartonia, but yellow bartonia is more stiffly upright and has opposite scale-like leaves which are 0.15 to 0.45 centimetres long. Flowers are straw yellow with oblong petals; anthers are yellow. The stigma is 0.15 to 0.23 centimetres long.

Top: Branched bartonia flowers, each with four tiny cream petals, are in racemes. Bottom: Yellow bartonia is stiffly upright; flowers are yellow-green.

62

Native Species

Fowler's knotweed

Polygonum fowleri

Marsh purslane, water purslane, common water-primrose

HABITAT: Fowler's knotweed is relatively common along gravelly to sandy coasts throughout Nova Scotia.

CHARACTERISTICS: There are eight similar species of creeping knotweeds in Nova Scotia. Fowler's knotweed is a bushy native species that has mostly creeping, often zigzagging, stems. Leaves and stems are succulent and blue- to grey-green or purple-tinted. Leaves are alternate and elliptical to obovate, with smooth edges. They measure 1 to 3 centimetres in length and are two to three times as long as they are wide. All leaves are essentially the same size.

Produced in axillary clusters, flowers are tiny, just 0.3 to 0.6 centimetres wide, with five green petal-like sepals which have thin white to pink edges. Its coastal habitat preference distinguishes this species from others in the province.

Perhaps the most common introduced species found along roadsides and in waste places of the province is the annual common knotweed, *P. aviculare*. It is similar in appearance to Fowler's knotweed, but the leaves on its side branches are significantly smaller than those on the main stems.

VITAL STATISTICS

Maximum height: 50 centimetres
Flowering season: Mid-July to September

Top: Tiny axillary flowers of Fowler's knotweed have five green sepals with white or pink-tinted edges. Middle: Fowler's knotweed's trailing stems often have a zigzag pattern. Bottom: Common knotweed flowers have deep pink sepals.

Coastal

Coniferous Forest

Mixed Forest

Deciduous Forest

Heath family / Ericaceae

One-sided wintergreen

Orthilia secunda (formerly *Pyrola secunda*)

One-sided pyrola

Native Species

VITAL STATISTICS

Maximum height: 20 centimetres
Flowering season: July

HABITAT: One-sided wintergreen grows in woodlands throughout Nova Scotia.

CHARACTERISTICS: One-sided wintergreen's creeping rhizomes form a groundcover in both shaded and sunny woodland areas. The leathery shiny evergreen leaves are hairless and elliptical to round in outline, have finely toothed or wavy edges, and reach 2 to 6 centimetres in length. Most leaves are basal and rosette-like but some may be found on the lower flower stems.

Flowering stems arise 7 to 20 centimetres and have a few small 0.2- to 0.4-centimetre-long alternate bracts. Flowers are produced in a strongly one-sided raceme of six to 20 greenish-white flowers. Each bell-like flower has five petals; the central style is straight and extends beyond the petals. Flowers rarely open fully.

Green-flowered pyrola, *Pyrola chlorantha*, another localized woodland species, also produces basal rosettes of leathery evergreen leaves from a creeping rhizome. Round hairless leaves are 1.5 to 3.5 centimetres wide with long petioles; their edges may be smooth or have a few slightly rounded teeth. Flower stems arise to 7 to 20 centimetres in height and produce a loose cylindrical raceme of two to 13 flowers. Individual bell-like flowers have five waxy greenish-white petals. The style extends beyond the petals and appears hook-shaped: it curves downward and has an upward-turning tip.

Top: One-sided wintergreen flowers are held in one-sided racemes. Middle: The round basal leaves of one-sided wintergreen are shiny and smooth. Bottom: Green-flowered pyrola has bell-like flowers with five waxy greenish-white petals.

Native Species

Saxifrage family / Saxifragaceae
Naked mitrewort
Mitella nuda
Naked bishop's-cap, bare-stemmed bishop's-cap

HABITAT: Naked mitrewort inhabits mostly cool mossy coniferous forests but is occasionally found in mixed or hardwood forests. It occurs throughout Nova Scotia, although it is uncommon along the Atlantic coast.

CHARACTERISTICS: Naked mitrewort forms small clumps of evergreen basal rosettes that arise from threadlike rhizomes. The 2- to 5-centimetre-wide leaves are heart-shaped with rounded teeth and scattered stiff hairs. This plant is often overlooked as it is mixed among other woodland wildflowers.

Thin wiry flower stems, each 3 to 20 centimetres long, produce a loose raceme of two to 13 minute flowers. Each flower is only 0.4 centimetres wide and has five rounded green sepals. Petals are unmistakable and deeply divided into four pairs of threadlike lobes, which gives them an antennae-like appearance.

VITAL STATISTICS

Maximum height: 20 centimetres
Flowering season: June to July

Top: The unmistakable petals are deeply divided into four threadlike lobes. Middle: Flowers are produced in loose racemes. Bottom: Round leaves have scattered stiff hairs.

65

Sandalwood family / Santalaceae

Northern comandra

Geocaulon lividum
False toadflax

Native Species

VITAL STATISTICS
Maximum height: 25 centimetres
Flowering season: June to July

HABITAT: Northern comandra inhabits sterile acidic sites in open coniferous woodlands, barrens, or, more rarely, sphagnum bogs. It is rare in Nova Scotia, restricted primarily to northern Cape Breton Island.

CHARACTERISTICS: Northern comandra produces several upright unbranched stems which are 10 to 25 centimetres in length. Thin-textured oblong leaves are bright green and alternate along the stem; they are often purple-tinted when they first emerge, turning purple by late summer. Leaves measure 1 to 3 centimetres in length, are hairless and smooth-edged, and have a short petiole.

Plants are usually monoecious. From the leaf axils partway up the stems, plants produce small clusters of two to four flowers on 1- to 3-centimetre-long stems. Individual flowers are 0.4 to 0.5 centimetres wide, green or tinted purple-brown, and star-shaped with five pointed sepals. Petals are small and undistinguished. The middle flowers of the cluster are usually female; the outer, male. Female flowers develop into dull orange-red berry-like fruit which is 0.5 to 0.8 centimetres in diameter. Remnants of the calyx create a crown-like projection at the end of each fruit. Although the fruit is juicy, it is not considered edible.

Northern comandra, a hemiparasitic plant, obtains some nutrients from neighbouring plants.

Top: The axillary starlike flowers have five green sepals.
Bottom: Female flowers develop into dull orange-red berry-like fruit.

Bristly sarsaparilla

Aralia hispida

Bristly spikenard, dwarf elder

Native Species

HABITAT: Common throughout Nova Scotia, bristly sarsaparilla occurs in open dry sandy barren areas and forest areas disturbed by clearing or burning.

CHARACTERISTICS: Bristly sarsaparilla is a shrub-like wildflower that grows up to 90 centimetres tall. Lower stems are slightly woody and covered in sharp bristles. Upper stems are branching, lack bristles, and are often red-tinted. Relatively large leaves are alternate, and bipinnate with ovate to elliptical sharply toothed leaflets.

Flowers are produced on long-stalked globular umbels which arise from the upper leaf axils and branch tips. Individual flowers are tiny, 0.3 to 0.5 centimetres wide, with five backward-curling greenish-white petals. These later develop into purple-black berries whose calyx remains as a crown-like tip. Although they are juicy, the berries are not considered edible.

American spikenard, *A. racemosa*, can reach 2 metres in height. It is found in calcareous rich hardwood forests from Annapolis to Victoria counties. This species lacks bristles on its stems. Leaves are similar to those of bristly sarsaparilla, but the leaflets are more heart-shaped. Flowers are also produced in globular umbels but are terminal on the stems in the form of an elongate panicle. The large clusters of reddish-black berries are conspicuous in the autumn.

VITAL STATISTICS
Maximum height: 90 centimetres
Flowering season: Late June to August

Barrens

Top: Bristly sarsaparilla flowers are in globular umbels. Middle: Flowers later develop into rounded clusters of black berries. Bottom: American spikenard has rounded umbels arranged in an elongate panicle.

Disturbed

67

Ginseng family / Araliaceae

Wild sarsaparilla

Aralia nudicaulis
Small spikenard

Native Species

VITAL STATISTICS

Maximum height: 40 centimetres
Flowering season: May to June

HABITAT: Wild sarsaparilla occurs primarily in shady woodlands or, less commonly, on barrens throughout Nova Scotia.

CHARACTERISTICS: Wild sarsaparilla grows on the forest floor. Each plant produces a single compound leaf. Although technically a basal leaf, it has a long stem that arises to 20 to 40 centimetres in height. The leaf is divided into three groups of three to five elliptical to ovate toothed hairless leaflets. Leaves are shiny and purple-brown when they emerge.

The leafless flower stem is solitary and arises directly from the base of the leaf. The flower stem is shorter than the leaf stalk, resulting in its being partly hidden; it is branched generally into three globular umbels, which are 3 to 5 centimetres in diameter. Individual flowers are only 0.3 to 0.5 centimetres wide with five strongly recurved greenish-white petals. Flowers later develop into blue-black berries whose calyx remains as a crown-like tip. Even though they are juicy, the berries are not considered edible.

Top: Flowers are in globular umbels. Middle: Leaves are shiny and purple-brown when they emerge. Bottom: Flowers later develop into rounded clusters of blue-black berries.

Native Species

Parsley family / Apiaceae

American water pennywort

Hydrocotyle americanum

Marsh pennywort

HABITAT: American water pennywort is found in wet forest depressions and ditches and along the edges of streams, usually in partly shaded locations, throughout Nova Scotia.

CHARACTERISTICS: American water pennywort forms creeping mats with thin trailing stems and rooting internodes. Leaves are alternate and round in outline, with six to 10 broad, rounded teeth or shallow, rounded lobes. Leaves measure up to 5 centimetres in width. All parts of the plant are hairless.

The five-petalled greenish-white flowers are inconspicuous. Two to seven flowers are arranged in small sessile umbels in the axils of the leaves. Individual flowers are only 0.2 centimetres in diameter.

Water pennywort, *H. umbellata*, a rare species restricted to the Atlantic coastal plain of Yarmouth and Queens counties, is more robust than American water pennywort. Leaf stalks are conspicuously attached to the centre of the leaf's underside. The umbel of white flowers is held on a relatively long stem just above the level of the leaves rather than being sessile.

VITAL STATISTICS
Maximum height: 20 centimetres
Flowering season: July to August

Top: American water pennywort produces tiny stemless umbels of green flowers in the leaf axils.
Middle: American water pennywort's round leaves have shallow rounded teeth and lobes.
Bottom: Water pennywort has elongate flower stems that hold the flowers above the level of the leaves.

Parsley family / Apiaceae

Purple-stemmed angelica

Angelica atropurpurea
Purple alexanders, great angelica

Native Species

VITAL STATISTICS
Maximum height: 3 metres
Flowering season: June to September

HABITAT: Purple-stemmed angelica is found along wet meadows, thickets, and streamsides primarily on Cape Breton Island and rarely in Antigonish and Guysborough counties.

CHARACTERISTICS: Purple-stemmed angelica is among the largest wildflowers in Nova Scotia with plants reaching to 3 metres in height. The unbranched stems are smooth, hollow, and typically purple with a waxy appearance. The hairless alternate leaves are large—up to 60 centimetres wide—triangular in outline, and bi- or triternately compound. Leaflets are elliptical to ovate and coarsely toothed. Emerging upper leaves and flowers are enclosed in distinctly veined inflated basal sheaths.

Plants produce large spherical umbels of many small spherical umbellets, creating a starburst effect. Individual flowers have five green petals and are about 0.6 centimetres in diameter. These flowers produce brown rolled-oat-like fruit in late summer.

Localized introductions of woodland angelica, *A. sylvestris*, occur along roadsides on Cape Breton Island. This species also has purple stems, but the main umbel is hemispherical, the leaves less coarse and shinier than those of purple-stemmed angelica, and the flowers white or pale pink. The stems of the umbellets are finely pubescent.

Top: Purple-stemmed angelica plants produce large spherical umbels with many smaller umbellets. Middle: Purple-stemmed angelica stems are often purple-tinted. Bottom: Woodland angelica produces flowers in hemispherical umbels.

 **Native Species**

Blue cohosh

Caulophyllum thalictroides
Papoose-root, squaw-root

HABITAT: Blue cohosh is occasionally found in rich deciduous forests and intervales primarily in central Nova Scotia from Kings to Cumberland counties.

CHARACTERISTICS: Blue cohosh is a clumping plant with several upright non-branching stems. Emerging stems and leaves are smoky purple but turn blue-green as they mature. Stems and leaves are hairless. Non-flowering stems terminate in a single triternately compound leaf with nine long-stemmed ovate leaflets whose edges are smooth but have two to five rounded cleft lobes at their ends. Flowering stems have two compound leaves. The entire lower "leaf" is composed of a whorl of three triternately compound leaves, each essentially looking like a single leaf of a non-flowering plant. From the centre of this whorl arises the second "leaf," which is a single biternately compound leaf.

A loose panicle of five to 30 flowers arises from the base of the leaflets on the second leaf. Individual flowers are about 0.8 centimetres wide and composed of six thick petaloid sepals which vary from yellow- to brown- to purple-green. The six true petals are tiny and insignificant. Flowers also have six stamens and a single beak-like pistil. Each flower develops into a single seed, which is covered in a bright blue seed coat.

VITAL STATISTICS
Maximum height: 90 centimetres
Flowering season: April to early June

Deciduous Forest

Top: Each flower has six petal-like sepals. Middle: Mature leaves have a blue-green tint. Bottom: Each flower develops into a single seed, which has a blue seed coat.

Gourd family / Cucurbitaceae

Wild cucumber

Echinocystis lobata

Prickly cucumber, wild balsam apple

VITAL STATISTICS

Maximum height: 3 metres
Flowering season: July to September

HABITAT: Wild cucumber appears on floodplains and in wet meadows, thickets, and waste places, primarily in central and southern Nova Scotia.

CHARACTERISTICS: Wild cucumber is an annual vine that climbs by twisting tendrils. Stems are smooth. Tendrils have three forks and are located opposite the leaves. Alternate leaves, which are up to 15 centimetres wide, are palmately lobed and similar in shape to those of a maple. They are finely toothed or smooth along their edges and generally hairless.

Plants are monoecious. Male flowers are produced in a loose 30- to 40-centimetre-long raceme along the upper leaf axils of the vine. Each blossom is about 1.5 to 2 centimetres wide with six narrow pubescent greenish-white petals. Solitary female flowers are located at the base of the male flower cluster. Female fruit is a 5-centimetre-long globular green gourd covered in soft spines. Superficially the fruit looks like a small spiny watermelon.

Top: Male flowers are in elongate racemes.
Middle: Plants produce maple-like leaves.
Bottom: Mature female fruit resemble a small spiny watermelon.

 **Native Species**

Asparagus family / Asparagaceae

Indian cucumber-root

Medeola virginiana

HABITAT: Indian cucumber-root grows in open hardwood forests throughout much of Nova Scotia.

CHARACTERISTICS: Indian cucumber-root's non-branching stems arise from an underground white tuber that tastes like cucumber. Stems reach 60 centimetres in height and are covered in white woolly hairs when young; these often erode as the season progresses. If flowering, plants will produce two whorls of leaves: the lower with five to nine leaves; the upper, three to five smaller leaves. Non-flowering stems produce only a single whorl of leaves. Leaves are elliptical to ovate in outline, hairless, and smooth-edged, with three to five parallel veins. They lack petioles and attach directly to the main stem.

Flowers are produced in a stemless umbel of three to nine blossoms immediately above the upper whorl of leaves. The greenish-yellow lily-like flowers are 1 centimetre in diameter and have six green recurved tepals. Each flower has six stamens and three rather long purple recurved stigmas. Flowers are nodding at or just below the level of the upper leaf whorl and later develop into globular dark purple berries. Leaves in the upper whorl are often tinted wine red at their bases as the fruit develop.

VITAL STATISTICS
Maximum height: 60 centimetres
Flowering season: June to July

Top: Individual nodding flowers have six green recurved tepals. Middle: Leaves are produced in whorls. Bottom: Flowers develop into dark purple berries.

Asparagus family / Asparagaceae

Hairy Solomon's-seal

Polygonatum pubescens
Downy Solomon's-seal

VITAL STATISTICS

Maximum height: 100 centimetres
Flowering season: June

HABITAT: Hairy Solomon's-seal is occasionally encountered in rich deciduous woodlands and shaded ravines and along riversides throughout Nova Scotia.

CHARACTERISTICS: Hairy Solomon's-seal produces non-branching stems that arise from a thick underground rhizome. Stems are smooth and arching. Alternate leaves are produced along the upper half of the stems. Leaves are waxy, smooth-edged, and lance-shaped to elliptical in outline and have several distinct parallel veins. On the underside of the leaves, fine soft hairs run along the veins. Leaves lack a petiole and attach directly to the main stem.

One or two, rarely three or four, tubular green or yellowish-green flowers are each 1 centimetre long and hang from the leaf axils on a forked flower stem. Each flower ends in six lobes. The six stamens are attached halfway down on the inside tube of the flower. In autumn, flowers develop into globular, fleshy blue-black berries, which may be mildly toxic.

Top: Tubular flowers hang from leaf axils.
Middle: Leaves are produced on the upper sides of the arching stems. Bottom: In autumn, flowers develop into blue-black berries.

Aster family / Asteraceae

Three-leaved rattlesnakeroot

Prenanthes trifoliolata
Gall-of-the-earth

Native
Species

HABITAT: Three-leaved rattlesnakeroot is common along roadsides and in open woods, barrens, and forested areas disturbed by clear-cutting or burning.

CHARACTERISTICS: Three-leaved rattlesnakeroot has upright non-branching green or purple-tinted stems. Plants are monocarpic, growing as a basal rosette for several years before flowering. After flowering, the plant dies. Long petioled basal leaves are deltoid, tri-lobed, or palmately lobed; lobes may be so deep that the leaves appear compound and may have a few large teeth. Lower leaves of blooming plants have similarly variable leaves; upper leaves are deltoid or elliptical and smooth-edged. The entire plant is hairless and, if cut, exudes a milky sap.

Nodding flowers are produced in an open panicle. Individual flower heads have seven to 10 phyllaries and a similar number of greenish-white or -yellow ray florets. Ripe seed heads resemble small cotton balls.

Tall rattlesnakeroot, *P. altissima*, can reach 2 metres in height and has tri-lobed to palmately lobed deltoid or ovate sharply toothed leaves. Each nodding flower head is composed of five phyllaries and five ray florets. It inhabits hardwood forests and is scattered throughout the province.

Purple rattlesnakeroot, *P. racemosa*, is very rare and restricted to Sydney Mines. Leaves are lance-shaped and coarsely toothed. Flowers are pink; phyllaries are covered in stiff hairs. Plants reach 150 centimetres in height.

VITAL STATISTICS
Maximum height: 120 centimetres
Flowering season: August to September

Top: Three-leaved rattlesnakeroot has nodding flowers in open panicles. Middle: Tall rattlesnakeroot flowers have five ray florets. Bottom: Purple rattlesnakeroot has pink flowers and hairy phyllaries.

75

Buttercup family / Ranunculaceae

Red baneberry

Actaea rubra

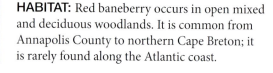

Native Species

VITAL STATISTICS
Maximum height: 90 centimetres
Flowering season: Mid-May to June

HABITAT: Red baneberry occurs in open mixed and deciduous woodlands. It is common from Annapolis County to northern Cape Breton; it is rarely found along the Atlantic coast.

CHARACTERISTICS: Red baneberry is a clumping wildflower with several non-branching stems that reach 60 to 90 centimetres in length. Alternate leaves are bi- or triternate with ovate, sharply toothed, or lobed leaflets. Leaves have scattered hairs.

Flowers are produced in a dense conical terminal raceme. Individual flowers are white and about 0.5 centimetres wide and consist of three to five sepals, five to 10 petals, and a mass of stamens, lending them a fluffy look. Flowers later become glossy red berries that sit at the ends of narrow green pedicles. White-fruited forms, which occur occasionally, belong to the variety *neglectum*.

Doll's-eyes, *A. pachypoda*, prefers rich deciduous forests and intervale regions and is uncommon across the province. Doll's-eyes and red baneberry are similar in appearance, but doll's-eyes' leaves are generally smooth. White berries with a black eye sit atop a thickened red pedicle.

The fruit of both species is mildly poisonous.

Top; Flowers are in a dense conical terminal raceme. Middle: Red baneberry produces red berries later in the season. Bottom: Doll's-eyes produces white berries with a central black spot.

Native Species

Buttercup family / Ranunculaceae

Tall meadow-rue

Thalictrum pubescens

Late meadow-rue, king-of-the-meadow, muskrat-weed

HABITAT: Tall meadow-rue is found along river and pond shorelines and in damp thickets, wet woods, ditches, swamps, fens, and damp meadows throughout Nova Scotia.

CHARACTERISTICS: Tall meadow-rue is among the tallest wildflowers in the province. Clumping plants produce both basal and stem leaves. Basal leaves have long petioles and each compound leaf is multi-divided into 15 to 27 stalked leaflets. Each leaflet is round with smooth edges and one to three rounded lobes. They are grey-green and smooth on top but may be finely pubescent on the lower surface. Leaves on the flower stalks are smaller than the basal leaves, sessile, and alternately arranged.

Plants are dioecious. Individual flowers lack petals but have four to five sepals that fall soon after the flowers open. The most noticeable part of the flower is the starburst of stamens (male) or pistils (female). Flowers are produced in a large panicle. Female flowers produce small spiky green to brown capsules.

VITAL STATISTICS
Maximum height: 250 centimetres
Flowering season: July to August

Top: Male flowers' starburst effect is created by many stamens. Middle: Close-up of female flowers. Bottom: Flowers are in large panicles.

77

Rose family / Rosaceae

Canada burnet

Sanguisorba Canadensis
Bottlebrush, wild burnet

Native
Species

VITAL STATISTICS

Maximum height: 120 centimetres
Flowering season: July to September

HABITAT: Canada burnet is found in peaty or boggy soils, commonly near the ocean. It is fairly common on Cape Breton Island but scattered elsewhere in Nova Scotia.

CHARACTERISTICS: Canada burnet is a relatively large leafy wildflower that arises from a thick rootstock. Stems are generally non-branching. Alternate leaves are hairless, pinnately compound with seven to 15 leaflets, and up to 45 centimetres in length. Leaflets are elliptical, coarsely toothed, and 3 to 6 centimetres long. Leaf tips are rounded and the base heart-shaped. Leaves are often waxy, imparting a blue- to grey-green colour.

Flowers are produced in multiple long-stemmed white-flowered cylindrical spikes which vary from 5 to 20 centimetres in length. Individual flowers are small, lack petals, and are essentially a mass of stamens and pistils.

Top: Flowers are in dense cylindrical spikes.
Bottom: Plants produce large clumps with pinnate leaves.

Native Species

Aster family / Asteraceae
Common boneset
Eupatorium perfoliatum
Boneset, thoroughwort

HABITAT: Common boneset occurs on the margins of streams and wetlands and in ditches throughout Nova Scotia, except northern Cape Breton.

CHARACTERISTICS: Common boneset is a stout wildflower with non-branching stems which reach 150 centimetres in length. The entire plant is covered in white hairs, particularly along the stems. Leaves are opposite and lance-shaped with finely scalloped edges and may reach 20 centimetres in length. The rugose pale green or yellow-green leaves are joined at the base; the stem passes through the centre.

Flat-topped loosely separated but dense corymbs of flowers are 5 to 20 centimetres wide. Corymbs have long stems and are produced both terminally and from the upper leaf axils. Each corymb is composed of multiple flower heads containing 10 to 40 tightly packed disc florets. They lack ray florets. Individual flowers are about 0.4 centimetres wide, with five small pointed petals and several elongate stamens. White or pink-tinted flower heads appear fluffy and are pleasantly fragrant.

Rare and restricted to one site on the Fundy coast of Cumberland County, white snakeroot, *Ageratina altissima* (formerly *Eupatorium rugosum*), grows in cool moist woods and thickets. It may reach 150 centimetres in height and has opposite long petioled ovate leaves with sharp teeth and fine hairs. Minute white flowers, in a loose terminal panicle, bloom in August and September.

VITAL STATISTICS
Maximum height: 150 centimetres
Flowering season: August to September

Wetlands

Top: Boneset flowers are in flat-topped loosely separated but dense corymbs. Middle: White snakeroot flowers are in loose terminal panicles. Bottom: White snakeroot has paired ovate leaves with long petioles.

Aster family / Asteraceae

Arctic sweet coltsfoot

Petasites frigidus

Arctic butterbur, northern sweet coltsfoot

Native Species

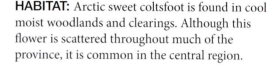

VITAL STATISTICS
Maximum height: 60 centimetres
Flowering season: May to early June

HABITAT: Arctic sweet coltsfoot is found in cool moist woodlands and clearings. Although this flower is scattered throughout much of the province, it is common in the central region.

CHARACTERISTICS: Arctic sweet coltsfoot is a perennial that spreads by creeping underground rhizomes, resulting in loose patches of colonies of plants. Leaves are basal and solitary. Each leaf is round in outline but palmately divided into five to seven deep lobes with coarsely toothed edges. When leaves emerge, they are covered in long white hairs; as leaves age, the upper surface becomes smooth, but the underside retains hairs. Leaves may reach 40 centimetres in diameter.

Flowers are produced before leaves emerge. Flower stems are leafless but have numerous green leafy bracts. When the flower first blooms, the stout stems are 10 to 20 centimetres high; they may elongate to 60 centimetres over time. Flowers are produced in globular clusters that elongate into a loose raceme. Fragrant flower heads are white or pale pink; each head is composed of many disc florets, which impart a fluffy look. Flowers are dioecious. Male flowers rapidly shrivel after blooming; females eventually produce numerous round seed heads that look like a miniature dandelion.

Top: Early flowers are in globular racemes. Middle: Less commonly, flowers may be pink. Bottom: The solitary flowers are palmately lobed with five to seven deep lobes.

Native Species

Wild calla
Calla palustris
Water arum

HABITAT: Wild calla is found in bogs and swamps and along marshy shorelines throughout Nova Scotia.

CHARACTERISTICS: A colonial plant, wild calla has alternate smooth heart-shaped leaves arising from a thick rhizome that creeps at or near the water's surface. Petioles may be 30 centimetres in length; the leaf, up to 15 centimetres. Leaves have smooth edges, parallel veins, and a waxy texture.

Plants produce solitary white ovate pointed spathes which are 3 to 6 centimetres in length. Within the spathe is a cylindrical thick 2-centimetre-long spadix which, later in the season, produces a dense cluster of red joined berries.

All parts of the plant are poisonous.

VITAL STATISTICS
Maximum height: 45 centimetres
Flowering season: June to July

Wetlands

Top: Wild calla produces its flowers in a solitary white spathe. Bottom: Plants produce smooth heart-shaped leaves.

Eriocaulaceae

Seven-angled pipewort

Native
Species

Eriocaulon aquaticum

White-buttons, common pipewort, duckgrass

VITAL STATISTICS

Maximum height: 20 centimetres
Flowering season: Mid-July to
September

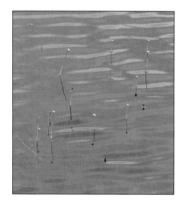

HABITAT: Seven-angled pipewort is an aquatic species found throughout Nova Scotia growing in still, clear water to a depth of 100 centimetres.

CHARACTERISTICS: Seven-angled pipewort is an aquatic species with tufted grass-like foliage. The only portion typically seen above water is the upper stem and flower. Leaves, which vary from 2 to 12 centimetres in length, are linear, blade-like, and translucent. Each leaf has three to seven distinct parallel veins.

Each rosette sends up a hollow angled stem that extends above the water's surface by 5 to 20 centimetres. Flowers are produced at the terminus of this stem. Individual flowers, stigma, and anthers are grey-black but tepal tips are covered by white cottony hairs. The overall effect is a pale grey-white button-like flower cluster which is 0.5 to 1 centimetres in diameter.

Top: Flowers are in a button-like head. Bottom: Generally only the upper flower stem and flower are above the water.

82

 **Native Species**

Dutchman's breeches

Dicentra cucullaria
Water arum

HABITAT: Dutchman's breeches, found in the shade of rich, often calcareous, deciduous woodlands, is widely distributed throughout Nova Scotia but is more common in Pictou and Colchester counties.

CHARACTERISTICS: Dutchman's breeches is a spring ephemeral. Plants arise in early spring but become dormant by early summer. Their hairless blue-green fern-like leaves are ternately compound and arise directly from a corm-like underground tuber. Leaf petioles are often brown-tinted. Leaflet edges are smooth but deeply lobed.

Up to 12 nodding dainty flowers are produced along a slender arching raceme. Flower stems are leafless. Individual flowers, each about 2 centimetres wide, are distinctive in shape, appearing, as the name suggests, like a pair of Dutchman's breeches or the wings of a butterfly. The "breeches" or "wings" are bright white; the spurs at the bottom of the flower are yellow.

All parts of this plant are poisonous if ingested.

VITAL STATISTICS
Maximum height: 25 centimetres
Flowering season: May to early June

Deciduous Forest

Top: Individual flowers are shaped like butterfly wings.
Bottom: The finely divided leaves are smooth and fern-like.

Violet family / Violaceae

European field pansy

Viola arvensis

Heart's ease, small wild pansy

VITAL STATISTICS

Maximum height: 40 centimetres
Flowering season:

HABITAT: European field pansy is a European species scattered in recently disturbed areas throughout Nova Scotia.

CHARACTERISTICS: European field pansy is a low matted leafy annual. Stems are prostrate to weakly ascending and multiple branching. Alternate leaves are elliptical to lanceolate with rounded teeth. Leafy stipules at the base of leaves are pinnately divided; the largest divisions have rounded teeth. Leaves and stems are hairless.

The long-stalked flowers are solitary from the upper leaf axils. Flowers are 1 to 1.5 centimetres wide with five creamy white (most common) to pale yellow or light purple petals. Two petals are held erect and two are lateral with long hairs on their inside bases. The lower petal is widest, with a short spur and a deep yellow, purple-striped patch at its base. The five narrow pointed sepals are almost as long as the petals. The seed capsule is globular with three longitudinal ridges.

Less common, and probably a garden escape, is Johnny-jump-up, *V. tricolor*. It looks much like European field pansy, but its leaves are larger and its flowers are 1.5 to 2.5 centimetres in diameter and more intensely coloured: upper petals are deeper shades of blue-violet, lateral petals lighter blue-violet, and the lower petal often entirely yellow. Lower and lateral petals may have purple stripes.

Top: Flowers have two erect petals, two lateral petals with hairy bases, and a lower lip with a deep yellow purple-striped patch. Middle: Flowers arise individually from the upper leaf axils. Bottom: Johnny-jump-up has larger flowers with usually blue or purple upper petals.

 **Native Species**

Lance-leaved violet

Viola lanceolata
Bog white violet

HABITAT: Lance-leaved violet occurs on boggy ground along damp roadsides and shorelines and in moist open woodlands and meadows. It is widespread in Nova Scotia, particularly in the southwest.

CHARACTERISTICS: Lance-leaved violet spreads by leafy mat-forming stolons. The 6- to 12-centimetre-long alternately arranged leaves are lance-shaped to elliptical, unlike any other violet in the province. Leaves are hairless on top but may have scattered hairs on the bottom. Leaf edges have a few rounded teeth.

Solitary flowers are 1.5 centimetres wide and usually held at or above the level of the leaves. Lateral petals are usually beardless; the lowest petal has purple veins and is often narrower and more pointed than the other petals. Flowers lack any fragrance. In areas where their distribution overlaps with that of *V. macloskeyi*, the hybrid *V. X sublanceolata* may be found. It is similar to *V. lanceolata* but its leaves are more elliptical or arrowhead-shaped.

VITAL STATISTICS

Maximum height: 12 centimetres
Flowering season: May to July

Top: The lateral petals lack hairs and the lower petal is longer than the other petals. Bottom: The lance-shaped leaves are unique among native violets.

Wetlands

Disturbed

Violet family / Violaceae

Small white violet

Viola macloskeyi (**formerly** *V. pallens*)

Northern white violet

Native Species

VITAL STATISTICS
Maximum height: 10 centimetres
Flowering season: May to July

HABITAT: Small white violet, common in various wetland habitats, usually in full sun, is found throughout Nova Scotia.

CHARACTERISTICS: Small white violet is the first of the white-flowered violets to bloom in the province and also the only one to prefer moist to wet sites. Tufted plants have alternate leaves that arise from slender stolons. Leaves are heart-shaped to round and hairless; leaf stalks may have a few hairs. Leaf edges have a few rounded teeth.

Flowers usually arise higher than the leaves. They are solitary, highly fragrant, and about 1 centimetre wide. Petals are white with distinct purple veins toward the centre. Lateral petals are beardless (lack hairs at their base).

Sweet white violet, *V. blanda*, grows in dry shady deciduous woodlands. Young leaves are pubescent but may retain hairs only on their undersides when older. Flowers are up to 1.5 centimetres wide and slightly fragrant, if at all. Lateral petals are heavily bearded. The plants are uncommon and localized.

Kidney-leaved violet, *V. renifolia*, another woodlander with pubescent young leaves, has beardless lateral petals and scentless flowers. The key distinguishing feature is its lack of stolons. It prefers coniferous and mixed forests over limestone and is most likely seen in the central regions of the province and on Cape Breton Island.

Top: Small white violet flowers are held just above the height of the leaves. Middle: Sweet white violet grows in lightly shaded woodlands. Bottom: Kidney-leaved violet leaves are wider than long.

 **Introduced Species**

White sweet-clover
Meliolotus albus (also known as *M. officinalis*)
Honey clover, Bokhara clover, white melilot

HABITAT: White sweet-clover, a European species, was probably introduced to Nova Scotia as a fodder crop. It is found in disturbed areas throughout the province, particularly in the calcareous central regions.

CHARACTERISTICS: White sweet-clover is a large bushy annual or biennial plant. Alternately arranged leaves are trifoliate with sharply toothed, oblong to obovate leaflets. Leaves are smooth or sparsely hairy. A pair of rounded stipules is at the base of each leaf.

Numerous white flowers are produced in 4- to 12-centimetre-long racemes located in the upper leaf axils. Flowers are sweetly fragrant. Individual flowers are 0.4 to 0.6 centimetres in length and pea-like in shape.

Botanists are undecided whether *M. albus* is simply a white-flowered version of *M. officinalis*. The latter species, commonly known as yellow sweet-clover, is also found throughout Atlantic Canada, often side by side with *M. albus*. It looks almost identical except for its yellow flowers. Tall yellow sweet-clover, *M. altissimus*, occasionally seen in Nova Scotia, is distinguished by seed pods with fine hairs.

VITAL STATISTICS
Maximum height: 150 centimetres
Flowering season: June to August

Top: Flowers are in narrow racemes. Middle: Leaves are trifoliate with finely toothed margins. Bottom: Yellow sweet-clover looks like white sweet-clover but has yellow flowers.

Disturbed

Pea family / Fabaceae

White clover

Trifolium repens
Dutch clover, creeping white clover

Introduced
Species

VITAL STATISTICS

Maximum height: 20 centimetres
Flowering season: June to September

HABITAT: A European introduction, white clover was cultivated initially in the province as a fodder crop and then as a lawn species. It is now a common species along roadsides and on lawns, meadows, and other disturbed areas throughout Nova Scotia.

CHARACTERISTICS: White clover is a low mat-forming plant with long creeping stems. The hairless leaves have long petioles and are alternate along the stems. Each leaf is trifoliate with heart-shaped tooth-edged leaflets, which end in a notch and usually have a pale green crescent in their middles.

Fragrant flowers are held just above the leaves at the ends of long flower stalks. They are produced in a globular 2-centimetre-long head of many small pea-like flowers. When flowers open, they are a creamy white but as they age they may develop a pink tint. Individual flowers are 0.5 to 0.9 centimetres long, narrow, and almost tubular.

Alsike clover, *T. hybridum*, is similar but its leaves are plain green and the flowers are two-toned pink and white. Alsike clover grows taller than white clover and is more clumping than creeping. It is found throughout Nova Scotia and is often grown as a fodder crop.

Top: White clover produces a globular head of many tiny pea-like flowers. Middle: The trifoliate leaves have a pale central crescent. Bottom: Alsike clover has pink and white flowers and green leaves.

Disturbed

Native Species

Northern water-horehound

Lycopus uniflorus

Northern bugleweed, tuberous water-horehound

HABITAT: Northern water-horehound prefers wet seepages, woods, meadows, and shorelines, often growing into the water. It occurs throughout the province.

CHARACTERISTICS: Northern water-horehound has non-branching square stems that arise from a tuberous-like root. Light green or purple-tinted leaves are opposite and elliptical to lance-shaped and usually have coarsely toothed edges, although plants in the shade may have smooth-edged leaves. Leaves vary from 2 to 11 centimetres in length and have short leaf stalks. Both stems and leaves are hairless. Plants are fragrant when bruised.

Tiny 0.3-centimetre-long flowers are produced in clusters along the upper leaf axils. Usually only a few flowers in each cluster are open at the same time. Each flower has a two-lipped appearance with two upper and three lower petals. The lowermost petals often have a few fine purple spots.

American water-horehound, *L. americanus*, is almost as common as northern water-horehound and grows in similar habitats. It reaches 90 centimetres tall and its leaves are deeply lobed or dissected at their bases while sharply toothed toward their tips. Leaves are generally hairless but have a few fine hairs along their lower leaf veins. Plants are not fragrant when bruised. Unlike *L. uniflorus*, which has five petals, this species has four petals.

VITAL STATISTICS
Maximum height: 60 centimetres
Flowering season: Late June to September

Wetlands

Top: The tiny five-petalled flowers of northern water-horehound are in axillary clusters. Middle: Plants produce coarsely toothed paired lanceolate leaves. Bottom: American water-horehound flowers have four rather than five petals.

Plantain family / Plantaginaceae

White turtlehead

Chelone glabra
Smooth balmony

Native
Species

VITAL STATISTICS

Maximum height: 90 centimetres
Flowering season: Mid-July to August

HABITAT: White turtlehead is found in swamps, wet meadows, and ditches and along streamsides throughout the province.

CHARACTERISTICS: White turtlehead has non-branching 60- to 90-centimetre-tall stems, which are square in cross-section. Opposite leaves are lance-shaped to elliptical, with toothed edges and short petioles. Each set of leaves is often at right angles to the next set. Stems and leaves are hairless.

Pleasantly fragrant flowers are held in a dense terminal spike. Individual flowers are creamy white, less commonly tinted pink, and two-lipped and measure 2.5 to 3.5 centimetres in length. The upper lip has two fused petals which form a hoodlike structure; the lower lip is made of three fused petals. The interior of the lower lip is hairy.

Top: The two-lipped flowers are in dense terminal spikes. Bottom: The paired leaves are lanceolate to elliptical and finely toothed.

Common eyebright

Euphrasia nemorosa
Hairy eyebright

Native Species

HABITAT: Common eyebright is a common species found in disturbed habitats and barren rocky areas throughout the province.

CHARACTERISTICS: Common eyebright is an annual with stiffly upright finely hairy stems which are 10 to 20 centimetres or, rarely, to 30 centimetres tall. Hairless glossy deep green opposite leaves are densely arranged along the stems. Leaves are 0.6 to 2.2 centimetres long and ovate with sharply toothed edges.

Flowers are arranged in terminal spikes. Individual flowers are about 1 centimetre wide. White or pale lavender flowers have five petals arranged in a two-lipped fashion. The upper two petals curl slightly backward; the lower three petals are more wide-spreading and are notched. Each petal has three purple veins; the lowermost also has a yellow patch in the middle. Each flower has a green bristle-tipped bract at its base.

Along the coast grows the diminutive Rand's eyebright, *E. randii*. It is usually less than 10 centimetres tall and has rounded teeth, variably hairy leaves, and tiny 0.3- to 0.4-centimetre-long white, pink, or purple flowers.

Hemiparasitic, eyebrights obtain nutrients by parasitizing neighbouring plants.

VITAL STATISTICS	
Maximum height:	30 centimetres
Flowering season:	July to September

Top: The striped flowers have a two-lipped appearance. Middle: Flowers are in terminal spikes and the opposite round leaves are coarsely toothed. Bottom: Rand's eyebright leaves have rounded teeth; flowers are often pink-tinted.

Barrens

Coastal

Disturbed

91

Broomrape family / Orobanchaceae

American cow-wheat

Native Species

Melampyrum lineare
Cow-wheat

VITAL STATISTICS
Maximum height: 40 centimetres
Flowering season: July to August

HABITAT: American cow-wheat is found on barrens and bogs and in open coniferous forests throughout the province.

CHARACTERISTICS: An annual, American cow-wheat has single stems or it may be multiple branching. The stem is square in cross-section with fine, often glandular, hairs. Linear to lance-shaped leaves are opposite and have short petioles. Leaves may be purple-tinted, hairless or slightly hairy, and slightly sticky on their upper surfaces. Leaf edges are mostly smooth but upper leaves have a few bristle-tipped teeth at their bases.

Flowers, solitary and produced in the upper leaf axils, are approximately 1 centimetre long and tubular with a two-lipped opening, reminiscent of a snake's head. The upper lip is shorter than the lower and curls back to reveal a hairy-fringed edge. The tube is white and the opening has a yellow patch.

Plants are hemiparasitic and obtain nutrients by tapping into the root systems of neighbouring plants.

Top: Each two-lipped flower is shaped like a snake's head. Bottom: Flowers are in the upper leaf axils.

Broomrape family / Orobanchaceae

One-flowered broomrape

 Native Species

Orobanche uniflora

Naked broomrape, one-flowered cankerroot

HABITAT: One-flowered broomrape is scattered in thickets, meadows, and open woodlands throughout the province.

CHARACTERISTICS: One-flowered broomrape is a parasitic plant that feeds off various plants. In Nova Scotia, goldenrods, *Solidago*, are a common host. Plants live for years as underground tuberous-like roots. When the conditions are right, plants will send up several leafless pale brown fleshy stalks topped by a single flower. Stalks and flowers are covered in fine sticky hairs.

Flowers have long curved tubes which are up to 2.5 centimetres long and which end in five petals: two upper and three lower. Flowers are typically white with pale lavender veins, but they may be entirely lilac. The middle of the three lower petals has two raised yellow beards that extend into the back of the flower. Flowers are delicately fragrant.

VITAL STATISTICS
Maximum height: 25 centimetres
Flowering season: June to July

Top: The middle of the three lower petals has two raised yellow beards. Middle: Less commonly, flowers are entirely lavender. Bottom: Plants are leafless and the flower stems covered in sticky hairs.

93

Orchid family / Orchidaceae

Showy lady's-slipper

Native Species

Cypripedium reginae
Pink and white lady's-slipper

VITAL STATISTICS
Maximum height: 80 centimetres
Flowering season: June to July

HABITAT: Showy lady's-slipper is restricted to calcareous wetlands and cedar swamps. It is localized in its distribution within Nova Scotia, primarily in the central region and on Cape Breton Island.

CHARACTERISTICS: Showy lady's-slipper is unmistakable: It produces clumps of non-branching stems that arise to 80 centimetres. Stems and leaves are fuzzy with short hairs. Plants produce three to five alternate overlapping leaves that are ovate in outline and clasp the stem. Leaves are smooth-edged and distinctly ribbed with parallel veins. The lowest leaves may reach up to 25 centimetres in length, but upper leaves are smaller.

Stems terminate in one, two, or, rarely, three large showy flowers measuring about 8 centimetres by 12 centimetres. Each flower is backed by a distinct green bract. Sepals and lateral petals are white. The dorsal sepal often leans forward; lateral petals arch slightly backward. The rounded pouch-like lip is in variable shades of pink or, rarely, white, and measures 3 to 5 centimetres in diameter.

Touching this orchid can cause dermatitis in people with sensitive skin.

Top: Flowers are white with a distinctive pink slipper-like pouch. Bottom: Its overlapping leaves clasp the stem.

Wetlands

 **Native Species**

Orchid family / Orchidaceae
Rattlesnake-plantain
Goodyera species

HABITAT: Rattlesnake-plantain grows in mossy shady areas in coniferous or mixed forests, or, less commonly, cedar swamps. Dwarf and checkered rattlesnake-plantain, *G. repens* and *G. tesselata*, are widespread; Menzie's rattlesnake-plantain, *G. oblongifolia*, is restricted to Cape Breton; downy rattlesnake-plantain, *G. pubescens*, is found in north-central Annapolis Valley.

CHARACTERISTICS: Nova Scotia's rattlesnake-plantains produce a basal rosette of alternate, egg-shaped, succulent evergreen leaves. Leaves are marked with silver-white veins.

Flowers of all species are pubescent and held on narrow leafless spikes. Individual flowers are white and about 0.3 centimetres wide. The dorsal sepal and lateral petals form a hood over the tiny pointed lip. Lateral sepals are usually strongly reflexed.

These features help distinguish among the four species:
- *G. oblongifolia*: off-white flowers on a loose one-sided spike; dull green leaves, each 4 to 10 centimetres long with a central silver-white stripe, with or without finer veins.
- *G. repens*: milk-white flowers on a loose one-sided raceme; dark green leaves, 1 to 3 centimetres in length, with large silver-white veins.
- *G. tesselata*: milk-white flowers spirally arranged; dull blue-green leaves, 2 to 7 centimetres in length, with pale green veins.
- *G. pubescens*: milk-white flowers held in a dense cylindrical spike; 3- to 6.5-centimetre-long leaves with a large central silver-white stripe and finer reticulated veins on the rest of the leaf.

Top: Flowers are in narrow spikes. Middle: All rattlesnake-plantains produce a basal rosette of leaves. Bottom: *Goodyera repens* has striking silver-veined leaves.

VITAL STATISTICS
Maximum height: 30 centimetres
Flowering season: July to August

Orchid family / Orchidaceae
White fringed orchid

Platanthera blephariglottis

Native Species

VITAL STATISTICS

Maximum height: 60 centimetres
Flowering season: July to August

HABITAT: White fringed orchid is encountered in wet meadows, fens, bogs, and roadside seepages. Scattered throughout much of Nova Scotia, it is fairly common in the southwest and on Cape Breton Island. It is an Atlantic Coastal Plain species.

CHARACTERISTICS: White fringed orchid produces stems which are 20 to 60 centimetres in length. Plants have two to four alternate lance-shaped leaves that clasp the stem; leaves are hairless and smooth-edged and become smaller as they ascend the stem.

Flowers are produced in a dense cylindrical spike. Individual flowers are bright white and about 2 centimetres in diameter. Dorsal sepals and lateral petals form a hood over the lip. Lateral sepals are ovate and often reflexed. The lip is narrow with heavily fringed edges. The nectar spur is 1.5 to 2 centimetres long.

Top: The narrow lip has heavily fringed edges.
Middle: Flowers are in a dense cylindrical spike.
Bottom: Plants commonly inhabit grassy fens.

Native Species

Tall white bog orchid

Platanthera dilatata

Bog candles, scent-bottle, leafy white orchid

HABITAT: Tall white bog orchid, a fairly common orchid throughout Nova Scotia, grows in wetland habitats.

CHARACTERISTICS: Tall white bog orchid is a tall, narrow plant with three to 12 alternate hairless smooth-edged lance-shaped leaves. Leaves become smaller farther up the stem.

Clove-scented snow-white flowers are produced in a dense narrow spike. Each flower has a narrow 2-centimetre-long leaf-like bract at its base. Individual flowers are about 2 centimetres wide. Dorsal sepal and lateral petals form a hood over the lip. Lateral sepals are wide-spreading and slightly reflexed, appearing like a tern in flight. The lip, rounded at the base, narrows toward the tip. The nectar spur is about the same length as the lip.

VITAL STATISTICS
Maximum height: 100 centimetres
Flowering season: Late June to August

Wetlands

Top: The dorsal sepal and lateral petals form a hood over the lip. Bottom: Flowers are in dense cylindrical spikes.

97

Orchid family / Orchidaceae

Nodding ladies'-tresses

Spiranthes cernua

White nodding ladies'-tresses, drooping ladies'-tresses

VITAL STATISTICS
Maximum height: 60 centimetres
Flowering season: July to August

HABITAT: Nodding ladies'-tresses grows in wetland habitats such as seepages, wet meadows, and moist sandy freshwater shorelines. Although distributed across the province, this plant is more common in the southwest.

CHARACTERISTICS: A slender plant, nodding ladies'-tresses produces several lanceolate hairless leaves near the base of the plant. Stem leaves are reduced to small bracts.

Flowers are held in three rows along a dense spike. The flower rows are slightly spiralled, but, less commonly, they may be parallel. Each flower has a short green bract at the base. Sepals and lateral petals are united to form an upward-arching hood. The lip arches downward. Individual flowers are about 1 centimetre wide and covered in fine hairs. Flowers have a slight vanilla scent.

Yellow ladies'-tresses, *S. ochroleuca*, is rare in Nova Scotia, preferring dry sandy sites in the southern half of the province. Flowers are pubescent and similar to nodding ladies'-tresses, but they are creamy yellow, especially in the throat, and have a strong fragrance.

Top: Flowers are covered in pubescent hairs. Middle: Nodding ladies'-tresses produces flowers in three parallel rows along a dense spike. Bottom: Yellow ladies'-tresses has creamy yellow flowers.

Orchid family / Orchidaceae

Northern slender ladies'-tresses

Spiranthes lacera

Bog candles, scent-bottle, leafy white orchid

Native Species

HABITAT: Scattered throughout Nova Scotia, northern slender ladies'-tresses grows in sandy to gravelly clearings along the edges of coniferous forests and in peaty meadows and old burn sites.

CHARACTERISTICS: Northern slender ladies'-tresses has slender leafless stems arising from one to four basal elliptical to oblong leaves that lie flat on the ground. Leaves are hairless with smooth edges and may be shrivelled at the time of blooming.

White flowers, produced in a dense spike, are strongly one-sided or widely spiralled along the stem. Individual flowers are about 0.5 centimetres in diameter. The lip, together with the dorsal sepal and lateral petals, has a tubelike appearance and an inside green patch. Lateral sepals are narrow and separated from the rest of the flower. The flower base is often sparsely pubescent.

Case's ladies'-tresses, *S. casei*, is rare in southwestern Nova Scotia. Densely pubescent flowers are creamy white and their lips lack a central green patch. Basal leaves are held erect and green at flowering during mid-August to September. It is an Atlantic Coastal Plain species.

Shining ladies'-tresses, *S. lucida*, is rare along the floodplains of the larger rivers of the province. Its white flowers, which bloom in late June and July, have a yellow lip on a three-rowed spiralled spike. Its oblong to oblanceolate leaves are not fully basal.

VITAL STATISTICS
Maximum height: 35 centimetres
Flowering season: Mid-July to August

Top: Northern slender ladies'-tresses flowers often spiral along the slender spike and have a distinct green patch at the lip base. Middle: Case's ladies'-tresses flowers also spiral along the stem but the lip does not have a green patch. Bottom: Shining ladies'-tresses has a yellow lip.

Orchid family / Orchidaceae

Hooded ladies'-tresses

Spiranthes romanzoffiana
White nodding ladies'-tresses, drooping ladies'-tresses

VITAL STATISTICS	
Maximum height: 35 centimetres	
Flowering season: Mid-July to September	

HABITAT: Hooded ladies'-tresses is scattered throughout the province, growing along shorelines and in damp meadows, clearings, seepages, shorelines, fens, and thickets.

CHARACTERISTICS: Hooded ladies'-tresses is a stout orchid which is 15 to 35 centimetres tall, with three to six alternate lance-shaped leaves that decrease in size up the stem. Leaves are hairless with smooth edges.

Flowers are held in three rows along a dense spike. Normally, flower rows are parallel, but they are sometimes spiralled. Each flower has a narrow green bract at the base that is nearly as long as, or longer than, the flower. Sepals and lateral petals unite to form an upward-arching hood. The lip arches downward. Individual flowers are about 1 centimetre wide and have a strong vanilla fragrance.

Top: Flowers are in three parallel rows along the dense cylindrical spike. Bottom: The narrow lance-shaped leaves decrease in size up the stem.

Wetlands

Barrens

Disturbed

Evening primrose family / Onagraceae

Small enchanter's-nightshade

 **Native Species**

Circaea alpina
Dwarf enchanter's-nightshade

HABITAT: Small enchanter's-nightshade inhabits cool moist shady woodlands, ravines, slopes, and wetland-forest borders throughout Nova Scotia.

CHARACTERISTICS: A common plant, small enchanter's-nightshade is often overlooked due to its small size and tiny flowers. While plants may reach 30 centimetres, they are more commonly 10 to 20 centimetres in height. Plants form large colonies, but individual stems are non-branching. Pale green succulent 2- to 5-centimetre-long leaves are opposite and heart-shaped. Leaves have coarsely toothed edges and hairs along their lower veins.

Flowers are held on slender racemes. Flower stems are covered in tiny sticky hairs. The flowers are only 0.2 centimetres wide, with two deeply lobed white petals (resembling four petals) that point forward, two petaloid white sepals that curl backward, one exerted style, and two exerted stamens. The base of the flower is covered in hooked hairs.

Large or broad-leaved enchanter's-nightshade, *C. canadensis* (formerly *C. lutetiana*) is scattered from Kings County to northern Cape Breton, growing in rich moist deciduous forests. Plants are generally over 30 centimetres tall with ovate leaves which grow up to 10 centimetres in length, twice as long as they are wide. Their petaloid sepals are generally green rather than white.

VITAL STATISTICS

Maximum height: 30 centimetres
Flowering season: June to September

Top: Individual flowers have two white sepals and two deeply lobed petals. Middle: Flowers are held in slender racemes. Bottom: Large enchanter's-nightshade has green rather than white sepals.

101

Water-plantain family / Alismataceae

Northern water-plantain

Alisma triviale

Native Species

VITAL STATISTICS

Maximum height: 80 centimetres
Flowering season: June to September

HABITAT: Northern water-plantain grows in muddy-bottomed shallow waters such as pond shorelines, streamsides, and ditches, and it is especially fond of calcareous muds. It is scattered throughout much of Nova Scotia but absent from the southwest and eastern shores.

CHARACTERISTICS: Northern water-plantain usually grows in shallow water. Leaves are basal but arise on long petioles. They are ovate to elliptical in outline, with parallel veins, smooth edges, and a slightly wrinkled appearance. Leaves on robust specimens may reach 18 centimetres in length. The entire plant is hairless.

Flowers are held in a large panicle. Branchlets arise in whorls well above the foliage. Individual flowers are about 0.5 centimetres in diameter with three white petals, three smaller green sepals, six stamens, and a globular green centre. A small yellow patch can be seen at the base of each petal. Seed heads look like small green buttons.

Top: A small yellow patch is visible at the base of the three white petals. Bottom: Plants produce a basal rosette of long petioled ovate leaves.

Native Species

Broad-leaved arrowhead

Sagittaria latifolia

Common arrowhead, duck potato, swamp potato, wapato

HABITAT: Broad-leaved arrowhead, which grows in muddy-bottomed shallow water such as stream and pond shorelines or mudholes, is common throughout the province.

CHARACTERISTICS: Broad-leaved arrowhead grows immersed in shallow water. Roots are tuberous and potato-like. Leaves are basal and arise on long petioles and measure 10 to 25 centimetres in length. Leaves have a triangular outline (called "sagittate") with three lobes: one large broad lobe at the top and two narrower, downward-pointing lobes on the bottom. Leaves are hairless with smooth edges and parallel veins. Stems and leaves exude a milky sap when cut.

Flowers are produced in whorls along the flower stems, which are held at the same level as the leaves or slightly above. Plants are monoecious; the lower flowers are female, the upper male. The 4-centimetre-wide flowers are satiny white with three rounded petals and three smaller green sepals. Male flowers have a cluster of golden stamens in the centre; female centres are green and burr-like.

Northern arrowhead, *S. cuneata*, looks like a half-sized version of broad-leaved arrowhead; it has 5- to 15-centimetre-long leaves and 2.5-centimetre-diameter flowers. It prefers calcareous muds.

Grass-leaved arrowhead, *S. graminea*, is scattered throughout Nova Scotia along silty and sandy pond margins. It is 20 to 50 centimetres in height and has narrow linear to lance-shaped leaves.

VITAL STATISTICS
Maximum height: 90 centimetres
Flowering season: July to September

Wetlands

Top: Individual flowers have three rounded white petals.
Middle: Leaves are distinctly arrowhead-shaped.
Bottom: Grass-leaved arrowhead has narrow linear to lance-shaped leaves.

103

Bunchflower family / Melantheaceae

Nodding trillium

Trillium cernuum
Nodding wakerobin

Native Species

VITAL STATISTICS

Maximum height: 30 centimetres
Flowering season: Mid-May to late June

HABITAT: Nodding trillium is found in mature deciduous forests and the floodplains of larger rivers. Scattered throughout the province, this flower is most likely to be seen in Pictou and Colchester counties.

CHARACTERISTICS: Nodding trillium forms loose colonies in the shade of deciduous trees. From an underground rhizome arises a single stem of 15 to 30 centimetres, topped with a whorl of three ovate leaves. The smooth-edged hairless leaves have obscure petioles.

A solitary 3- to 5-centimetre-diameter flower arises from the junction of three leaves. The flower stem is bent downward such that the flower is nodding below the leaves. The flower is composed of three elliptical white petals, three lance-shaped green sepals, six anthers, and a three-lobed stigma. Petals and sepals have recurving tips. Flowers develop into 3-centimetre-diameter fleshy red berries later in the season. The fruit is poisonous if eaten.

In one locality within Kings County grows a population of white trillium, *T. grandiflorum*. This species has large 10-centimetre-diameter white flowers held a few centimetres above a whorl of stemless leaves.

Top: Each flower has three white petals and three green sepals. Middle: The nodding flowers are held below the whorl of leaves. Bottom: Leaves are in a whorl of three.

Native Species

Bunchflower family / Melanthiaceae
Painted trillium
Trillium undulatum
Painted lady, painted wakerobin

HABITAT: Painted trillium is found mostly in dry coniferous woods but may occur in any woodland location, including cutover areas. It is scattered over much of the province but extremely rare on Cape Breton Island.

CHARACTERISTICS: Painted trillium forms a loose colony of solitary stems that arise from an underground rhizome. Stems are often purple-tinted early in the season. Elliptical to ovate leaves have long pointed tips and are produced in a whorl of three; they have short but obvious petioles and are also often purple-tinted, especially early in the season. Leaves are hairless and smooth-edged.

A solitary flower arises from the junction of the three leaves. Each flower is 5 to 7 centimetres in diameter and composed of three white tongue-shaped petals, three green lance-shaped sepals, six stamens, and a three-lobed stigma. Each petal has a pink-stained base, giving a pink centre to each flower. Later in the season, flowers develop into 1- to 2-centimetre-diameter poisonous red berries.

VITAL STATISTICS	
Maximum height:	40 centimetres
Flowering season:	Late May through June

Top: Each petal has a pink-stained base. Middle: Plants produce a whorl of three leaves. Bottom: Flowers develop into a red berry.

105

Mustard family / Brassicaceae

Drummond's rockcress

Boechera stricta (formerly *Arabis drummondii*)

Native Species

VITAL STATISTICS

Maximum height: 80 centimetres
Flowering season: May to July

HABITAT: Drummond's rockcress is a rare calciphile in Nova Scotia mostly confined to limestone or gypsum gravels of northern Cape Breton and the head of the Bay of Fundy.

CHARACTERISTICS: Drummond's rockcress, a slender plant with non-branching stems, is a biennial or a short-lived perennial. The rosette leaves are oblanceolate, usually hairless, and smooth-edged. The numerous stem leaves are alternate and lance-shaped but widest at their bases. Two backward-pointed lobes are found at the base of each stem leaf.

Flowers are produced in strongly erect racemes which are up to 80 centimetres tall. Opening flowers, each 1 to 2 centimetres wide, are white but age to lavender. The narrow seed capsules, or siliques, are held stiffly erect and are up to 10 centimetres long.

Barrens

Top: White four-petalled flowers age to lavender.
Bottom: Basal and stem leaves are narrow, hairless, and smooth-edged.

Native Species

Shepherd's-purse

Capsella bursa-pastoris

HABITAT: Shepherd's-purse, a European introduction, is commonly found in disturbed habitats throughout the province.

CHARACTERISTICS: Shepherd's-purse is an annual that often overwinters as an evergreen rosette. Basal leaves are elliptical to lance-shaped, have a petiole, and are pinnately lobed. The alternately arranged stem leaves are scattered and elliptical to lance-shaped with smooth or slightly toothed edges. These leaves are sessile and clasp the stem, often with a pair of ear-like lobes at their base. The entire plant may be hairless or have scattered stiff hairs.

Flowers are produced in a raceme. Individual flowers are about 0.5 centimetres wide with four white petals. Flower stems significantly elongate as they set seed. Seed pods are heart-shaped and flattened.

Field pennycress, *Thlaspi arvense*, which often grows with shepherd's-purse, is an annual with a few petioled basal leaves that are elliptical and widest at their tip. Flower stems are ribbed. The numerous stem leaves are elliptical to lance-shaped with sparingly toothed edges. They are alternately arranged and sessile, either clasping the stem or with a pair of ear-like lobes at its base. The entire plant is hairless. Its flowering habit is virtually identical to that of shepherd's-purse, but its seed pods, although flattened, are rounded with a notch at the top.

VITAL STATISTICS
Maximum height: 60 centimetres
Flowering season: May to November

Top: Seed pods of shepherd's-purse are heart-shaped and flattened. Middle: Narrow leaves clasp the stem. Bottom: Field pennycress has rounded flattened seed pods with a notch at their ends.

Disturbed

Mustard family / Brassicaceae

Two-leaved toothwort

Native Species

Cardamine diphylla

Broad-leaved toothwort, crinkleroot

VITAL STATISTICS

Maximum height: 40 centimetres

Flowering season: April to early June

HABITAT: Two-leaved toothwort occurs in wet hollows and along brooks in deciduous and mixed forests. It is confined to the northern half of Nova Scotia.

CHARACTERISTICS: Two-leaved toothwort is a spring ephemeral that disappears by mid-summer. Leaves are trifoliate with elliptical to ovate leaflets that are hairless and coarsely toothed. Non-flowering plants have a single basal leaf on a long petiole. Flowering stems have a pair of opposite or sub-opposite leaves with shorter petioles. Each leaflet has a short petiole.

Flowers are produced in a loose raceme. Individual flowers have four white, sometimes lilac, petals and are 2 to 3 centimetres in diameter. They develop into long thin siliques.

Top: Flowering plants have trifoliate leaves and a loose raceme of flowers. Bottom: Each flowering plant produces a pair of trifoliate leaves.

Mustard family / Brassicaceae

Pennsylvania bittercress

Cardamine pensylvanica

Native Species

HABITAT: Pennsylvania bittercress, which grows along muddy pond and stream shorelines as well as in ditches and swamps, is common throughout Nova Scotia.

CHARACTERISTICS: Pennsylvania bittercress is a biennial species. Plants overwinter as an evergreen rosette and bloom early in the second year. The base of the stem has stiff hairs but the rest of the plant is hairless. Leaves are pinnately compound. Basal and lower stem leaves have rounded leaflets; leaves farther up the stem have more linear leaflets. The terminal leaflet is usually the largest. Leaflet edges may be shallowly lobed or have a few rounded teeth.

Flowers are produced in racemes. Individual flowers are 0.3 to 0.8 centimetres in diameter with four white petals and six stamens. The fruit is an elongate narrow silique up to 3.5 centimetres long.

Watercress, *Nasturtium officinale*, a similar-looking introduced species found along slow-moving streams, is a perennial with stems that root in the water or mud. The fleshy, pinnately compound leaves have round leaflets with a few rounded teeth.

VITAL STATISTICS
Maximum height: 45 centimetres
Flowering season: May to July

Wetlands

Top: Pennsylvania bittercress flowers develop into long slender siliques. Middle: The upper stem leaves of Pennsylvania bittercress have pinnate leaves with narrow leaflets. Bottom: The pinnate leaves of watercress have round leaflets.

Mustard family / Brassicaceae

Rock draba

Draba arabisans
Rockcress whitlowgrass

Native
Species

HABITAT: Rock draba, a rare calciphile, is found on the limestone gravels and cliffs of northern Cape Breton and the head of the Bay of Fundy.

CHARACTERISTICS: Rock draba produces a loose mat of evergreen rosettes. Leaves are oblanceolate to spatulate with toothed edges. Flower stems are slender with a few alternate, ovate to oblong leaves.

Flowers are produced in a branched raceme. Individual flowers are 0.5 to 1 centimetre in diameter with four white petals and six anthers. Sepals, flower stems, and stalks are densely pubescent. Seed capsules are narrow and teardrop-shaped, and distinctly flattened but twisted.

Smooth draba, *D. glabella*, is a small matted plant with evergreen basal rosettes. The spatulate leaves, covered in white star-shaped hairs, may have a few coarse teeth toward their tip. Flowers are similar to those of rock draba, but stems are usually less than 20 centimetres long and seed capsules are not twisted. Smooth draba is also rare, and it is found in similar habitats to those of rock draba.

The rarest *Draba* is Norway draba, *D. norvegica*, which is confined to the calcareous gravels of northern Cape Breton. It has small, pubescent evergreen rosettes and a much-tufted appearance. Norway draba has fewer flowers than the other species, on shorter, up to 15 centimetres long, stems. Seed capsules are oval.

Top: Rock draba often has flowers in branched racemes.
Middle: Smooth draba is a small matted plant.
Bottom: Norway draba has fewer and smaller flowers than other native draba.

 **Introduced Species**

Field peppergrass

Lepidium campestre
Field cress

HABITAT: Field peppergrass, a European introduction, is found in disturbed habitats, such as roadsides, gardens, and waste places, throughout Nova Scotia.

CHARACTERISTICS: Field peppergrass is a winter annual or biennial plant that overwinters as an evergreen rosette. Leaves are elliptical but widest at their tips. They have petioles; leaf edges are smooth toward the tip but undulating and sharply toothed or lobed toward their base. The alternately arranged stem leaves are sessile and numerous. The slightly triangular leaves clasp the stem with two ear-like lobes; leaves are often toothed or undulating at the base but become smooth-edged toward the tip. The entire plant is covered in fine hairs.

Flowers are produced in dense branching racemes. Individual flowers are 0.3 centimetres wide with four white petals. Seed pods are flattened, concave, and ovate in outline with a small notch at the tip.

Common peppergrass, *L. densiflorum*, is also found in waste areas throughout the province. It has pinnatifid basal leaves but linear to lance-shaped stem leaves. It is essentially hairless. Flowers are in dense branching racemes, but the petals are minute, each only about 0.1 centimetre long, or may be missing; flowers appear green due to the presence of sepals.

VITAL STATISTICS
Maximum height: 60 centimetres
Flowering season: May to September

Top: Field peppergrass flowers are in dense branching racemes. Bottom: Common peppergrass has lobed leaves and nearly non-existent petals.

Disturbed

111

Heath family / Ericaceae

Creeping snowberry

Gaultheria hispidula

Capillaire, magna-tea berry

Native Species

VITAL STATISTICS
Maximum height: 5 centimetres
Flowering season: June

HABITAT: Creeping snowberry, scattered throughout Nova Scotia, grows in shady mossy coniferous to mixed forests or, less commonly, on open barrens, bogs, and headlands.

CHARACTERISTICS: This plant is a broad-leaved trailing evergreen sub-shrub. Thin stems of creeping snowberry are brown with short stiff hairs. Its ovate leaves are alternate and stiff with smooth revolute edges. The upper surfaces of the leaves are glossy, bright green, and hairless; the undersides are pale with a few short stiff hairs.

Plants produce tiny bell-shaped white or almost transparent solitary flowers with four petals. Blossoms are usually hidden under the foliage. In August and September, solitary white egg-shaped berries are produced. These edible winter-green-flavoured berries have a few short brown hairs.

Creeping snowberry is sometimes confused with twinflower (*Linnaea borealis*)—but twinflower's leaves are opposite (not alternate) on the stem, and twinflower lacks a wintergreen fragrance when its leaves are crushed.

Top: Tiny bell-like flowers are hidden under the leaves.
Middle: Plants form evergreen mats of round leaves.
Bottom: Later in the season, flowers become white egg-shaped berries.

 **Native Species**

Dogwood family / Cornaceae

Bunchberry

Cornus canadensis

Crackerberry, creeping dogwood, dwarf cornel

HABITAT: Bunchberry, common throughout Nova Scotia, occurs in many habitats including forests, barrens, and wetlands.

CHARACTERISTICS: This sub-shrub often forms large colonies that grow from semi-woody subterranean rhizomes. Bunchberry stems (10 to 25 centimetres tall) are topped by three pairs of closely spaced leaves that initially appear whorled; the lowest pair is largest. Leaves are mostly ovate to obovate, less commonly elliptical with un-toothed edges. They are often evergreen through winter, replaced by new shoots in spring.

What appear to be white flowers are sets of four white petal-like leaves (bracts). The actual flowers are tiny with four creamy white petals, four anthers, and a single style. They are produced in a cluster at the bract's centre. By August, flowers develop into a dense cluster of orange-red drupes. The fruit is edible but has little taste.

Swedish bunchberry, *C. suecica*, is rare and local-ized primarily in Cape Breton and Queens coun-ties. It resembles bunchberry but its paired leaves do not appear whorled, its flowers are purple with white bracts, and its red fruit has larger but fewer drupes.

VITAL STATISTICS
Maximum height: 25 centimetres
Flowering season: June

Top: "Flowers" are four white bracts surrounding a central head of tiny central flowers. Middle: Flowers develop into a raspberry-like cluster of orange-red berries. Bottom: Swedish bunchberry's true flowers are purple.

Madder family / Rubiaceae

Bedstraw

Galium species

Cleavers

Native Species   Introduced Species

VITAL STATISTICS
Maximum height: 50 centimetres
Flowering season: June to September

HABITAT: A dozen species of bedstraw occur throughout Nova Scotia in disturbed habitats, woodlands, wetlands, or barrens (depending on the species).

CHARACTERISTICS: All *Galium* produce thin trailing stems which are square in cross-section. Small leaves grow in whorls of four to eight. Flowers, less than 0.5 centimetres wide, have four, less often three, white petals and are usually in cymes. Here the similarities end. Plants may be smooth or have short stiff hairs, leaves lance-shaped to round, and flowers in threes or large panicles.

The six most frequently encountered species are
- Rough bedstraw, *G. asprellum*: six elliptical leaves per whorl; stems with stiff backward-facing hairs; flowers in loose open panicle; wetlands.
- Smooth bedstraw, *G. mollugo*: introduced species with six to eight lance-linear leaves per whorl; greenish-white flowers in large dense panicles; disturbed areas.
- Marsh bedstraw, *G. palustre*: four to six elliptical to spatulate leaves per whorl; flowers in large open panicles; wetlands.
- Dyer's bedstraw, *G. tinctorium*: five or six oblanceolate to spatulate leaves per whorl; flowers solitary or in groups of threes; wetlands.
- Three-petalled bedstraw, *G. trifidum*: four lance-linear leaves per whorl; flowers solitary or in groups of three; three-petalled flowers; wetlands.
- Three-flowered bedstraw, *G. triflorum*: six lance-elliptical leaves per whorl; greenish-white flowers in threes; mixed or deciduous woodlands.

Top: Smooth bedstraw has large panicles.
Middle: Smooth bedstraw's leaves are in whorls of six to eight. Bottom: Three-petalled bedstraw has leaves in whorls of four.

 **Native Species**

Madder family / Rubiaceae

Partridgeberry

Mitchella repens

Running box, two-eyed berry

HABITAT: Partridgeberry favours coniferous and mixed forests throughout Nova Scotia.

CHARACTERISTICS: A prostrate evergreen sub-shrub, partridgeberry may grow 1 to 2 centimetres tall. Opposite, round leaves are shiny green, leathery in texture, and hairless. Only about 1 centimetre wide, leaves have smooth or wavy edges and pale central veins. Stems are smooth.

Small white hairy four-petalled flowers are produced in pairs at the ends of the stems. Each flower has four stamens and a single style with four stigmas. Some flowers have exerted stamens; others have exerted stigmas. This irregularity is botanically referred to as having dimorphous flowers. Distinctively, each pair of flowers shares a single ovary. The paired flowers develop into conjoined red berries in September; berries persist through winter.

VITAL STATISTICS
Maximum height: 2 centimetres
Flowering season: July

Top: The four-petalled flowers are in pairs. Bottom: Later in the season, flowers become red berries with two eyes.

Coniferous Forest

Mixed Forest

Deciduous Forest

Wetlands

Barrens

Coastal

Disturbed

Asparagus family / Asparagacae

Wild lily-of-the-valley

Native Species

Maianthemum canadense

Canada mayflower, false lily-of-the-valley

VITAL STATISTICS

Maximum height: 15 centimetres
Flowering season: Mid-May to June

HABITAT: Wild lily-of-the-valley, which grows in both sun and shade in a variety of habitats, including forests, barrens, dry wetland hummocks, clearings, old burn sites, and dunes, is common throughout Nova Scotia.

CHARACTERISTICS: Wild lily-of-the-valley forms large colonies which spread by thin underground rhizomes. Plants produce two types of leaves. Non-flowering plants produce a single basal heart-shaped leaf with a distinct petiole; flowering plants produce two or three alternate leaves that are heart-shaped and clasp the stem. Leaves are shiny, bright green, hairless, and smooth-edged. Veins are parallel.

Flowers are produced in a dense raceme which is 2 to 3 centimetres long. The tiny 0.4-centimetre-diameter flowers have four white petals and four stamens and are sweetly fragrant. Flowers develop into brown-speckled 0.4-centimetre-diameter berries that turn shiny red when fully ripe. Berries are poisonous.

Top. Individual flowers have four petals and four exerted stamens. Middle: Flowers are in short dense racemes. Bottom: Later in the season, plants produce speckled berries, which eventually turn red.

116

 **Native Species**

Buttercup family / Ranunculaceae

Canada anemone

Anemone canadensis
Canada windflower, meadow anemone

HABITAT: Canada anemone grows along streamsides and in moist meadows, woodland borders, and the floodplains of large rivers. It is rare, primarily confined to calcareous soil.

VITAL STATISTICS

Maximum height: 60 centimetres
Flowering season: May to July

CHARACTERISTICS: Canada anemone forms large colonies; plants spread rapidly from underground rhizomes. Basal leaves have long hairy petioles, which reach 20 centimetres in length; stem leaves are opposite and have no petioles. The palmately lobed leaves have scattered hairs and are deeply cut into five to seven parts; each segment is also deeply cut or toothed.

Each stem produces one to three 3- to 4-centimetre-diameter flowers with five rounded petaloid sepals and a mass of yellow stamens and green pistils. Seed heads are globular and spiky.

Virginia anemone, *A. virginiana* (also known as *A. riparia*), is stout with palmately, deeply lobed leaves. Stem leaves are paired or in whorls of three; each leaf has a petiole. Plants produce a few 2-centimetre-diameter flowers with five white petaloid sepals. Seed heads are thimble-shaped and woolly. This rare calciphile is restricted to Hants, Inverness, and Victoria counties.

Cut-leaved anemone, *A. multifida*, another calciphile, grows in only one site in Inverness County. It is tufted, reaches 30 centimetres in height, and has bi- to triternate, deeply divided, almost feathery leaves. The entire plant is densely pubescent. Its off-white flowers are 1 to 2 centimetres wide.

Top: Canada anemone has palmately lobed, deeply cut leaves; flowers have five rounded white petaloid sepals. Middle: Virginia anemone flowers have globular spiky centres. Bottom: Cut-leaved anemone is densely pubescent, including its flowers.

117

Buttercup family / Ranunculaceae

Woodland anemone

Anemone quinquefolia
Wood anemone

Native Species

VITAL STATISTICS

Maximum height: 20 centimetres
Flowering season: Late May to early June

HABITAT: Woodland anemone grows in wooded ravines and along riverbanks. It is rare in Nova Scotia, restricted to Annapolis, Hants, Colchester, Guysborough, and Victoria counties.

CHARACTERISTICS: Woodland anemone is a spring ephemeral, germinating and flowering early in the spring then becoming dormant and disappearing by early summer. The slender flowering stem has a whorl of three petioled trifoliate leaves. Outer leaflets are so deeply divided that the leaves appear palmate. Leaflets have toothed edges and are hairless. Immature shoots produce a single basal leaf, similar in shape to the stem leaves.

A solitary 2.5-centimetre-diameter white flower with five to nine white petaloid sepals is produced at the junction of the stem leaves. Sepal undersides may be tinted pink or lilac. The flower stem is generally hairless.

Small-flowered anemone, *A. parviflora*, is a tufted 10- to 20-centimetre-diameter calciphile. It is very rare, found only in Inverness County. Basal leaves are trifoliate with round leaflets, dark green, and shiny. Leaflets are lobed or have rounded teeth at their tips. Stem leaves are in a whorl of three with each leaf nearly stemless and deeply tri-lobed. Leaves are smooth or have varying amounts of fine hairs. Flowers are solitary, 2 centimetres in diameter, with five to seven rounded white petaloid sepals. Sepal undersides are hairy and may be tinted blue.

Top: Woodland anemone has a whorl of three trifoliate leaves; each deeply lobed leaflet appears to have five leaflets. Bottom: Small-flowered anemone has dark green shiny foliage; stem leaves are a whorl of three tri-lobed leaves.

Native Species

Buttercup family / Ranunculaceae
Goldthread
Coptis trifolia (formerly *C. groenlandica*)
Canker-root, goldenroot

HABITAT: Goldthread is common in mossy coniferous forests but it also occurs in mixed or deciduous forests as well as on open barrens, bogs, cutovers, and recent burn sites. It is well distributed throughout Nova Scotia.

CHARACTERISTICS: Goldthread forms small colonies that spread by golden yellow threadlike rhizomes: hence the common name. Leaves are basal and trifoliate with round leaflets; each leaflet has three obscure lobes and several teeth. Leaves are evergreen, leathery, shiny, and hairless, arising on a 5- to 10-centimetre-long petiole.

Flowers arise from the ground on thin leafless stems that are up to 13 centimetres long. The solitary starlike flowers have five (most common) to seven white petaloid sepals and a central cluster of stamens and pistils. Each flower is about 1 centimetre in diameter.

VITAL STATISTICS
Maximum height: 13 centimetres
Flowering season: Mid-May to mid-June

Top: Goldthread produces solitary starlike flowers.
Bottom: The basal leaves are shiny, hairless, and trifoliate with round leaflets.

119

Buttercup family / Ranunculus

White water buttercup

Ranunculus aquatilis
White water-crowfoot, common water-crowfoot

VITAL STATISTICS
Maximum height: 5 centimetres Flowering season: July to August

HABITAT: White water buttercup grows in shallow muddy-bottomed pools in fresh or brackish water or along slow-moving streams. Within Nova Scotia, it occurs from Digby County to northern Cape Breton, but it is absent along the Atlantic coast.

CHARACTERISTICS: White water buttercup forms floating mats. Plants have two types of leaves, both of which are alternately arranged and hairless. Submerged leaves are finely dissected and feather-like, promptly collapsing when removed from the water. Floating leaves, if present, are stiffer and kidney-shaped with three main lobes and several minor lobes, with or without additional rounded teeth. Overall the leaves appear tri-lobed to palmately lobed.

Solitary flowers, which are 1 to 1.5 centimetres in diameter, arise from the leaf axils and extend a few centimetres above the water's surface. They have five shiny white petals, each with a yellow base and a cluster of yellow stamens in the middle.

Small yellow water buttercup, *R. gmelinii*, is also aquatic with a similar mat-like habit and submerged and emergent leaves. It has 1- to 1.5-centimetre-diameter flowers, which may be solitary or in a cluster of up to four flowers. The number of yellow petals varies from four to 14. Because this species prefers calcareous substrates, it is scattered in central Nova Scotia and on Cape Breton Island.

Top: The shiny white flowers have a yellow patch at the base of each petal. Bottom: Small yellow water buttercup is also aquatic but has yellow flowers.

 **Introduced Species**

Green carpetweed

Mollugo verticillata
Indian carpetweed, carpetweed

HABITAT: Green carpetweed, native to the southern areas of North America, has been introduced to Kings and Hants counties, where it grows along moist sandy roadsides and river-banks as well as in gardens.

CHARACTERISTICS: Green carpetweed is a low creeping matted annual with multiple branching stems. Young plants have a basal rosette, but plants quickly begin to branch, and the basal leaves then fade. Sessile leaves are linear, lanceolate, elliptical, or spatulate and are held in whorls of three to eight. Leaf edges are smooth; the plant is hairless. Plants are superficially similar to bedstraw or *Galium*.

Flowers are produced in axillary umbels with two to six 0.3- to 0.4-centimetre-diameter blossoms. Each flower has five petaloid white sepals, and three (rarely four) stamens, which meet at the top of the green globular ovary.

VITAL STATISTICS
Maximum height: 5 centimetres
Flowering season: June to October

Top: Stamens meet at the top of the globular ovary.
Bottom: Leaves are whorled but variable shapes.

Disturbed

121

Pink family / Caryophyllaceae

Field chickweed

Native Species

Cerastium arvense

Meadow chickweed, field-mouse-ear chickweed

VITAL STATISTICS

Maximum height: 30 centimetres
Flowering season: June to July

HABITAT: Field chickweed is scattered along roadsides and in gravelly or turfy barrens, headlands, and old pastures throughout Nova Scotia.

CHARACTERISTICS: Field chickweed's trailing stems grow to 30 centimetres in length, but plants form a matted clump about 10 to 15 centimetres tall. The opposite sessile leaves vary in shape from linear to elliptical and have smooth edges. The entire plant is covered in soft pubescent hairs. Tufts of small leaves are often present in the lower leaf axils.

Two to 20 flowers are produced in a loose cyme at the ends of wiry stems. The 2-centimetre-diameter flowers have five white petals with two-lobed tips, 10 stamens, and five styles. Petals are two to three times longer than the narrow green sepals.

Snow-in-summer, *C. tomentosum*, an occasional garden escape in the province, resembles field chickweed but has distinctive silver-white foliage due to the long white silky hairs which cover the plant.

Top: Flowers have five notched petals. Middle: Plants form matted clumps. Bottom: Snow-in-summer has silver hairy foliage.

Barrens

Disturbed

122

Common mouse-ear chickweed

Introduced Species

Cerastium fontanum subsp. *vulgare* (formerly *C. vulgatum*)
Mouse-ear chickweed

HABITAT: Common mouse-ear chickweed is an introduced European species found on moist disturbed areas and in meadows throughout Nova Scotia.

CHARACTERISTICS: Common mouse-ear chickweed has trailing matted stems that reach 45 centimetres in length. The entire plant is covered in fine, occasionally sticky, pubescent hairs. The opposite sessile leaves are elliptical to ovate in outline with smooth edges.

Flowers are produced in a loose cluster or cyme. Each blossom is 1 to 1.5 centimetres in diameter and has five white cleft petals, 10 stamens, and five styles. Petals are the same length as or slightly longer than the green elliptical sepals.

Five-stamen mouse-ear chickweed, *C. semidecandrum*, is another European introduction recently found in several campgrounds throughout Nova Scotia. It is more compact than common mouse-ear chickweed and the entire plant is covered in glandular hairs. Flowers, which are 0.5 to 0.7 centimetres in diameter, have five rather than 10 stamens and the petals are a little shorter than the sepals.

VITAL STATISTICS
Maximum height: 45 centimetres
Flowering season: June to September

Top: Common mouse-ear chickweed's white petals are only slightly longer than the green sepals.
Bottom: Five-stamen mouse-ear chickweed's white petals are a little shorter than the green sepals.

Disturbed

Pink family / Caryophyllaceae

Seabeach sandwort

Honckenya peploides

Seaside sandwort, sea chickweed, sea purslane

VITAL STATISTICS
Maximum height: 30 centimetres
Flowering season: May to September

HABITAT: Seabeach sandwort is restricted to sandy and fine gravelly beaches along the coast of Nova Scotia.

CHARACTERISTICS: Seabeach sandwort forms clumps or mats with multiple branching trailing stems. The base of the stems may be considerably buried in sand. Leaves are sessile, opposite, and egg-shaped to elliptical with a pointed tip. They are fleshy, shiny, and hairless and have crenate edges. Each pair of leaves is often at right angles to the next.

Honey-scented flowers are produced terminally and are axillary, solitary, or in small cymes. Sepals and petals are about the same length but the egg-shaped sharp-pointed sepals are broader than the rounded petals. Individual flowers measure 1 to 1.5 centimetres in diameter. Each flower has 10 stamens and three styles. The globular yellow-green seed capsule resembles a berry.

Coastal

Top: Petals and sepals are about the same length.
Bottom: Plants form mats of opposite egg-shaped pointed leaves.

Pink family / Caryophyllaceae

Native Species

Grove sandwort

Moehringia lateriflora (formerly *Arenaria lateriflora*)
Blunt-leaved sandwort

HABITAT: Grove sandwort is found along gravelly or turfy shores and in damp thickets and meadows, dry heaths, and open woodlands throughout Nova Scotia.

CHARACTERISTICS: Grove sandwort has weak stems and commonly rambles through surrounding vegetation. Stems have backward-facing hairs that impart a roughness when the stem is rubbed. Leaves are opposite, sessile or with a very short pedicle, elliptical, and smooth-edged; they are hairless on the top surface but may have a few fine hairs on the underside.

Flowers may be solitary or in a loose cyme with two to five blossoms from the leaf axils. Individual flowers have five rounded white petals, which are twice as long as the sepals. Flowers are each about 1 centimetre in diameter with 10 stamens and three styles.

Greenland stitchwort, *Minuartia groenlandica* (formerly *Arenaria groenlandica*), forms a small tufted plant. The overlapping leaves are opposite and needle-like and often covered in sticky glandular hairs. Leaves have three distinct ribs.

Flowers are produced in loose terminal clusters with 0.5-centimetre-diameter flowers. The five petals, which are uncleft, are nearly twice the length of the sepals. This species is found on the granitic gravels of Halifax, Lunenburg, and Inverness counties.

VITAL STATISTICS	
Maximum height: 30 centimetres	
Flowering season: June to September	

Top: Individual flowers have five rounded petals, ten stamens, and three styles. Middle: Grove sandwort's weak stems ramble through neighbouring vegetation. Bottom: Greenland stitchwort forms a small tufted plant with terminal flower clusters.

125

Pink family / Caryophyllaceae

Bladder campion

Silene vulgaris (formerly *S. cucubalus*)
Maiden's tears

VITAL STATISTICS

Maximum height: 60 centimetres
Flowering season: June to August

HABITAT: Bladder campion, a European introduction, is occasionally found in fields and waste places, generally near larger towns and cities, throughout Nova Scotia.

CHARACTERISTICS: Bladder campion is a clumping plant with multiple branched stems. Smooth-edged fleshy leaves are opposite and sessile to almost clasping the stem; the waxiness of the grey-green leaves imparts a dull texture. Leaves are oblong, oblanceolate to lanceolate in outline and can reach 8 centimetres in length.

Flowers are produced in a loose panicle. Individual flowers are about 2.5 centimetres wide and composed of five deeply cleft white petals, which give the appearance of 10 petals. Each flower has 10 stamens and three pistils. The calyx is bladder-like and pale green to pink-tinted, with noticeable net-veins. Flowers are mostly nodding.

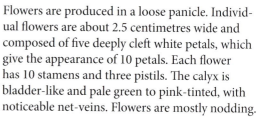

Night-flowering catchfly, *S. noctiflora*, another European introduction occasionally found in the province, is an annual covered in sticky glandular hairs. Lower leaves are oblanceolate but upper leaves are elliptical to lanceolate. White flowers are in small cymes. The calyx is more ellipsoid and not as inflated as that of bladder campion.

White campion, *S. latifolia*, is similar to *S. noctiflora* but its flowers are dioecious. Male flowers have 10 stamens; female flowers have five styles. All flowers are fragrant.

Top: The five petals of each bladder campion flower are so deeply cleft they appear to be 10 petals. Middle: Night-flowering catchfly's stems have fine glandular hairs. Bottom: White campion's flowers are similar to those of night-flowering catchfly but close examination reveals stamens or styles, not both.

Disturbed

126

Corn spurrey
Spergula arvensis
Stickwort, starwort

Introduced Species

HABITAT: Corn spurrey is a European species commonly found in newly disturbed sites throughout the province.

CHARACTERISTICS: Corn spurrey is a low bushy branching annual. Leaves, which are up to 5 centimetres long, are linear and in whorls and have a narrow channel at their base. Leaves and stems are smooth or, less commonly, stems have glandular hairs.

Flowers are produced in loose terminal cymes. Individual flowers, each about 0.3 centimetres wide, consist of five green sepals, five white petals, five or 10 stamens, and five pistils. Sepals and petals are about the same length. Flower stems are often purple-tinted and covered in glandular hairs. Flower stems angle downward as the seed capsules develop.

VITAL STATISTICS
Maximum height: 40 centimetres
Flowering season: June to October

Top: Petals and sepals are the same length.
Bottom: The linear leaves are whorled.

Disturbed

Pink family / Caryophyllaceae
Grass-leaved starwort

Stellaria graminea
Grass-leaved stitchwort, common stitchwort

VITAL STATISTICS

Maximum height: 45 centimetres
Flowering season: May to October

HABITAT: Grass-leaved starwort is a European introduction and a weedy species in disturbed areas throughout Nova Scotia.

CHARACTERISTICS: Grass-leaved starwort is a delicate species which rambles through surrounding vegetation or forms mats on its own. Stems are square in cross-section. The plant is nearly hairless except for a few hairs located near the base of each leaf. Opposite leaves are sessile and lance to linear-shaped with pointed tips and smooth edges.

Flowers are produced in loose terminal cymes. Individual flowers are 0.5 to 1 centimetre in diameter; petals are slightly longer than the sepals. Each has 10 stamens and three styles.

Long-leaved starwort, *S. longifolia*, is a native species. Its lance to linear leaves are widest at the tip and narrow to the base. Flowers are in small loose clusters from the upper leaf axils. It is localized in damp meadows and along shores primarily in Hants County.

Native boreal starwort, *S. borealis*, and bog stitchwort, *S. alsine*, appear in seepages throughout Nova Scotia. The former has solitary flowers in the leaf axils; the latter, small clusters. On both species, petals are shorter than sepals.

Top: The five petals of each grass-leaved starwort flower are so deeply cleft they appear to be 10 petals. Middle: Grass-leaved starwort flowers are in loose cymes; narrow leaves have pointed tips. Bottom: Boreal starwort's solitary flowers have petals that are shorter than the sepals.

Common chickweed

Stellaria media

Chickweed, common starwort

Introduced Species

HABITAT: A European introduction, common chickweed is found in disturbed habitats throughout Nova Scotia. It can be a pest in agricultural regions.

CHARACTERISTICS: Common chickweed, an annual plant, has trailing stems which reach 50 centimetres in length, resulting in a clumping or matted habit. Leaves are opposite, round to elliptical in outline, and smooth-edged. Lower leaves have petioles; upper leaves are sessile. One or two rows of hairs grow along the stem; sometimes hairs also grow along leaf edges.

Flowers are produced in cymes, both terminal and from the upper leaf axils. Flower stems and sepals have short hairs. Individual flowers, each about 1 centimetre in diameter, have five white petals that are so deeply lobed that they appear to be 10 petals. These petals are shorter than the green sepals. Flowers generally have five stamens and always three styles, which separates common chickweed flowers from those of the similar genus *Cerastium*, which have five styles.

VITAL STATISTICS
Maximum height: 50 centimetres
Flowering season: April to November

Top: The flower stems have short hairs.
Middle: The deeply cleft petals are shorter than the sepals. Bottom: The ovate leaves are opposite and the stems have scattered long hairs.

Disturbed

129

Knotweed family / Polygonaceae

Eurasian black bindweed

Fallopia convolvulus

Black bindweed, climbing buckwheat, wild buckwheat

VITAL STATISTICS

Maximum height: 150 centimetres
Flowering season: June to October

HABITAT: Eurasian black bindweed is a European introduction often found in waste areas and, less commonly, on gravelly beaches throughout Nova Scotia.

CHARACTERISTICS: Eurasian black bindweed is a twining annual vine. Thin stems are light green or tinted red. Alternate leaves are widely spaced and long petioled. Leaves are heart- or arrowhead-shaped with smooth edges. Stems may be finely pubescent; leaves are hairless. The largest leaves are up to 7 centimetres long. The base of each leaf has a membranous sheath (ocrea), which is also hairless.

Tiny 0.3- to 0.5-centimetre-wide flowers are produced in thin 2- to 10-centimetre-long axillary spikes. Individual flowers have five petaloid sepals, which are white, less commonly tinted pink, with a green central stripe. Sepals are keeled when in fruit.

Fringed black bindweed, *F. cilinodis*, is perennial, native to Nova Scotia, and grows to 5 metres. The distinguishing feature is the ocrea, which has a ring of fringed hairs. Leaves have slightly hairy undersides. Axillary flowers are in open spiked panicles. Fringed black bindweed inhabits waste areas, rocky slopes, and clearings; it is more scattered than Eurasian black bindweed.

Climbing false buckweed, *F. scandens*, is an uncommon native species localized in wet streamside meadows. Sepals are strongly winged when in fruit.

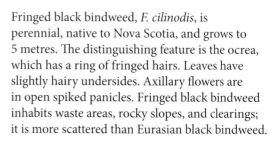

Top: The tiny flowers are in narrow racemes.
Middle: Eurasian black bindweed's twining stems produce arrowhead-shaped leaves. Bottom: Climbing false buckweed has winged sepals.

Buckwheat family / Polygonaceae

Japanese knotweed

Fallopia japonica (formerly *Polygonum cuspidatum* or *Reynoutria japonica*)

Mile-a-minute, September mist

HABITAT: Japanese knotweed, an invasive species found throughout Nova Scotia, occurs in disturbed areas such as roadsides, waste areas, and neglected gardens.

CHARACTERISTICS: Japanese knotweed is unmistakable simply because of its size. Spring foliage is red-tinted. Stout stems are hollow, smooth, and often mottled red. They are swollen at the joints where leaves or branches arise. Plants are multiple branching; overall, the plant is shrub-like. The alternately arranged leaves are round to triangular, hairless, and smooth-edged with a distinct narrow tip. They may reach up to 15 centimetres in diameter.

During late summer, flowers are produced in upright spray-like forking panicles among the upper leaf axils. Individual flowers are minute, each 0.2 to 0.3 centimetres wide, with five white tepals. Plants are dioecious with male and female parts. Male flowers are distinguished by their eight stamens.

Giant knotweed, *F. sachalinensis*, is less common than Japanese knotweed but also found throughout Nova Scotia. It is similar but overall larger, reaching to 4 metres in height. The plant is sparingly branched. Leaves are heart-shaped and up to 30 centimetres in length, with hairs along the main veins on the undersides. Panicles are bushier than those of Japanese knotweed. A hybrid between these two species, *F. X bohemica*, has intermediate characteristics.

VITAL STATISTICS
Maximum height: 2.5 metres
Flowering season: August to September

Top: Flowers are in axillary narrow panicles.
Middle: Plants have a shrub-like habit. Bottom: Giant knotweed has larger heart-shaped leaves and bushier panicles than Japanese knotweed.

Disturbed

131

Buckwheat family / Polygonaceae

Arrow-leaved smartweed

Native Species

Persicaria sagittata

Arrow-leaved tearthumb, arrow-leaved knotweed

VITAL STATISTICS
Maximum height: 150 centimetres
Flowering season: July to October

HABITAT: Arrow-leaved smartweed is found along shorelines and in rich alluvial thickets, bottomlands, shorelines, ditches, and wet meadows. It is common throughout Nova Scotia.

CHARACTERISTICS: Arrow-leaved smartweed is a weakly ascending multiple branching annual. Stems are square in cross-section and covered in downward-pointing stiff prickles that help it climb neighbouring plants. Alternate leaves, each 3 to 10 centimetres long, are mostly elliptical with two downward-pointing lobes at the base, which results in an arrowhead shape. Leaves are hairless with smooth edges. Lower leaves have a petiole; upper leaves clasp the stem.

Flowers are produced in long-stemmed globular racemes, both terminally and from the upper leaf axils. Individual flowers are 0.4 centimetres long, with five white or pink-tinted petaloid sepals, eight stamens, and three stigmas.

Halberd-leaved smartweed, *P. arifolia*, is rare and confined to central Nova Scotia. Appearing in similar habitats to arrow-leaved smartweed, halberd-leaved smartweed also has prickles on its stems. Two diverging lobes on its lower leaves impart a triangular outline. Leaves are smooth-edged and pubescent. Globular flower clusters have white or pink flowers with four sepals, six stamens, and two stigmas. Flower stems are glandular.

Top: Arrow-leaved smartweed flowers, in globular racemes, are often pink-tinted. Middle: Stems have backward-pointing prickles; leaves have a pair of downward-pointing basal lobes. Bottom: Each halberd-leaved smartweed leaf has two diverging lobes at its base, creating a triangular outline.

Sundew family / Droraceae

Round-leaved sundew

Drosera rotundifolia

Native Species

HABITAT: Round-leaved sundew, common throughout Nova Scotia, grows in damp to wet habitats.

CHARACTERISTICS: An insectivorous plant, round-leaved sundew produces a rosette of ground-hugging, round leaves which have long hairy petioles. Leaves are covered in red hairs with distinctive glandular tips; these glands exude a clear glutinous fluid that appears like dewdrops. Insects are attracted to, and become trapped by, the sticky fluid and are gradually digested by the plant, providing an essential source of nitrogen. Leaves partially enfold larger insect prey.

Flowers are produced on a one-sided raceme upon a wiry erect leafless stalk; each flower has five white petals and is about 0.5 to 0.8 centimetres in diameter.

Spoon-leaved sundew, *D. intermedia*, has spatulate leaves and hairless petioles. It is nearly as common as round-leaved sundew.

The endangered thread-leaved sundew, *D. filiformis*, has elongate narrow leaves and purple flowers. This Atlantic Coastal Plain species is restricted to Shelburne County.

Wetlands

Top: Flowers are on a leafless one-sided raceme.
Middle: Round leaves are covered in sticky red hairs.
Bottom: Spoon-leaved sundew has narrow leaves and hairless petioles.

133

Heath family / Ericaceae

One-flowered wintergreen

Moneses uniflora

One-flowered pyrola, one-flowered shinleaf

Native
Species

VITAL STATISTICS
Maximum height: 10 centimetres
Flowering season: Mid-June to July

HABITAT: One-flowered wintergreen inhabits mossy, shady forest floors throughout Nova Scotia.

CHARACTERISTICS: One-flowered wintergreen is a delicate forest-floor wildflower which forms small colonies or mats from underground rhizomes. Leaves, either paired or in a whorl of three, are located at ground level—thus appearing basal. The round to egg-shaped leaf is evergreen and veiny, with fine teeth along its edges.

Flowers are solitary and nod at the end of 5- to 10-centimetre-long leafless stems. Fragrant flowers are 1.5 to 2.5 centimetres in diameter with five waxy wavy-edged white petals, 10 stamens, and a relatively large five-lobed stigma. The flower is held parallel to the ground.

Top: The solitary flowers have a relatively large five-lobed stigma. Middle: Flowers are distinctly nodding. Bottom: Leaves are often in a whorl of three.

Heath family / Ericaceae

Indian pipe

Monotropa uniflora

Ghostflower, ghost pipe, corpse plant

Native Species

HABITAT: Indian pipe grows in mossy shady woodlands, especially coniferous woodlands, throughout Nova Scotia.

CHARACTERISTICS: Indian pipe is a non-photosynthetic plant that survives by parasitizing mushrooms from the genus *Russula*. The plant has no green leaves and appears more like a fungus than a plant. Indian pipe may live for years underground but, when conditions are optimal, several waxy hairless stems appear above ground. Although leafless, the plants do have white or translucent alternately arranged 1-centimetre-long fleshy flaps along the stems—their answer to leaves.

Flowers are solitary, nodding, and bell-shaped, measuring 1.5 to 2.5 centimetres in length. They have five fleshy white or pink-tinted petals. The flowers become erect once they set seed.

Pinesap, *Hypopitys monotropa* (formerly *Monotropa hypopitys*), is less common than Indian pipe in Nova Scotia. It, too, is a parasitic plant. It is similar to Indian pipe but flowers are smaller, up to 1 centimetre in diameter, and are in a nodding or upright raceme with two to 11 flowers. Flowers appear slightly different depending on whether they bloom in mid-summer or fall: Summer flowers are cream or yellow-tinted with a slight pubescence; fall flowers are tinted red-pink and densely pubescent.

VITAL STATISTICS
Maximum height: 30 centimetres
Flowering season: July to September

Top: Indian pipe has white or translucent stems and solitary nodding flowers. Bottom: Pinesap has yellow-tinted stems and produces clusters of flowers.

Heath family / Ericaceae

Shinleaf

Pyrola elliptica

Wax-flowered pyrola, white-flowered pyrola, wax-flowered wintergreen, waxflower

Native Species

VITAL STATISTICS
Maximum height: 25 centimetres
Flowering season: July to August

HABITAT: Shinleaf prefers open mixed woodlands but is occasionally seen along roadsides and in pastures, bogs, and fens. It is well distributed throughout the province.

CHARACTERISTICS: Shinleaf has a basal rosette of evergreen thin-textured and elliptical, oblong, or obovate leaves. Leaves, commonly 5 to 8 centimetres long, are dull green with a few shallow teeth along their edges. The leaf tip is rounded and the base tapers into the petiole, which is generally shorter than the length of the blade.

Flowers are produced in a cylindrical raceme on a leafless stem. Up to 15 nodding 1-centimetre-wide flowers are produced; each flower has five ovate waxy white petals and a curved style reminiscent of an elephant's trunk. Sepals are triangular in shape and about as long as they are wide.

The uncommon but widespread round-leaved pyrola, *P. americana*, occurs in both wetlands and woodlands. It has round leathery evergreen leaves which are fairly shiny. The 1.5-centimetre-diameter flowers are highly fragrant and milky white. The style is arched down and out like an elephant's trunk. The egg-shaped sepals are twice as long as they are wide.

Top: Shinleaf produces a cylindrical raceme of flowers on a leafless stem. Middle: Shinleaf's curved style is reminiscent of an elephant's trunk. Bottom: Round-leaved pyrola has a long raceme of flowers and leathery round leaves.

Bittersweet family / Celastraceae

Small-flowered grass-of-Parnassus

Native Species

Parnassia parviflora
Small northern grass-of-Parnassus

HABITAT: Small-flowered grass-of-Parnassus prefers wet calcareous soil. Rare, it is restricted to Cape Breton.

CHARACTERISTICS: Small-flowered grass-of-Parnassus produces a basal rosette of elliptical to egg-shaped hairless smooth-edged leaves.

Plants produce several flower stems, each topped with a solitary flower. A single sessile leaf is produced near or below the middle of the flower stem. Flowers, which are 1 to 1.5 centimetres in diameter, have five white petals with faint green veins; petals are slightly longer than the sepals. Flowers have five stamens, which alternate with the petals, and four stigmas. They also have five false stamens, called staminodia, which are green-yellow and shiny. In this species, each staminodia has five to seven glandular-tipped hairs.

VITAL STATISTICS
Maximum height: 30 centimetres
Flowering season: July

Wetlands

Barrens

Top: The solitary flowers have white petals with faint green veins. Bottom: Plants produce a basal rosette of leaves from which arise several solitary flowers.

Saxifrage family / Saxifragaceae

White mountain saxifrage

Saxifraga paniculata
Encrusted saxifrage, alpine saxifrage

Native Species

VITAL STATISTICS	
Maximum height:	15 centimetres
Flowering season:	June to July

HABITAT: White mountain saxifrage, a calciphile restricted to calcareous gravels, ledges, and cliffs, is found on northern Cape Breton Island as well as Cape Blomidon, Cape D'Or, and Cape Split.

CHARACTERISTICS: White mountain saxifrage is a tufted evergreen plant with basal rosettes of stiff leathery oblong to spatulate leaves. Leaves are silvery green with white lime-en-crusted finely toothed edges. Flower stems have alternately arranged leaves.

Flowers are produced in a small panicle. Individual flowers, each up to 1 centimetre wide, are white, often with fine red spotting. They have five petals, 10 stamens, and two pistils.

Barrens

Coastal

Top: Flowers are in small panicles. Bottom: Plants produce rosettes of silvery green leaves with lime-encrusted white edges.

Native Species

Heart-leaved foamflower
Tiarella cordifolia
Creeping foamflower, false mitrewort

HABITAT: Heart-leaved foamflower is found in lush, primarily deciduous, woods and intervales. Rare in the province, it is restricted to Hants, Kings, and Colchester counties.

CHARACTERISTICS: Heart-leaved foamflower has a tufted to mat-forming habit. Leaves are basal and also alternately arranged along the length of running stolons; leaves are heart- to egg-shaped, sparsely hairy on their upper surfaces, and pubescent on their undersides. Their petioles are densely pubescent. Leaves are palmately lobed and their edges have sharp teeth.

Plants produce several leafless 10- to 30-centimetre-high flower stalks. Flowers are produced in a cylindrical raceme which is up to 15 centimetres in length. Individual white or pale pink starlike flowers are tiny, just 0.25 to 0.5 centimetres wide. They have five petals and five petaloid sepals, which give the impression that the flowers have 10 petals. They also have 10 stamens and two styles.

VITAL STATISTICS	
Maximum height: 30 centimetres	
Flowering season:	

Deciduous Forest

Top: Flowers are in cylindrical racemes. Bottom: The heart-shaped leaves are palmately lobed and toothed along their margins.

Rose family / Rosaceae

Queen-of-the-meadow

Filipendula ulmaria
Meadowsweet

Maximum height: 150 centimetres
Flowering season: July to August

HABITAT: Queen-of-the-meadow, a European species introduced as a garden ornamental, has become naturalized along roadsides and thickets, albeit locally, throughout the province.

CHARACTERISTICS: Queen-of-the-meadow is a clumping plant with many non-branching stems that arise from a thick rhizome. Stems, often tinted purple or red, are stiff, erect, and furrowed. The basal and alternate stem leaves are pinnately compound with alternating large and small leaflets. The terminal leaflet is the largest and is often tri-lobed. Leaflets are sharply and coarsely toothed. The upper leaf surface is dark green; the lower is whitened with dense, soft pubescent hairs. Basal leaves have long petioles; upper stem leaves are short petioled but have a pair of kidney-shaped toothed stipules at their base.

The fragrant flowers are produced in irregularly branched cymes, creating a fluffy panicle of blooms. Individual flowers are about 0.5 centimetres wide with five creamy white petals and 20 or more stamens. Rarely, a double-flowered form is encountered.

Queen-of-the-prairie, *F. rubra*, is another occasional garden escape found in Yarmouth, Halifax, and Victoria counties. It may reach 2 metres in height with unbranched stems. Its large leaves resemble those of queen-of-the-meadow, except their undersides are green. Fluffy panicles of minute flowers are various shades of pink.

Top: Queen-of-the-meadow flowers are in fluffy irregular panicles. Bottom: Queen-of-the-prairie also produces fluffy panicles of bloom but in shades of pink.

Disturbed

Native Species

Rose family / Rosaceae

Wild strawberry

Fragaria virginiana
Common strawberry

HABITAT: Wild strawberry grows along roadsides and trailsides and in old meadows and pastures throughout Nova Scotia.

CHARACTERISTICS: Wild strawberry is a mat-forming plant that spreads by stolons. Leaves, often evergreen with a bluish tint, are basal and trifoliate with ovate sharply toothed leaflets. Leaf top surfaces are hairless; undersides may have silky hairs. The terminal tooth of the middle leaflet is shorter than the adjacent teeth.

Flowers are produced in clusters on leafless stems. Individual flowers have five white petals and are 1.5 to 2 centimetres wide. Flower stems are generally shorter than the leaf petioles. Seeds of the ovate fruit are embedded within pits on the fruit surface. The fruit is fleshy and sweet-tasting.

The less common woodland strawberry, *F. vesca*, is usually found in slightly shadier locations than wild strawberry, such as open woodlands, slopes, and ravines. It prefers, but is not restricted to, calcareous soils. Plants have long petioled leaves and the terminal tooth of the middle leaflet is longer than the adjacent teeth. The flower stem is longer than the leaf petioles. One to 1.5-centimetre-wide flowers are smaller than those of wild strawberry and are produced on a raceme. Seeds on the fruit are not embedded in a pit.

VITAL STATISTICS
Maximum height: 15 centimetres
Flowering season: May to June

Top: Flowers have five petals and a central cluster of stamens and styles. Middle: Seeds are embedded in pits on the ovate fruit's surface. Bottom: Woodland strawberry's long flower stems result in flowers being held above the leaves.

141

Rose family / Rosaceae

White avens

Geum canadense

Canada avens

Native Species

VITAL STATISTICS

Maximum height: 80 centimetres
Flowering season: July

HABITAT: White avens is found in rich woodlands, thickets, and intervales throughout Nova Scotia.

CHARACTERISTICS: White avens is a leafy plant with slender coarsely hairy stems. Plants have both basal leaves and alternately arranged stem leaves. Basal leaves, often evergreen over the winter, vary in shape from round with three to five shallow lobes to trifoliate or pinnately compound with five, rarely seven, leaflets, always with sharply toothed edges. Basal leaves may be smooth or have a few hairs, especially along the lower veins. Lower stem leaves are often trifoliate with short petioles; the upper are deeply tri-lobed and sessile. At the base of all stem leaves is a pair of stipules.

Flowers are solitary or in a loose cluster of up to three; each flower has five white petals and is 1 to 1.5 centimetres in diameter. Flower stems are finely pubescent. Seeds are produced in a spiky rounded head.

Less common than white avens, rough avens, *G. laciniatum*, prefers similar, but wetter, habitats; it is coarser and stouter, with rough hairy leaves. Basal leaves are commonly pinnate with five leaflets; stem leaves are trifoliate or tri-lobed. White petals are only half the length of the sepals; flower stems have long hairs. Seeds are produced in a spiky globular head.

Top: Flowers have five white petals and finely pubescent stems. Middle: Lower leaves are commonly trifoliate with sharply toothed edges. Bottom: Rough avens' small petals are shorter than the sepals.

 **Native Species**

Rose family / Rosaceae
Cloudberry
Rubus chamaemorus
Bakeapple, salmonberry, jonesberry

HABITAT: Cloudberry grows in acidic bogs and, less commonly, on rocky coastal headlands. Widespread in Nova Scotia, it occurs primarily near the coast.

CHARACTERISTICS: This plant is a low deciduous sub-shrub with unbranched stems arising from subterranean and semi-woody rhizomes. Non-flowering stems often have a solitary leaf; flowering stems may have two or three alternate leaves. The leaves—palmate with five lobes and sharply toothed edges—resemble a cloak in shape. Leathery and rugose, leaves are slightly glossy, often bronzy green (especially in exposed locations), and turn bronzy purple in autumn.

Plants are dioecious. Separate male and female plants bloom in June and early July. Solitary white flowers (2 to 4 centimetres in diameter) have four to seven petals and many stamens. The calyx tightly encloses developing fruit. On ripening (August and September), it curls back to reveal the solitary orange to amber raspberry-like fruit, which is edible and highly prized for jams and jellies.

VITAL STATISTICS
Maximum height: 25 centimetres
Flowering season: June to early July

Wettlands

Barrens

Top: Male flowers have a central cluster of many stamens. Middle: Leaves are cloak-like in shape. Bottom: Flowers develop into an orange raspberry-like fruit.

Rose family / Rosaceae

Dewberry

Rubus pubescens

Dwarf raspberry

Native Species

VITAL STATISTICS

Maximum height: 25 centimetres
Flowering season: June

HABITAT: Dewberry prefers damp forests but also grows on damp rocky slopes, at wetland edges, and along shorelines. It is well distributed throughout the province.

CHARACTERISTICS: A sub-shrub with short slender stems, dewberry can be either flowering or vegetative. It appears to be herbaceous, but look closer: the loosely upright flowering stems (10 to 25 centimetres long) are somewhat woody at the base. Trailing vegetative stems can grow to 100 centimetres or more in length; their tips often root to create new plants. Both stem types are softly hairy. The alternate thin leaves are trifoliate or palmately compound with double-toothed edges. Trifoliate leaves often have lower leaflets that are lobed as well as toothed.

Dewberry produces five-petalled flowers that are white or pale pink. The petals, held at right angles to the calyx, meet at the tips or can be recurved; flowers appear singly or in a loose cluster of two to five blossoms. They develop into small sweet-tasting translucent shiny red raspberry-like fruit.

Top: Petals often meet at the top of the flower; leaves are often bronzy when exposed to full sun. Middle: Leaves are either trifoliate or palmately compound. Bottom: Flowers develop into shiny raspberry-like fruit.

 **Native Species**

Dewdrop

Rubus repens (formerly *Dalibarda repens*)

Robin-run-away, false violet, star violet

HABITAT: Dewdrop, found in moist deciduous or mixed woodlands, is distributed mostly in the southern part of Nova Scotia.

CHARACTERISTICS: Dewdrop is a low tufted to creeping plant. Leaves are basal as well as alternate along the creeping rhizomes. Individual leaves, which are 3 to 5 centimetres wide, are round to heart-shaped with scalloped edges. Petioles are densely hairy; leaves are less hairy than the petioles.

Flowers are solitary and of two types. Typical flowers, which are 0.8 to 1.6 centimetres in diameter, are produced on thin hairy stems and held just above the leaves. Although they have five white petals and numerous stamens, they are sterile. Fertile flowers lack petals and are held on curving stems hidden beneath the leaves. Although now classified as a *Rubus*, this plant does not produce a fleshy raspberry-like fruit.

VITAL STATISTICS
Maximum height: 10 centimetres
Flowering season: August

Mixed Forest

Deciduous Forest

Top: Held above the leaves, sterile flowers have five petals and a central cluster of stamens. Bottom: Leaves are round with scalloped edges.

Rose family / Rosaceae

Three-toothed cinquefoil

Sibbaldiopsis tridentata (formerly *Potentilla tridentata*)

Native Species

VITAL STATISTICS

Maximum height: 25 centimetres
Flowering season: June to July

HABITAT: Three-toothed cinquefoil occurs primarily on exposed rocky barrens, mountains, and coastal headlands. Less commonly, it may be encountered in open coniferous woodlands, along roadsides, or on mature meadows and sand dunes. It is found throughout Nova Scotia but more frequently along the coast.

CHARACTERISTICS: Three-toothed cinquefoil is a tufted or mat-forming plant with leathery evergreen basal leaves and alternately arranged stem leaves along creeping stems. Each leaf is trifoliate with elliptical leaflets and a pair of stipules at the base of the petiole. Edges are smooth except for three terminal teeth. The upper surface is glossy and generally hairless, but the underside has fine hairs. Winter foliage is often tinted red.

Flowers are produced in loose clusters of up to 25 flowers. Individual flowers have five white petals, are 1 to 1.5 centimetres wide, and have 20 to 30 stamens, which form a central pincushion effect. Flower stems are pubescent and often tinted red.

Top: A central cluster of stamens create a pincushion effect. Middle: Plants produce loose clusters of flowers. Bottom: The trifoliate leaves have three terminal teeth.

Native Species

Sandalwood family / Santalaceae

Bastard toadflax

Comandra umbellata
Common comandra

HABITAT: Bastard toadflax prefers sandy calcareous soils on dunes and exposed headlands and in open coniferous forests. Rare in Nova Scotia, it is found primarily on Cape Breton Island and in neighbouring Antigonish County.

CHARACTERISTICS: Bastard toadflax is a smooth leafy plant with branched or unbranched stems. Hemiparasitic, it obtains nutrients from neighbouring plants. The alternately arranged leaves are elliptical to spatulate, thick-textured, hairless, and smooth-edged. They are pale green but sometimes tinted olive-brown. They are either sessile or have short petioles.

Flowers are produced in a terminal corymb. Individual flowers are about 0.6 centimetres wide and have five or, rarely, six white or pale pink pointed petaloid sepals which impart a starlike appearance. Plants commonly have non-flowering branches located immediately below the flower clusters.

VITAL STATISTICS
Maximum height: 30 centimetres
Flowering season: June to July

Barrens

Coastal

Top: Small starlike flowers are in a terminal corymb.
Bottom: The unbranched stems have pale green leaves.

147

Flax family / Linaceae

Fairy flax

Linum catharticum

Dwarf flax, white flax

Introduced
Species

VITAL STATISTICS

Maximum height: 25 centimetres
Flowering season: June to August

HABITAT: Fairy flax, a European plant, is occasionally seen in disturbed areas such as roadsides, trails, and gravel pits. It is predominately localized to limestone substrates on Cape Breton Island and in Antigonish County.

CHARACTERISTICS: Fairy flax is a delicate, slender annual or biennial. Late germinating plants overwinter as a small rosette. The opposite stem leaves, which are generally 1 to 2 centimetres long, are lanceolate to elliptical, smooth-edged, and sessile. The entire plant is hairless.

The long-stalked flowers are produced in open cymes. Flower buds are nodding, becoming erect when they open. Individual flowers are about 1 centimetre wide and have five white petals that are yellow at the base as well as five narrow pointed green sepals. Each petal has three to five parallel veins. Flowers also have five stamens and three styles. The seed capsule is rounded with distinct grooves.

Top: Long-stemmed flowers are in open cymes.
Bottom: Plants have thin wiry stems and opposite leaves.

 **Native Species**

Dwarf ginseng

Panax trifolius
Groundnut, fairy spuds

HABITAT: Dwarf ginseng is found in rich deciduous forests and intervales from Kings and Cumberland counties east to Guysborough County.

CHARACTERISTICS: Dwarf ginseng is a spring ephemeral that forms loose colonies. Plants produce tuberous roots and go dormant, disappearing by mid-summer. Plants send up a single stem that ends in a whorl of three to five long petioled, trifoliate, or palmately compound leaves. Each compound leaf has three to five lance-shaped to elliptical toothed leaflets, which are sessile and 2 to 4 centimetres in length. All parts of the plant are hairless.

Flower stems arise from the top of the whorl of leaves. Flowers are produced in a rounded umbel. Individual flowers are about 0.3 centimetres wide with five white petals. Flowers may be male or bisexual; the former has five stamens and a single non-functional pistil. Bisexual flowers have five stamens and three pistils. The sex of the plants can change from year to year. Flower stems are often white. Bisexual flowers develop berries that change colour from green to yellow. Berries are dry and contain three seeds.

VITAL STATISTICS
Maximum height: 20 centimetres
Flowering season: June

Deciduous Forest

Top: Flowers are held in a round umbel.
Bottom: Compound leaves (trifoliate shown) have toothed elliptical leaflets.

149

Parsley family / Apiaceae

Goutweed

Aegopodium podagraria
Bishop's goutweed, ground elder

Introduced
Species

VITAL STATISTICS

Maximum height: 100 centimetres
Flowering season: June to August

HABITAT: Goutweed, a European plant, is now a troublesome weed in many gardens, especially if the soil is moist and shaded. It grows in waste areas throughout the province.

CHARACTERISTICS: Goutweed, an aggressive groundcover plant, spreads rapidly by underground rhizomes. Most leaves are basal and solitary, arising directly from the rhizome. Leaves have long petioles, which are 30 centimetres or more in length. Each leaf is biternate; the short-stemmed leaflets are ovate and sharply toothed or lobed. Flowering stems have alternately arranged leaves. Lower stem leaves are similar to the basal leaves, but upper stem leaves are smaller and may be simply trifoliate. Stems and leaves are hairless.

The lower portion of flowering stems is generally unbranched, but the upper portion may branch to produce several leafless hemispherical compound umbels. Individual flowers, each about 0.3 centimetres wide, have five white petals, five stamens, and two pistils.

Occasionally, the variegated ornamental form is encountered as a garden escape.

Top: Flowers are in hemispherical umbels.
Bottom: Leaves are biternately compound with ovate toothed leaflets.

 **Introduced Species**

Parsley family / Apiaceae

Wild caraway

Carum carvi

Caraway, common caraway

HABITAT: A European introduction, wild caraway is found in waste places and neglected lawns and pastures throughout Nova Scotia.

CHARACTERISTICS: Wild caraway is a biennial plant. In the first season, plants produce a basal rosette of finely dissected bi- to tripinnately compound leaves. In the second season, plants produce multiple branches with alternately arranged carrot-like leaves. Stems and leaves are hairless.

Branches terminate in flat-topped compound umbels. Individual flowers, about 0.3 centimetres in diameter, have five white or pale pink petals, five stamens, and two pistils. The crescent-shaped ribbed caraway seeds are commonly used as a spice in cooking.

Burnet saxifrage, *Pimpinella saxifraga*, is less common in Nova Scotia than wild caraway and is most frequently found in Yarmouth County. This introduced perennial, which reaches to 60 centimetres in height, has coarse basal leaves that are pinnately compound with sessile oblong to obovate toothed leaflets. The upper stem leaves are smaller than those of wild caraway, with narrow leaflets which may have deep narrow lobes. The compound umbels of flowers are like those of wild caraway but they do not bloom until August to September.

VITAL STATISTICS
Maximum height: 60 centimetres
Flowering season: June

Top: Wild caraway flowers are held in flat-topped compound umbels. Middle: The finely dissected leaves of wild caraway are similar to carrot leaves. Bottom: Burnet saxifrage has pinnate leaves with rounded toothed leaflets.

Disturbed

151

Carrot family / Apiaceae

Bulbous water-hemlock

Cicuta bulbifera

Native Species

VITAL STATISTICS

Maximum height: 100 centimetres
Flowering season: August

HABITAT: Bulbous water-hemlock grows in shallow water along streams, ponds, and cattail marshes throughout Nova Scotia, except in the southwest.

CHARACTERISTICS: Bulbous water-hemlock is a tall, slender member of wetland communities. Alternately arranged leaves are finely dissected. Lower leaves have long petioles and are bipinnately compound; linear leaflets are narrowly lobed and/ or sharply toothed. Upper leaves are short petioled to sessile and pinnately compound. The plant is hairless. Upper leaf axils produce bulblets in late summer.

Terminal flowers are in compound umbels, often consisting of eight flat umbellets of about 16 tiny flowers. Each 0.3-centimetre-diameter blossom has five white petals, five stamens, and two styles.

Widely distributed and growing in similar habitats is the biennial spotted water-hemlock, *C. maculata.* It has basal leaves in the first year and flowering stems in the second. The stout stems often have purple mottling. Leaves are bipinnate with lance-shaped to elliptical leaflets. Their compound umbels each consist of 10 to 20 slightly domed umbellets. Both water-hemlocks are poisonous if ingested.

Another wetland plant found throughout Nova Scotia, common water-parsnip, *Sium suave,* has ribbed stems and pinnate leaves with seven to 17 lance-shaped to elliptical sharp-toothed leaflets. Their compound umbels consist of 10 to 25 umbellets. The base of each umbel has six to 10 narrow downward-curving bracts.

Top: Flowers are in compound umbels. Middle: The bipinnate leaflets of spotted water-hemlock are lance-olate to elliptical. Bottom: Common water-parsnip has pinnate leaves with elliptical leaflets.

Native
Species

Parsley family / Apiaceae

Hemlock-parsley

Conioselinum chinense

HABITAT: Hemlock-parsley inhabits cool wet coniferous forests, shady ravines, and wet peaty slopes. This plant is scattered in Nova Scotia and has a strong preference for coastal areas.

CHARACTERISTICS: Hemlock-parsley is a slender upright plant with basal and alternately arranged stem leaves that are finely dissected and carrot-like. Stems and leaves are hairless but hairs are usually present on the flower stems.

Flowers are terminal, in compound umbels. Individual flowers are 0.3 to 0.5 centimetres in diameter with five white notched petals, five stamens, and two pistils. The round but flattened seeds have two distinct wings.

VITAL STATISTICS

Maximum height: 100 centimetres
Flowering season: August to October

Wetlands

Coastal

Top: Flowers are in flattened compound umbels.
Bottom: The finely dissected leaves are similar to those of carrots.

153

Parsley family / Apiaceae

Queen Anne's lace

Daucus carota
Wild carrot

VITAL STATISTICS

Maximum height: 100 centimetres
Flowering season: July to September

HABITAT: Queen Anne's lace, a European species, is found in waste places throughout Nova Scotia.

CHARACTERISTICS: Queen Anne's lace is a biennial. In the first season, plants produce a basal rosette of bi- to tripinnately compound leaves whose toothed leaflets are narrow and threadlike; they resemble carrot leaves. In the second season, plants produce one to several upright stems with alternately arranged leaves. Stems, petioles, and the veins on leaf undersides are covered in soft hairs.

Flowers are produced in a terminal flat-topped compound umbel. The base of the primary umbel has a skirt of threadlike divided bracts. Individual flowers are 0.3 to 0.5 centimetres wide with five white, rarely pink, petals (two smaller and three larger). Umbellet stems arch inward as ovate bristly seeds develop, creating what looks like a bird's nest.

Wild chervil, *Anthriscus sylvestris*, is uncommon and localized. It blooms much earlier than Queen Anne's lace, from late May through June. Plants are biennial or short-lived perennials and hairless except for some pubescent hairs at the base of the strongly ribbed stems. Primary umbels have no leafy bracts; the bases of umbellets have a small ring of green bracts. Umbellet stems do not curl in on themselves as the narrow ribbed seeds develop.

Top: Flowers are in flat-topped compound umbels. Middle. Because Queen Anne's lace umbellets curl inward as seeds develop, the seed heads appear like a bird's nest. Bottom: Wild chervil resembles Queen Anne's lace but blooms in late spring-early summer.

Disturbed

Parsley family / Apiaceae

American cow parsnip

Heracleum maximum
Cow parsnip

Native
Species

HABITAT: American cow parsnip grows along streams and roadsides and in wet meadows and intervales throughout Nova Scotia. It is most likely encountered along the coast.

VITAL STATISTICS

Maximum height: 2.8 metres
Flowering season: June to August

CHARACTERISTICS: American cow parsnip forms a large clump. Stems are hairy, grooved, and hollow. Leaves are basal on non-flowering plants but alternately arranged along flowering stems. Leaves are trifoliate with palmately lobed, coarsely toothed leaflets. Leaves, often 60 centimetres long, are covered in short hairs, especially on the undersides. Stem leaves, enlarged at the base, sheathe the stem.

Several hemispherical umbels of flowers may reach 30 centimetres in diameter; each is composed of many umbellets. Each 1-centimetre-wide flower has five white petals, one or two of which are twice as large as the others and deeply cleft. Seed capsules are ovate to round and flat.

Common hogweed, *H. sphondylium*, a rare intro-duction, is distinguished by pinnately compound blunt-toothed lobed hairy leaves and confined to Hants and Lunenburg counties.

Giant hogweed, *H. mantegazzianum*, found in a few restricted locations on Cape Breton Island, grows to over 3 metres in height. Smooth stems have hairs at the leaf nodes; leaves are smooth, shiny, and toothed. Purple blotches and warts differentiate this species.

The sap of these three species can cause severe blis-tering on skin exposed to sun.

Top: American cow parsnip's large trifoliate leaves have palmately lobed leaflets; flowers are in large hemispher-ical umbels. Middle: Common hogweed leaves are pinnate with blunt-toothed and lobed leaflets.
Bottom: Giant hogweed has large flat-topped umbels, shiny deeply cut leaves, and stems with purple blotches.

Wetlands

Coastal

Disturbed

155

Parsley family / Apiaceae

Scotch lovage

Ligusticum scoticum
Beach lovage, sea lovage

Native Species

VITAL STATISTICS

Maximum height: 60 centimetres
Flowering season: July to August

HABITAT: Scotch lovage is scattered throughout Nova Scotia, growing along rocky or peaty headlands, saline marshes, and gravelly beaches.

CHARACTERISTICS: Scotch lovage is a clumping plant with many upright non-branching stems. Both the basal and alternately arranged stem leaves are biternate and celery-like, with ovate leaflets which grow to 5 centimetres in length. The leaflets are coarsely toothed, sometimes lobed, shiny, and fleshy. The stems and leaf petioles are often tinted red, especially at the base of the petiole. The entire plant is hairless.

Flowers are produced in terminal compound umbels and have five stamens and two pistils. Individual flowers, each 0.3 to 0.5 centimetres wide, have five white petals that curl inward at the tip, showing a green stripe on the underside. The seeds are ovate with strong ribs.

Seacoast angelica, *Angelica lucida*, reaches 150 centimetres in height and has dense umbels of greenish-white flowers. It has globose seeds with ribs and broader, more distinctly veined leaves than Scotch lovage. Leaves are often triternate. Although this plant is scattered in coastal areas throughout the province, it is not as common as Scotch lovage.

Top: Flowers are in flat-topped compound umbels and stems are often tinted red. Middle: The biternate leaves of Scotch lovage are smooth and celery-like. Bottom: Seacoast angelica has green-tinted flowers and veiny leaves.

Coastal

Native Species

Carrot family / Apiaceae

Hairy sweet cicely

Osmorhiza claytonii
Clayton's sweetroot

HABITAT: Hairy sweet cicely grows in semi-shady sites in moist rich deciduous or mixed woodlands throughout Nova Scotia. It is uncommon along the Atlantic coast.

CHARACTERISTICS: Hairy sweet cicely has slender stems and basal and alternately arranged stem leaves. Leaves are hairy and biternately compound with ovate toothed and lobed leaflets. The petioles have long hairs. Plants may reach 90 centimetres but generally grow 40 to 60 centimetres in height.

Compound umbels of flowers have four to seven umbellets; each umbellet base has a ring of narrow hairy-fringed bracts. Each 0.3- to 0.5-centimetre-wide flower has five notched petals, five white stamens, and two pistils. Bristly seed pods are narrow, up to 1 centimetre in length, and split in two when ripe.

Smooth sweet cicely, *O. longistylis*, is uncommon, found primarily in deciduous forests along the North Mountain and on Cape Breton Island. It may reach 120 centimetres in height, with generally smooth stems and petioles; leaf axils may have scattered hairs and leaves may be pubescent. The sweet anise fragrance produced by the foliage when bruised will help differentiate it from hairy sweet cicely.

Mountain sweet cicely, *O. berteroi*, resembles hairy sweet cicely in habitat and appearance. Mountain sweet cicely's flowers are more greenish-white, its umbels are wider-spreading, and its narrow seed capsules reach 2 centimetres in length. Plants may reach 100 centimetres in height.

VITAL STATISTICS
Maximum height: 90 centimetres
Flowering season: May to June

Top: Hairy sweet cicely stems are finely pubescent; umbels have four to seven umbellets. Middle: Smooth sweet cicely usually has smooth stems.
Bottom: Mountain sweet cicely has green-tinted flowers in wide-spreading umbels.

157

Nightshade family / Solancaeae

European black nightshade

Solanum nigrum

Deadly nightshade, black nightshade

Introduced Species

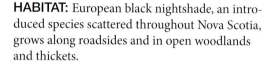

VITAL STATISTICS

Maximum height: 60 centimetres
Flowering season: June to September

HABITAT: European black nightshade, an introduced species scattered throughout Nova Scotia, grows along roadsides and in open woodlands and thickets.

CHARACTERISTICS: European black nightshade is a busy, coarse annual. Alternate dark green leaves are oval, up to 5 centimetres wide and 8 centimetres long, with irregular rounded teeth or smooth edges. Leaves are sparsely hairy; stems and petioles are more densely hairy.

Flowers are produced in axillary umbels of five to 10. Individual 1- to 1.5-centimetre-wide flowers have five recurved white pointed petals and five erect, conical yellow anthers surrounding the single style. Flowers develop into dull black berries, each 0.8 to 1.3 centimetres in diameter.

Eastern black nightshade, *S. ptycanthum*, is larger than European black nightshade, reaching to 100 centimetres in height with slightly larger leaves; it generally has two to four flowers per umbel. The shiny black fruit is 0.7 to 0.9 centimetres in diameter. This native species is occasionally encountered.

An introduced species, ground-cherry or hairy nightshade, *S. physalifolium*, is often considered a weed. This branching annual may reach 60 centimetres in height. Smooth-edged leaves are ovate to triangular. Leaves and stems are covered in soft, dense greyish hairs. White starlike flowers are in axillary umbels. Green to yellow berries are half-covered by the calyx.

Top: Individual European black nightshade flowers have five recurved white petals and conical anthers that surround a single style. Middle: Eastern black nightshade has glossy black fruit. Bottom: Ground-cherry fruit are partly covered by the large softly hairy calyx.

Hedge bindweed

Calystegia sepium (formerly *Convolvulus sepium*)
Wild morning-glory, larger bindweed

Introduced Species

HABITAT: Hedge bindweed has two forms in Nova Scotia: the European form grows primarily in waste areas; the native form grows along fresh- and saltwater marshes. Both are common throughout the province.

CHARACTERISTICS: Hedge bindweed is a twining plant that clambers over its neighbours. Plants many be hairless or finely pubescent. The smooth-edged leaves are alternate, 5 to 10 centimetres long, and arrowhead, triangular, heart-shaped, or egg-shaped, often with incised bases. Leaves have long petioles.

Solitary funnel-shaped flowers, each 6 to 7.5 centimetres in diameter, are produced from the upper leaf axils. Each flower has five shallow lobes—evidence of five fused petals—and a pair of green bracts. The introduced European form has white flowers; the native variation *americana* has pink flowers. Flowers open in the morning and close by late afternoon.

Field bindweed, *Convolvulus arvensis*, is a European introduction widely scattered and localized in disturbed areas. It is also a vine, but it more often grows along the ground, with stems reaching 100 centimetres in length. Leaves are similar to those of hedge bindweed but are smaller; flowers may also be white or pale pink but are less than 2.5 centimetres wide and lack the pair of green bracts present at the base of hedge bindweed flowers.

VITAL STATISTICS
Maximum height: 3 metres
Flowering season: July to September

Top: Hedge bindweed's unmistakable funnel-shaped white flowers. Middle: The native variety *americana* has pink-tinted flowers. Bottom: Field bindweed flowers are smaller than those of hedge bindweed and plants ramble along the ground.

Wetlands

Disturbed

159

Morning-glory family / Convolvulaceae

Swamp dodder

Cuscuta gronovii

Native Species

HABITAT: Swamp dodder is found in swamps, marshes, and wet thickets and along lakeshores throughout Nova Scotia.

CHARACTERISTICS: Swamp dodder is an annual parasitic vining plant that lacks leaves, although small scale-like bracts may be present. The tangled stems are smooth and gold, orange, or pink-tinted. The most frequent hosts include *Impatiens*, *Salix*, *Cephalanthus*, *Decodon*, and *Eupatorium*.

Flowers are produced in small dense panicles scattered along the upper stems. Individual flowers are 0.2 to 0.4 centimetres in diameter with five white triangular petals. Flowers, and especially the developing seed capsules, are covered in sticky glandular hairs.

Buttonbush dodder, *C. cephalanthi*, is a rare species found primarily in Pictou and Antigonish counties, where it occurs along low-lying coastal regions. It is distinguished by its flowers, which have four rather than five translucent white petals. It commonly parasitizes asters.

Wetlands

Top: Flowers are in small dense panicles.
Bottom: Dodder lacks leaves and forms a tangle of yellow or orange-tinted twining stems.

Bog buckbean

Menyanthes trifolata

Bogbean, buckbean

Native Species

HABITAT: Bog buckbean grows in the shallow water of various wetland habitats throughout Nova Scotia.

CHARACTERISTICS: Bog buckbean forms floating mats. Plants spread by a thick creeping rhizome located at or just below the water's surface. At the end of the rhizome arise a few long petioled trifoliate leaves whose bases sheathe the rhizome. Each leaf has three hairless ovate leaflets whose edges are smooth or have a few rounded teeth. Leaves are held 10 to 30 centimetres above the water's surface.

The cylindrical raceme of flowers arises to 30 centimetres on leafless stems. Individual flowers are intricate. From pink buds open 1.5-centimetre-diameter star-shaped flowers with five, rarely six or seven, white or pale pink petals. The upper surface of the petals is covered with long white hairs. The golden style in the centre is noticeable. Seeds are produced in globular capsules.

VITAL STATISTICS

Maximum height: 30 centimetres
Flowering season: June

Wetlands

Top: The long hairy blossoms of bog buckbean.
Bottom: Bog buckbean forms large colonies.

Buckbean family / Menyanthaceae
Little floatingheart
Nymphoides cordata
Floating hearts

Native
Species

VITAL STATISTICS

Maximum height: 2 metres
(water depth)
Flowering season: July to September

HABITAT: Little floatingheart is found along the shores of shallow mud-bottomed ponds and slow-moving streams. The species is well distributed across Nova Scotia; it is especially common in the southwest.

CHARACTERISTICS: Little floatingheart is an aquatic plant with long thin stems that arise from rhizomes growing in muddy-bottomed streams and ponds. A single floating leaf is produced on each stem. Leaves are heart-shaped, often purple-mottled, and 2 to 5 centimetres in length. They are smooth-edged and hairless and look like a smaller version of a water-lily leaf.

Flowers are produced in an umbel and held just above the water's surface. The flower stem arises where the leaf petiole joins the stem, usually a few centimetres below the water's surface. A cluster of fleshy spur-like roots often arise at this junction later in the season. Each 1-centimetre-diameter flower has five sepals, five petals, five stamens, and a single pistil. Sepals and petals are united at their base. Petals are white and hairy and have a yellow gland at their bases.

Top: The white petals have a yellow gland at their base.
Bottom: The small waterlily-like leaves are often mottled purple.

Wetlands

Aster family / Asteraceae

Common yarrow

Achillea millefolium
Milfoil, yarrow

Native Species Introduced Species

HABITAT: Common yarrow, both European and native forms, is found in disturbed habitats and, less often, in barrens and limestone barrens throughout Nova Scotia.

CHARACTERISTICS: Common yarrow is a mat-like or clumping plant with several non-branching stems and both basal and stem leaves. The alternately arranged narrow fern-like leaves are bipinnately compound with fine narrow leaflets which may be toothed or smooth-edged. Leaves are usually covered in fine white hairs. Basal leaves are larger with a petiole; upper stem leaves are smaller and sessile. The entire plant is aromatic when bruised.

Flowers are produced in dense flat-topped compound corymbs. Individual flower heads are about 0.5 centimetres wide and are composed of five white ray florets and 15 to 20 white disc florets. Each ray floret ends in three teeth. Less commonly, the ray and disc florets may be pink to rose-purple.

Woolly yarrow, *A. millefolium* var. *lanulosa*, is the native version of yarrow. Difficult to distinguish from the European form, it has more round-topped corymbs and densely white woolly stems and leaves.

Sneezeweed, *A. ptarmica*, a garden escape occasionally found along roadsides or trails near communities, has lance-shaped to linear leaves with finely toothed edges along non-branching upright stems. It is commonly hairless. Blooms are produced in a loose corymb; each flower head has eight to 12 white ray florets.

VITAL STATISTICS
Maximum height: 100 centimetres
Flowering season: July to September

Top: Flowers are in flat-topped clusters. Middle: Common yarrow foliage is finely dissected. Bottom: Sneezeweed flowers have eight to 12 ray florets in loose flat-topped corymbs.

Barrens

Disturbed

163

Aster family / Asteraceae

Hairy galinsoga

Galinsoga quadriradiata

Shaggy galinsoga, quicksilver, shaggy soldier, galinsoga cilié

Introduced
Species

HABITAT: Hairy galinsoga, a Mexican species, is scattered in the central counties of Nova Scotia.

CHARACTERISTICS: Hairy galinsoga is a loosely branched annual with sticky glandular hairs over almost the entire plant. The opposite oval to elliptical leaves are up to 7 centimetres long and have three distinct veins radiating from the base. Leaves are hairy and have coarsely serrated teeth. Lower leaves have petioles; the upper are often sessile.

Flowers are held on open few-flowered cymes among the upper leaf axils and at the ends of the upper branches. Individual flower heads, each about 0.6 to 0.8 centimetres wide, are usually composed of five small white three-toothed ray florets surrounding a cluster of yellow disc florets.

Top: Individual flowers have five small white petals with three terminal teeth. Bottom: Flowers are in open few-flowered cymes among the upper leaf axils.

Disturbed

Large false Solomon's-seal

Native Species

Maianthemum racemosum (formerly *Smilacina racemosa*)

False spikenard, false Solomon's-seal

HABITAT: Large false Solomon's-seal is found in rich deciduous or mixed forests throughout Nova Scotia, especially in the northern half of the province.

VITAL STATISTICS
Maximum height: 90 centimetres
Flowering season: June

CHARACTERISTICS: Large false Solomon's-seal has non-branching slightly zigzagging stems that often lean to one side. Parallel-veined, alternately arranged leaves are elliptical with smooth but undulating edges. Reaching up to 15 centimetres in length, leaves are usually sessile, although lower leaves may have a short petiole. The upper leaf surface is smooth; the lower, finely pubescent.

Flowers are produced in plume-like branching panicles which are up to 15 centimetres long. Individual flowers are only about 0.5 centimetres in diameter with six narrow white tepals, six stamens, and one style. Stamens are a little longer than tepals. Later in summer, flowers develop into smooth globular red-speckled berries that ripen to bright red. Berries are inedible.

Top: Flowers are held in plume-like panicles.
Bottom: The alternately arranged elliptical leaves have distinct parallel veins.

165

Asparagus family / Asparagaceae

Star-flowered false Solomon's-seal

Maianthemum stellatum (formerly *Smilacina stellata*)
Starry false Solomon's-seal, starry false lily-of-the-valley

VITAL STATISTICS

Maximum height: 40 centimetres
Flowering season: June to July

HABITAT: Star-flowered false Solomon's-seal is found along coastal headlands and swales, and, less commonly, in wet meadows and marshes. It is scattered primarily along the coast, especially in northern Cape Breton.

CHARACTERISTICS: Star-flowered false Solomon's-seal is a colonial species which spreads by thin underground rhizomes. The alternate leaves, which are up to 12 centimetres long, are elliptical and sessile and clasp the stem. The smooth-edged leaves have prominent parallel veins and finely pubescent undersides. The upper surface is dull and waxy. The unbranched stem slightly zigzags between the leaves and has a tendency to lean to one side.

Flowers are a terminal raceme with three to 20 flowers. Each flower is about 1 centimetre wide with six white tepals, six stamens, and a single three-parted style. They later develop into maroon-striped berries that turn bright red when ripe. Berries are inedible.

Top: Flowers are held in a few-flowered terminal raceme. Middle: The alternately arranged elliptical leaves clasp the stem. Bottom: In late summer, plants produce maroon-striped berries.

166

 **Native Species**

Asparagus family / Asparagaceae

Three-leaved false Solomon's-seal

Maianthemum trifolium (formerly *Smilacina trifolia*)
Three-leaved false lily-of-the-valley, three-leaved Solomon's plume

HABITAT: Three-leaved false Solomon's-seal is found in bogs and wet meadows across the province.

CHARACTERISTICS: Three-leaved false Solomon's-seal is a colonial plant which spreads by thin underground rhizomes. Leaves are elliptical and sessile and clasp the stem. Non-blooming plants often have just one or two leaves; flowering plants produce three alternate leaves. Leaves, which may reach 10 centimetres in length, are usually held erect. They are hairless and shiny with smooth edges and parallel veins.

Five to 15 flowers are produced on a terminal raceme. Individual flowers have six white tepals, six stamens, and a single three-parted style. Flowers are about 0.5 to 0.7 centimetres in diameter; they become green berries with fine red spots which fully ripen into bright red berries.

VITAL STATISTICS
Maximum height: 20 centimetres
Flowering season: June

Top: Flowers are in a few-flowered terminal raceme. Middle: Flowering plants typically produce three alternately arranged elliptical leaves. Bottom: In late summer, plants produce green berries, which later turn red.

Wetlands

167

Lily family / Liliaceae

Clasping-leaved twisted-stalk

Streptopus amplexifolius

White mandarin, clasping twisted-stalk, liverberry

Native Species

VITAL STATISTICS
Maximum height: 90 centimetres
Flowering season: Late May to July

HABITAT: Clasping-leaved twisted-stalk, relatively common in Nova Scotia, grows in damp woodlands and intervales.

CHARACTERISTICS: Clasping-leaved twisted-stalk has a stout stem with a few zigzagged stemmed branches. The elliptical to ovate leaves are alternate and sessile and clasp the stem. The 5- to 12-centimetre-long leaves have parallel veins and are hairless and smooth-edged; leaf undersides are often waxy grey-green.

One-centimetre-long flowers are solitary and hang from the upper leaf axils on thin kinked stems. Each flower has six white strongly reflexed tepals that have a few fine purple speckles at their base. Flowers become bright red elliptical juicy berries that taste like cucumber.

Top: Individual flowers have six tepals, which are variously spotted purple at their base. Middle: Plants produce a stout stem with a few zigzagging branches. Bottom: In late summer, flowers become elliptical red berries; note the kinked pedicle.

Native Species

Waterlily family / Nymphaceae
Fragrant water-lily

Nymphaea odorata
Fragrant white water-lily

HABITAT: Fragrant water-lily prefers still clear acidic water with a muddy bottom. It occurs around the margins of ponds or in wetland pools across Nova Scotia.

CHARACTERISTICS: Fragrant water-lily is an aquatic plant which produces floating leaves from a thick, horizontal rhizome. Leaf petioles can extend up to 3 metres to accommodate the water depth. The 10- to 30-centimetre-diameter leaves are smooth, leathery, and round, with a cleft from the middle on one side. The top surfaces of the leaves are deep green; their undersides are mottled purple.

Solitary floating flowers are produced at the ends of long stalks. Flowers are 8 to 15 centimetres in diameter with 20 to 30 pointed upward-curving white petals. The centre of the flower has multiple yellow stamens and a single large pistil. The fragrant flowers open in the morning and close by late afternoon. The globular seed capsule bends down under the water, where it matures and releases floating seeds.

VITAL STATISTICS
Maximum height: 3 metres
Flowering season: June to September

Wetlands

Top: Solitary floating flowers have multiple petals and a central cluster of yellow stamens. Bottom: The floating leaves are round with a cleft at one end.

169

Poppy family / Papaveraceae

Bloodroot

Sanguinaria canadensis
Pucoon-root

 **Native Species**

VITAL STATISTICS
Maximum height: 30 centimetres
Flowering season: May

HABITAT: Bloodroot grows in rich deciduous or mixed forests, especially in intervale areas. Although this plant is scattered from Hants County to Cape Breton, it is more common in Colchester County.

CHARACTERISTICS: Bloodroot is among the earliest of wildflowers to bloom in Nova Scotia. Plants form colonies with solitary basal leaves arising from a thick rhizome. The rhizome oozes red sap when broken, giving the plant its common name. The single leaf is round, hairless, and palmately lobed with five to seven rounded lobes. The divisions are also shallowly lobed or have a few rounded teeth. The base of the leaf is heart-shaped; its underside has raised veins and a waxy appearance. The leaf curls around the developing flower and unfurls after the bloom has opened.

The solitary flower arises on a leafless stalk to a height just above the level of the leaf, usually around 15 centimetres at blooming time, although the stem may elongate to 30 centimetres as seeds develop. The 2.5- to 3.5-centimetre-diameter flower is composed of eight to 12 elliptical to lance-shaped white tepals and a mass of golden yellow stamens. The flower lives only a few days and then develops into an elliptical to lance-shaped seed capsule.

Top: Solitary flowers with eight to 12 petals are held just above the leaves; note how the leaves curl around the flower. Bottom: The round leaves are palmately lobed.

 **Native Species**

Myrsine family / Myrsinaceae

Northern starflower

Trientalis borealis
Starflower

HABITAT: A common plant, northern starflower grows in woodland settings and on barrens and limestone barrens throughout Nova Scotia.

CHARACTERISTICS: Northern starflower forms loose colonies as plants spread by slender underground rhizomes. Each stem is solitary with a terminal whorl of five to nine (usually seven) lance-shaped hairless leaves. Leaf edges may be smooth or faintly toothed.

Just above where the leaves join together, plants produce a solitary star-shaped flower or an umbel of two or three flowers at the end of thin stems. Individual flowers are about 1 centimetre in diameter with five to nine (usually seven) petals and an equal number of stamens.

VITAL STATISTICS

Maximum height: 20 centimetres
Flowering season: May to July

Top: The starlike flowers typically have seven petals.
Bottom: Plants produce a whorl of lance-shaped leaves.

Aster family / Asteraceae

Pearly everlasting

Anaphalis margaritacea

VITAL STATISTICS

Maximum height: 80 centimetres
Flowering season: August to October

HABITAT: Pearly everlasting grows in disturbed habitats such as roadsides, forest clearings, meadows, open barrens, and open woodlands throughout Nova Scotia.

CHARACTERISTICS: Pearly everlasting forms bushy clumps of pale grey-green foliage. Stems are mostly non-branching and covered in dense soft white hairs. The lance-shaped to linear leaves are densely woolly on the undersides but less so on the upper surfaces. Leaves are alternate on the stem and lack petioles. They have smooth edges that are often rolled under.

Flowers are produced in flat-topped panicles. Individual flower heads are about 1 centimetre wide; they have no petals but the many white papery phyllaries are petal-like. The central disc florets are yellow.

Top: Flowers are in flat-topped panicles. Bottom: Plants form bushy clumps with narrow silvery green foliage.

Native Species

Aster family / Asteraceae

Flat-top white aster

Doellingeria umbellata (formerly *Aster umbellatus*)

Tall white aster

HABITAT: Flat-top white aster grows in damp habitats, including the edges of ponds and streams, ditches, swamps, marshes, meadows, and damp woodlands. It is common throughout the province.

CHARACTERISTICS: Flat-top white aster is a tall wildflower with many non-branching stout stems that are mostly smooth and often tinted purple. The elliptical to lance-shaped leaves are alternate along the stem and smooth or stiffly hairy, with distinct veins. Leaf edges are also smooth but fringed in fine hairs. Leaves are either sessile or have a short petiole.

Flowers are produced in a series of corymbs which, together, form a flat-topped panicle up to 30 centimetres in diameter. Individual flower heads are about 2 centimetres wide, consisting of five to 15 white ray florets and 12 to 35 yellow disc florets; the latter turn off-white after blooming. Flower stems and base are covered in fine grey-white hairs.

VITAL STATISTICS
Maximum height: 2 metres
Flowering season: August to September

Top: Daisy-like flowers are in flat-topped clusters.
Bottom: Stems are unbranched with alternately arranged narrow leaves and purple-tinted stems.

Aster family / Asteraceae

Hyssop-leaved fleabane

Erigeron hyssopifolius

Native Species

VITAL STATISTICS

Maximum height: 25 centimetres
Flowering season: June to July

HABITAT: Considered rare, hyssop-leaved fleabane, a calciphile restricted to limestone and gypsum cliffs, outcrops, and shores, is confined primarily to Hants County and northern Cape Breton.

CHARACTERISTICS: Hyssop-leaved fleabane forms a tufted plant with numerous thin non-branching stems. The linear to lance-shaped leaves are alternately arranged and crowded along the stems. They are smooth-edged and hairless or may have a few scattered hairs.

Flower heads are usually solitary and terminal. Individual heads are about 2 centimetres wide with 20 to 30 white ray florets, which often turn pink as they age, and numerous yellow disc florets.

Top: Plants produce solitary daisy-like flowers.
Bottom: Plants form tufted clumps with crowded narrow leaves on unbranched stems.

174

 **Native Species**

Rough fleabane

Erigeron strigosus

Whitetop fleabane, rough daisy fleabane

HABITAT: Rough fleabane is commonly found in disturbed areas throughout Nova Scotia.

CHARACTERISTICS: Rough fleabane is an annual or, less commonly, a biennial species. Plants produce several non-branching stems that arise to 100 centimetres and have scattered white hairs. The alternately arranged leaves are oblanceolate, oblong, or spatulate. They are minutely hairy and mostly smooth-edged, although larger basal leaves have a few coarse teeth along their outer edges.

Flowers are produced in a loose corymb. Individual daisy-like flowers are 1 to 2 centimetres wide with 40 to 100 white or pale lavender ray florets and numerous yellow disc florets. Flowers are mildly fragrant.

Annual or daisy fleabane, *E. annuus*, is found in similar habitats as rough fleabane but differs in having stouter, leafier stems and leaves which are more regularly coarsely toothed.

Horseweed, *Conyza (Erigeron) canadensis*, is another annual species which looks superficially similar to rough fleabane but has crowded linear leaves, conspicuously hairy stems, and smaller white flowers in many-branched terminal clusters. Its ray florets are very short, sometimes inconspicuous.

VITAL STATISTICS
Maximum height: 100 centimetres
Flowering season: July to September

Top: Rough fleabane produces a loose corymb of flowers; each flower head has numerous narrow petals. Middle: Annual fleabane has leafy stems with coarsely toothed leaves. Bottom: Horseweed's numerous small flower heads' ray florets are very short.

Disturbed

175

Aster family / Asteraceae

Oxeye daisy

Introduced Species

Leucanthemum vulgare (formerly *Chrysanthemum leucanthemum*)
Marguerite daisy, field daisy

VITAL STATISTICS

Maximum height: 80 centimetres
Flowering season: June to July

HABITAT: Oxeye daisy is a European species commonly found along roadsides and on pastures, meadows, and other disturbed areas across the province.

CHARACTERISTICS: Oxeye daisy is a clumping plant with numerous non-branching stems. Plants have both evergreen basal leaves and alternately arranged stem leaves. The oblanceolate basal leaves have distinct petioles and may reach 12 centimetres in length; they become smaller and oblong up the stem, where they are sessile or may even clasp the stem. They are coarsely toothed, fleshy, and generally hairless. The furrowed stem may have scattered hairs.

The 4- to 5-centimetre-diameter flower heads are solitary, with 15 to 35 white ray florets and numerous yellow disc florets.

Feverfew, *Tanacetum parthenium* (formerly *Chrysanthemum parthenium*), is a widespread European garden escape most commonly encountered in the central region of Nova Scotia. It is a short-lived bushy perennial with light green pinnate leaves whose leaflets are coarsely toothed and lobed. Plants reach 80 centimetres in height and have a loose leafy corymb of flowers. Individual flower heads are about 1 centimetre in diameter with many white ray florets and yellow disc florets. The plant has a rank smell when bruised.

Top: Oxeye daisy's unmistakable white flowers have many flat white ray florets surrounding a button of yellow disc florets. Middle: Oxeye daisy forms a clump of many unbranched stems; each stem is topped by a single flower. Bottom: Feverfew has pale green pinnate leaves; flowers are in loose corymbs.

 **Native Species**

White goldenrod

Solidago bicolor
Silverrod

HABITAT: White goldenrod occurs in disturbed areas such as roadsides, old fields, and recent burn sites, as well as in open woodlands and on open barrens and seaside cliffs. It is common throughout Nova Scotia.

VITAL STATISTICS
Maximum height: 100 centimetres
Flowering season: August and September

CHARACTERISTICS: White goldenrod plants produce solitary or a few generally non-branching erect stems ranging from 30 to 50 centimetres, exceptionally to 100 centimetres, in height. Stems and leaves are covered in soft hairs which impart a grey-green appearance. Plants produce both basal and stem leaves. Basal leaves are relatively large, thick, oblanceolate to spatulate, and pubescent with finely toothed edges. They gradually taper into elongate petioles. Stem leaves are elliptical, smooth-edged, and without petioles; they rapidly become smaller up the length of the stem.

Flowers are produced in a solitary or cluster of wand-like panicles which are 10 to 15 centimetres in length. Flower stems are covered in fine hairs. Individual flower heads are only 0.4 centimetres wide and have seven to nine white to cream ray florets and nine to 12 yellow disc florets.

Hairy goldenrod, *S. hispida*, is virtually identical to white goldenrod in form and habitat; it has yellow rather than white flowers. It is uncommon and localized within the province.

Top: Individual flowers have seven to nine narrow ray florets and nine to 12 disc florets. Middle: White goldenrod flowers are in narrow wand-like panicles. Bottom: Hairy goldenrod resembles white goldenrod but has yellow flowers.

Barrens

Coastal

Disturbed

177

Aster family / Asteraceae

Rush aster

Native Species

Symphyotrichum boreale (formerly *Aster borealis*)
Northern bog aster

VITAL STATISTICS

Maximum height: 100 centimetres
Flowering season: August to
September

HABITAT: Rush aster prefers the sandy and gravelly shorelines of lakes and rivers as well as calcareous bogs and swamps. It is an uncommon species scattered throughout the province.

CHARACTERISTICS: Rush aster is a slender plant with non-branching stems which are 40 to 60 centimetres, rarely to 100 centimetres, in length. The lance-shaped to linear leaves are hairless with smooth edges that are rolled under. They are alternately arranged and lack petioles.

Flowers are produced in a loose panicle or may be solitary. Individual flower heads are 1.5 to 2 centimetres in diameter and have 25 to 35 white ray florets and a similar number of disc florets which change from pale yellow to purple-brown as they age.

Tradescant's aster or shore aster, *S. tradescanti*, has a similar habit as rush aster, but is often more bushy and commonly 20 to 40 centimetres in height. It also grows along gravelly shorelines. Leaves are lance-shaped to elliptical with smooth or slightly toothed edges. Flowers are produced in narrow loose panicles but are rarely solitary; individual flower heads have 15 to 25 ray florets and a similar number of disc florets. This species is uncommon across the province; it is more likely to be seen in the southwest. It is an Atlantic Coastal Plain species.

Top: Rush aster often produces solitary flower heads. Middle: Rush aster is a slender plant with narrow hairless sessile leaves. Bottom: Tradescant's aster is often bushy with loose panicles of flower heads.

Native Species

Aster family / Asteraceae
Calico aster

Symphyotrichum lateriflorum (formerly *Aster lateriflorus*)
White woodland aster, one-sided aster

HABITAT: Calico aster, found along roadsides and in old fields, woodland borders, and barrens throughout Nova Scotia, is perhaps the most common aster in the province.

CHARACTERISTICS: Calico aster is a clumping plant with many slender multiple branching stems. The stems, and the veins on the undersides of the leaves, are hairy. Otherwise, the leaves are smooth with toothed edges. Leaf shape varies from lance-shaped to spatulate. Plants produce overwintering basal leaves which have shrivelled by the time the plants bloom. Stem leaves are alternately arranged and vary from 5 to 15 centimetres in length.

Flowers are produced in an open panicle of one-sided racemes. Individual flower heads are 1 to 1.5 centimetres in diameter and have eight to 15 white ray florets and a similar number of mauve to purple disc florets.

White panicled aster, *S. lanceolatum*, is encountered throughout the province but most often in the central region in damp woodlands, intervales, and thickets and along roadsides. Plants are stouter than calico aster and reach 150 centimetres in height. Lance-shaped leaves are 10 to 20 centimetres long, smooth, and with or without toothed edges. Flowers are produced in a leafy pyramidal panicle. Individual flower heads are 1.5 to 2 centimetres in diameter with 20 to 40 white ray florets and a similar number of yellow disc florets.

VITAL STATISTICS
Maximum height: 80 centimetres
Flowering season: July to October

Top: Individual calico aster flower heads have white ray florets and purple disc florets. Middle: The narrow smooth-edged leaves are alternate along the stem. Bottom: White panicled aster produces flower heads in leafy pyramidal panicles; its flower heads have white ray florets and yellow disc florets.

179

Aster family / Asteraceae
Scentless chamomile

Introduced Species

Tripleurospermum inodorum (formerly *Matricaria maritima*)
False chamomile, scentless mayweed

VITAL STATISTICS
Maximum height: 60 centimetres
Flowering season: June to September

HABITAT: Scentless chamomile, a European introduction which grows in disturbed areas, usually near the coast, is well distributed across Nova Scotia.

CHARACTERISTICS: Scentless chamomile is a bushy annual or biennial with wide-spreading upright branches and fine feathery leaves. The entire plant is essentially hairless and lacks any scent when bruised. The alternately arranged leaves are bipinnately dissected with linear lobes. They are not particularly fleshy.

Solitary flower heads are produced at the ends of the many branches. Each flower head is 3 to 4 centimetres in diameter with 10 to 25 white ray florets and numerous yellow disc florets. The flower head becomes conical as the flower ages.

Stinking chamomile, *Anthemis cotula*, a European species also found in waste places in the province, appears similar to scentless chamomile but this plant is rank-smelling when bruised. It often has fine hairs on its stems.

Top: Scentless chamomile produces solitary white daisies at the ends of its many branches. Middle: Scentless chamomile has finely dissected foliage. Bottom: Stinking chamomile also has solitary white daisies and finely dissected leaves.

Disturbed

Aster family / Asteraceae

Devil's beggarticks

Introduced Species

Bidens frondosa

Common beggarticks, leafy beggarticks, large-leaved beggarticks

HABITAT: Devil's beggarticks, a European introduction, inhabits damp waste places and is common throughout Nova Scotia.

CHARACTERISTICS: Devil's beggarticks is an erect annual with branched smooth stems, which are often tinted purple. Its opposite leaves are trifoliate or pinnately compound with five lance-shaped sharply toothed leaflets. Leaflets, each 5 to 10 centimetres long, have distinct stalks; the terminal leaflet is larger than the other leaflets. Leaves are smooth, with fine hairs on their undersides. Uppermost leaves are often simple and lance-shaped.

The long-stalked 1- to 2-centimetre-wide flower heads are solitary or in groups of three at the ends of the branches. Flowers, composed of many orange-yellow disc florets, generally lack ray florets. Below the flowers is a whorl of six to 10 unequal-sized green leafy bracts with hairy edges. Two barbed awns on the seeds allow them to stick to fur and clothing.

Tall beggarticks, *B. vulgata*, is less common than devil's beggarticks but it is found in similar habitats, generally confined to central Nova Scotia. These robust plants reach 150 centimetres in height; their stems and petioles are finely hairy. Leaflets from the trifoliate or pinnately compound leaves are almost sessile and flower heads lack ray florets. The base of the flower heads has a whorl of 11 to 20 green leafy bracts with hairy edges.

VITAL STATISTICS

Maximum height: 100 centimetres
Flowering season: Late July to September

Top: Below the petal-less flower heads of devil's beggarticks is a whorl of six to 10 irregular green bracts. Middle: Plants commonly have trifoliate leaves with sharply toothed leaflets. Bottom: The base of the rayless tall beggarticks flowers has a whorl of 11 or more hairy-edged green bracts.

Disturbed

181

Aster family / Asteraceae

Grass-leaved goldenrod

Euthamia graminifolia (formerly *Solidago graminifolia*)
Lance-leaved goldenrod, flat-topped goldentop

Native Species

VITAL STATISTICS

Maximum height: 150 centimetres
Flowering season: August to September

HABITAT: Grass-leaved goldenrod commonly grows in disturbed sites such as clearings, roadsides, ditches, and old meadows throughout Nova Scotia.

CHARACTERISTICS: Grass-leaved goldenrod is a clump-forming plant with upright, slender leafy stems. Stems are mostly non-branching except near the top, where they branch into many flowering corymbs; stems may be hairless but often have lines of fine hairs along their length. Leaves, which are up to 10 centimetres long, are alternately arranged and linear to lance-shaped with smooth edges. The upper surface is often smooth, while the underside has short fine hairs along the one to three main veins.

Numerous flowers are produced in many corymbs, which may be densely or loosely arranged or more open. Overall, flower clusters have a flat-topped appearance. Individual flowers are about 0.5 centimetres wide with 20 to 35 disc and ray florets. This species does not have recognizable "petals" as do other goldenrods.

Slender-leaved goldenrod, *E. caroliniana* (*Solidago galetorum/tenuifolium*), a plant of the Atlantic Coastal Plain flora, is found primarily in the southwest and southern parts of the province, where it prefers moist sandy, peaty, or gravelly shorelines. This slender plant has wiry, mostly non-branching, stems which reach 100 centimetres in height. Leaves are more linear than those of the grass-leaved goldenrod, with three to five veins, and are often curled. The plant blooms from August to September.

Top: Flowers are in a cluster of flat-topped corymbs. Middle: The linear to lance-shaped leaves of grass-leaved goldenrod have smooth edges. Bottom: Slender-leaved goldenrod has narrow leaves that are often curled.

Disturbed

182

 **Introduced Species**

Common tansy

Tanacetum vulgare
Golden buttons

HABITAT: Common tansy, a European introduction originally grown as an ornamental or medicinal plant in Nova Scotia, is occasionally seen along roadsides and in waste areas.

CHARACTERISTICS: A clumping plant, common tansy has many hairless leafy stems and a strong, rank odour when bruised. The hairless alternate leaves have an elliptical outline but are bipinnately divided and appear fern-like.

Flowers are produced in terminal flat-topped corymbs. Each flower head is 0.5 to 1 centimetre in diameter and contains many yellow disc florets but lacks ray florets; this gives the flowers a button-like appearance.

VITAL STATISTICS

Maximum height: 150 centimetres
Flowering season: July to August

Top: The petal-less flower heads look like yellow buttons. Bottom: The finely dissected bipinnate leaves are fern-like.

Disturbed

Downy yellow violet

Native
Species

Viola pubescens

Common yellow violet, smooth yellow violet

VITAL STATISTICS

Maximum height: 45 centimetres
Flowering season: April to May

HABITAT: Downy yellow violet occurs in cool, damp, mostly deciduous forests and shady rocky slopes. It is common in central Nova Scotia and on Cape Breton Island.

CHARACTERISTICS: Downy yellow violet forms a small clump with several thin, leafy, and softly hairy stems. Some leaves may be basal but most are alternate along the stems. The leaves, which are up to 7 centimetres long, are broadly cordate with toothed or scalloped edges. The leaf stalk is also softly hairy. The base of each leaf has a pair of ovate stipules. Emerging leaves have fine hairs but are less obviously hairy as they mature.

The 2-centimetre-diameter flowers are solitary and arise on thin stems from the upper leaf axils. They have five yellow petals with fine purple-brown lines at their bases, especially on the lowermost lip-like petals. The fruit is an egg-shaped capsule that, when mature, shoots seeds several feet from the parent plant.

Top: Flowers are solitary; the lowest petals have distinctive purple stripes at their bases. Bottom: Heart-shaped leaves have scalloped edges.

Meadow pea

Lathyrus pratensis
Meadow vetchling, yellow vetchling

Introduced Species

HABITAT: Meadow pea, a European species, is occasionally found along the edges of fields or roadsides, most frequently along the Northumberland shore.

CHARACTERISTICS: Meadow pea is a slender vine with multiple branches and ridged stems. The alternate leaves are compound with a pair of lance-shaped smooth-edged leaflets. The tip of the leaf has a single or a forked tendril; the base has a pair of arrow-shaped stipules. The entire plant is hairless.

Flowers are produced in axillary, usually one-sided, racemes with four to 10 yellow pea-like flowers measuring 1.5 to 2 centimetres in length. Seeds are produced in a 4-centimetre-long narrow pod.

VITAL STATISTICS

Maximum height: 80 centimetres
Flowering season: July

Top: Flowers are held on one-sided racemes.
Middle: Leaves terminate in a twining tendril.
Bottom: Each leaf has a single pair of narrow leaflets and a pair of narrow stipules at its base, giving the appearance of four leaflets.

Disturbed

Pea family / Fabaceae

Bird's-foot trefoil

Lotus corniculatus
Garden bird's-foot trefoil

VITAL STATISTICS

Maximum height: 60 centimetres
Flowering season: July to September

HABITAT: A European species, bird's-foot trefoil is now naturalized along roadsides and in waste areas throughout Nova Scotia.

CHARACTERISTICS: Bird's-foot trefoil, a clumping plant with many prostrate stems, often occurs in large colonies. Its stems may be smooth or hairy. The alternately arranged leaves are pinnately compound with three to five elliptical to oblong leaflets. The lowest pair of leaflets is basal, giving the appearance of stipules; the upper three leaflets resemble a trifoliate leaf. Leaflet edges are finely toothed and often fringed with hair.

Flowers are produced in a long-stemmed umbel among the upper leaf axils. Each umbel is composed of three to 15 yellow pea-like flowers. Flower buds, and sometimes the flowers themselves, have a red tint. Individual flowers are 0.8 to 1.5 centimetres long. The fruit is a small pea pod containing up to 25 brown-black seeds.

Top: The pea-like flowers are held in a rounded umbel.
Bottom: Plants appear clumped with trailing stems; its flowers are among the upper leaf axils.

Disturbed

 **Introduced Species**

Pea family / Fabaceae

Yellow clover

Trifolium aureum (formerly *T. agrarium*)
Yellow hop clover, large hop clover

HABITAT: Yellow clover, a European species, grows in disturbed habitats such as roadsides, waste places, and gardens throughout Nova Scotia.

CHARACTERISTICS: An annual or biennial, yellow clover forms a low mat-like growth with wide-spreading lateral branches. Stems may be smooth or have short flattened hairs. Alternately arranged leaves are trifoliate with ovate stemless leaflets. Leaflets have toothed edges except at their bases. Each leaf has a pair of stipules which are almost as long as its petiole.

Axillary flowers are produced in rounded head-like clusters, each about 2 centimetres wide, sitting atop 2- to 5-centimetre-long stems. Each flower cluster is composed of many small yellow pea-like flowers that change to cream and then to rusty brown as they set seed.

Low hop clover, *T. campestre*, a similar species found throughout the province, is generally shorter than yellow clover and is distinguished by its terminal stalked leaflet.

Small hop clover, *T. dubium*, is the smallest of the three yellow clovers, with three to 15 flowers per flower cluster. Its terminal leaflet has a short stalk. The upper petal is barely striated, whereas it is clearly striated on low hop clover.

Black medick, *Medicago lupulina*, is a province-wide yellow clover look-alike. It has small 1-centimetre-diameter flower heads, prostrate hairy stems, and trifoliate leaves with hairy undersides. The terminal leaflet is stalked. Its curled seed pods distinguish black medick from the yellow clovers, whose seed pods are straight.

VITAL STATISTICS
Maximum height: 45 centimetres
Flowering season: June to September

Top: Yellow clover flowers turn rusty brown as they age. Middle: The terminal leaflet of low hop clover has a distinct short petiole. Bottom: Black medick has tiny rounded heads of pea-like flowers.

Disturbed

Balsam family / Balsamaceae

Spotted jewelweed

Impatiens capensis

Orange jewelweed, spotted touch-me-not

VITAL STATISTICS

Maximum height: 120 centimetres
Flowering season: July to August

HABITAT: Common throughout Nova Scotia, spotted jewelweed prefers damp locations such as streamsides, wet thickets, and ditches.

CHARACTERISTICS: Spotted jewelweed is an upright annual with single stems and scattered branches. It often grows in self-seeding colonies. The entire plant is smooth, fleshy, and brittle. Stems are shiny and may be tinted red. The alternate leaves are ovate, thin-textured, and dull, pale green. Leaves have low broad teeth.

Flowers are produced among the upper leaf axils, usually solitary but sometimes in clusters of two or three. The conical flowers, located at the ends of thin drooping stems, are held horizontal. Flowers are about 2.5 centimetres long and orange with yellow and red markings and composed of three sepals and three petals. Two of the sepals are small; the third is modified to form a backward-projecting nectar spur with a curled tip. The uppermost petal and the lower two petals are larger than the two lateral petals, giving an upper and lower lipped appearance. Flowers produce an ovate seed capsule that explodes when ripe, shooting seeds several feet.

Pale jewelweed, *I. pallida*, is less common and found primarily on Cape Breton, neighbouring Antigonish and Guysborough counties, and around the Minas Basin. It is distinguished by its yellow flowers, which are finely spotted with red in the throat, its elliptical blue-tinted leaves, and its preference for alkaline substrates.

Top: The conical orange flowers are mostly solitary among the upper leaf axils. Middle: The flower's side-profile reveals the backward-pointing but curl-tipped nectar spur. Bottom: Pale jewelweed has yellow flowers.

 **Introduced Species**

Musk monkeyflower

Erythranthe moschata (formerly *Mimulus moschatus*)

Muskflower

HABITAT: A western North American species now naturalized in the province, musk monkeyflower occasionally grows in stream margins, damp ditches, and areas which have natural springs.

CHARACTERISTICS: A creeping plant, musk monkeyflower has weakly upright stems; its stems and leaves are covered in sticky hairs. Stems that extend along the ground often root at their nodes. The opposite leaves are ovate to oblong and may have smooth or toothed edges.

The funnel-shaped bright yellow flowers are solitary and produced on a thin pedicle from the upper leaf axils. Up to 2-centimetre-long flowers have two petals that form an upper lip and three petals that form a lower lip. The throat of the lower lip is finely veined in red and has two densely hairy lines. The flower may or may not have a musky scent.

VITAL STATISTICS

Maximum height: 30 centimetres
Flowering season: July to August

Wetlands

Top: The flower's throat has fine red spots and two hairy lines. Bottom: The solitary flowers are among the upper leaf axils.

189

Plantain family / Plantaginaceae

Golden hedge-hyssop

Gratiola aurea

Golden pert

Wetlands

VITAL STATISTICS

Maximum height: 40 centimetres
Flowering season: July to August

HABITAT: Golden hedge-hyssop grows along the sandy freshwater shorelines of southwestern Nova Scotia, sometimes partially submerged in water up to 15 centimetres deep. It is an Atlantic Coastal Plain species.

CHARACTERISTICS: Golden hedge-hyssop is a semi-aquatic low bushy plant with several upright mostly unbranched stems arising from fleshy rhizomes. Stems are square in cross-section. The opposite leaves, which are up to 3 centimetres long, vary from linear to ovate and are stem-clasping with smooth or slightly toothed edges. The entire plant is hairless, but leaves have glandular spots, which impart a slightly sticky feel. Plants produce purple-tinted stolons.

Flowers are solitary among the upper leaf axils. They are about 1.5 centimetres in diameter with five yellow petals, two of which are fused to form a cleft upper lip; the other three are partly fused and form a three-lobed lower lip. The inside base of the upper lip has a cluster of hairs.

Clammy hedge-hyssop, *G. neglecta*, is a rare annual, found in only a few muddy locations within Hants, Colchester, and Cumberland counties. Leaves are lanceolate, opposite, and sessile; leaves and stems are clammy and sticky. The solitary flowers are smaller than those of the golden hedge-hyssop. The upper lip may be a single lobe or two-lobed; the lower lip has three distinct lobes. The upper lobe has an interior yellow beard. Flowers are white with yellow bases and floral tubes.

Top: The flower's notched upper lip has hairs at its base.
Middle: Flowers are solitary among the upper leaf axils.
Bottom: Clammy hedge-hyssop's solitary flowers have four white yellow-throated petals.

Introduced Species

Plantago family / Plantaginaceae

Butter and eggs

Linaria vulgaris

Common toadflax, yellow toadflax

HABITAT: Butter and eggs, a European introduction, is common in disturbed habitats throughout Nova Scotia.

CHARACTERISTICS: A suckering plant, butter and eggs has non-branching upright stems and often forms extensive colonies. The entire plant is essentially hairless. Its smooth-edged leaves are numerous, linear, and a waxy pale green. Leaves are mostly alternate, although, due to denseness, some may appear opposite or whorled.

Flowers are produced in a dense raceme. The pale to deep yellow tubular flowers are about 2.5 centimetres long and composed of an upper and lower lip, both of which are two-lobed. The palette between the two lips is orange-yellow. The flowers look like snapdragon flowers. A narrow nectar spur extends behind each flower.

Dalmatian toadflax, *L. dalmatica*, another European introduction occasionally found in disturbed areas, is not as common as butter and eggs. Dalmatian toadflax is distinguished by its waxy blue-tinted ovate to oblong clasping leaves and large (to 4 centimetres wide) deep yellow flowers.

VITAL STATISTICS

Maximum height: 80 centimetres
Flowering season: July to August

Top: Butter and eggs' snapdragon-like flowers are in dense racemes. Middle: Some butter and eggs plants produce pale yellow flowers. Bottom: Dalmatian toadflax has ovate blue-tinted foliage and large flowers.

Disturbed

191

Broomrape family / Orobanchaceae
Little yellow rattle
Rhinanthis minor (formerly *R. crista-galli*)
Common yellow rattle, rattlebox, yellow rattle

Native Species

VITAL STATISTICS

Maximum height: 60 centimetres
Flowering season: June to July

HABITAT: Little yellow rattle occurs on old meadows, roadsides, barrens, and coastal headlands. It is well distributed throughout Nova Scotia.

CHARACTERISTICS: Little yellow rattle is a single-stemmed upright loosely branched annual. It is hemiparasitic, parasitizing nearby grasses. The plant is mostly hairless; its stems are often tinted or streaked with red or brown. The opposite, sessile leaves are dark green, often tinted bronze. They are lance-shaped with sharp bristle-tipped teeth and distinct veins.

Flowers are arranged in a leafy one-sided raceme. The inflated calyx is rounded with flat sides; initially green, it becomes brown and papery when mature. Each tubelike flower has five yellow petals: the upper two are fused, forming a hood; the lower three form a three-toothed lip. Seeds are produced inside a flattened capsule within the inflated calyx. When mature and dry, the plants "rattle," giving them their common name.

Top: Plants have a flattened inflated calyx behind the tubular flowers. Bottom: The opposite narrow leaves have sharp teeth, distinctive veins, and often a bronzy tint.

Bladderwort family / Utriculariaceae

Horned bladderwort

Utricularia cornuta
Common toadflax, yellow toadflax

Native
Species

HABITAT: Horned bladderwort is an aquatic species found in shallow muddy bogs and fen pools throughout Nova Scotia.

CHARACTERISTICS: An aquatic plant, horned bladderwort has fine threadlike leaves which are generally concealed by the muddy bottoms of the pools they inhabit. Leaf tips have minute bladders which trap and digest planktonic organisms.

The fragrant flowers are held just above the water's surface at the tips of wiry stems. These stems may reach 30 centimetres from the base of the plant to the water's surface. The bright yellow flowers are solitary or produced in a raceme of up to six flowers (two or three flowers are most common). Individual flowers are about 2 centimetres long and have an upper and lower lip, reminiscent of a snapdragon flower. The lower lip is relatively large and helmet-shaped; the upper lip is small and held more erect. A pointed spur extends below the flower.

Lesser bladderwort, *U. minor*, is an uncommon species found in similar habitats. It looks like horned bladderwort but its flowers are paler yellow and lack an obvious spur. Seven additional species of yellow-flowered bladderworts occur in the province. They are challenging to identify.

Wetlands

Top: Horned bladderwort flowers are reminiscent of a snapdragon's. Middle: Flowers are held atop leafless wiry stems. Bottom: Lesser bladderwort has pale yellow flowers and lacks the horned bladderwort's spur.

Orchid family / Orchidaceae
Yellow lady's-slipper

Cypripedium parviflorum
American yellow lady's-slipper, small yellow lady-slipper

VITAL STATISTICS

Maximum height: 60 centimetres
Flowering season: June to July

HABITAT: Yellow lady's-slipper grows on limestone wetlands, shorelines, thickets, and barrens throughout Atlantic Canada; it is less common in deciduous forests. It is threatened in Nova Scotia and, while scattered, it is found primarily in Hants and Kings counties and on Cape Breton.

CHARACTERISTICS: Yellow lady's-slipper forms a low clump with non-branching stems. The alternate leaves are ovate to lance-shaped with pointed tips and distinct parallel ribs. Up to six smooth-edged leaves are produced; each leaf is smaller than the one below it. Leaves are covered in fine hairs on the variety *pubescens* but nearly smooth on the variety *makasin*.

Flowers are usually solitary but rarely up to three are produced per stem. Sepals vary from yellow to green to mahogany and may be variously spotted purple-brown. Lateral petals, also variable in colour, are usually twisted. The lip is yellow and distinctly pouched or slipper-like. The variety *makasin* has a 2- to 3-centimetre-long lip and is sweetly fragrant; *pubescens* has a larger lip, is 2.5 to 5 centimetres in length, and is only slightly fragrant.

Top: The sepals and twisted lateral petals are commonly mahogany with a distinct yellow slipper-like lip. Middle: Plants form clumps with alternate ribbed leaves. Bottom: Sepals and lateral petals are sometimes greenish-yellow.

Yellow iris

Iris pseudacorus

Yellow flag iris, yellow flag

Native
Species

HABITAT: Yellow iris, a European species, was originally grown in Nova Scotia as a garden ornamental. It is now widely scattered and naturalized throughout the province in marshes, along streams and ponds, and in roadside ditches.

CHARACTERISTICS: Yellow iris is a clumping grass-like plant. Leaves are strap- or sword-like and all basal; central median ridges help differentiate yellow iris from other "wild" irises in the province. Leaves are hairless with smooth edges and their bases are often pink-tinted.

Flowers are produced on stout leafless stems. These stems may be single or have two to three branches, each producing one to three flowers. The bright yellow flowers are showy and about 8 centimetres wide. Flowers have three downward-arching, broad sepals (the falls) and three small, erect, narrow petals (the standards). Sepals and petals are bright yellow. The base of the falls has a brown ring as well as brown veins. The falls are 5 to 7.5 centimetres long; standards are 2 to 3 centimetres long. The thick cylindroid seed capsule is three-angled and 4 to 7 centimetres long, with a nipple-like beak at its terminus.

VITAL STATISTICS
Maximum height: 100 centimetres
Flowering season: Late June to July

Top: The three broad downward-arching sepals are the flower's most significant feature. Bottom: Plants produce sword-like foliage.

Disturbed

195

Poppy family / Papaveraceae

Greater celandine

Chelidonium majus

Swallowwort, rock poppy, celandine

VITAL STATISTICS

Maximum height: 100 centimetres
Flowering season: July to August

HABITAT: Greater celandine is a European plant originally introduced in Nova Scotia as a garden ornamental. It is now naturalized in disturbed areas, thickets, and roadsides near coastal communities, primarily in the southern half of the province.

CHARACTERISTICS: Greater celandine is an upright bushy plant with ribbed stems. Plants have basal leaves in winter and early spring, then alternate leaves on the flowering stems. Leaves, which are up to 20 centimetres long, are pinnately compound, with five to nine oval leaflets which are variously lobed with round-toothed edges. Although most leaves are hairless, they are often covered in a blue-green wax. Petioles and stems have long white hairs, especially near the base. When cut, the plant exudes orange-coloured sap.

The long-stemmed flowers are produced in axillary umbels of three to eight flowers. Individual flowers, each about 2 centimetres wide, have four yellow petals, numerous stamens, and a single stout green style. Black seeds are produced in slender cylindrical capsules that are 3 to 5 centimetres long.

Top: Individual flowers have four yellow petals, a cluster of stamens, and a single stout green style. Bottom: Leaves are pinnate with variously lobed and round-toothed oval leaflets.

Disturbed

196

Introduced Species

Bitter wintercress

Barbarea vulgaris

Common wintercress, yellow rocket, garden yellow rocket

HABITAT: Bitter wintercress is a European introduction commonly seen in disturbed habitats, including roadsides, waste areas, and cultivated grounds, throughout Nova Scotia.

CHARACTERISTICS: Bitter wintercress is a biennial plant. In the first season, plants produce a basal rosette of evergreen dark green leaves. These leaves are elliptical in outline and lyrate: deeply lobed with a large rounded lobe at the end and one to four pairs of small rounded lobes toward the base. Shiny hairless leaves may reach 15 centimetres in length. Leaf edges may be smooth, coarsely toothed, or wavy.

In its second season, bitter wintercress produces several upright leafy stems with alternately arranged leaves. Stems are ridged and often tinted purple. Stem leaves are similar to basal leaves, but smaller. The uppermost stem leaves may be simply rounded with coarse teeth.

Flowers are produced in multiple racemes, which are globular when they first bloom but elongate as the flowering season progresses. The 1-centimetre-wide flowers have four yellow petals and six stamens. Their seed capsules are narrow, upwardly curved, and up to 3 centimetres long.

VITAL STATISTICS

Maximum height: 60 centimetres
Flowering season: Late May to June

Top: Early blossoms are held in globular racemes. Middle: In their second season, plants produce multiple racemes on upright leafy stems. Bottom: First-season plants produce a low rosette of deeply lobed smooth leaves.

Disturbed

197

Mustard family / Brassicaceae

Black mustard

Brassica nigra

Introduced Species

VITAL STATISTICS

Maximum height: 2.5 metres
Flowering season: June to October

HABITAT: A European introduction, black mustard is found in disturbed habitats, usually near towns and farms, throughout Nova Scotia.

CHARACTERISTICS: Black mustard is a tall, slender to bushy annual. Its alternate leaves are covered in short bristly hairs; leaves are up to 20 centimetres long at the stem base but smaller toward the summit. Lower leaves are oblanceolate to spatulate, pinnately lobed with a large terminal lobe and smaller lateral lobes, and coarsely toothed. Upper leaves are lance-shaped to elliptical and coarsely toothed, with or without lobes. All leaves have slender petioles. Stems have a few stiff hairs at the base. Plants often wilt during the day but stiffen at night.

Flowers are produced in multiple narrow elongate racemes up to 60 centimetres long. Each 2-centimetre-wide flower has four yellow petals, four yellow-green sepals, six stamens (four long and two short), and a single pistil. The seed capsules are narrow, cylindrical, stiffly upright, and often overlapping.

Field mustard, *B. rapa*, and Chinese mustard, *B. juncea*, are also nearly hairless. Field mustard's upper stem leaves are clasping; its narrow wide-spreading seed capsules have an elongate beak-like tip. The upper leaves of Chinese mustard are short petioled or sessile.

The leaves of wild radish, *Raphanus raphanastrum*, are covered in stiff hairs; its branched stems are more sprawling than those of black mustard. Emerging flowers are pale yellow then turn dirty white with violet veins.

Top: Robust black mustard plants can produce multiple racemes. Middle: Field mustard has the yellow four-petalled flowers typical of all mustards. Bottom: Wild radish has pale yellow flowers and a sprawling habit.

 **Introduced Species**

Flixweed

Descurainia Sophia
Common tansy mustard, herb Sophia

HABITAT: A European species, flixweed is uncommon and widely dispersed in waste areas throughout Nova Scotia.

CHARACTERISTICS: Flixweed is a leafy branching annual. The alternate leaves are lance-shaped in outline but dissected with bipinnate lobes which have narrow divisions. Overall, they appear fern-like or similar to real tansy, *Tanacetum*; however, the foliage is not rank-smelling like tansy's. Under a magnifying glass, the hairs on stems and leaves are star-shaped; to the naked eye, hairs appear pubescent and greyish.

Flowers are produced in narrow racemes. Unlike the petals of most yellow "mustards," flixweed petals are narrow and held erect, not wide-spreading. Individual flowers are about 0.5 centimetres in diameter. The greenish-yellow petals are shorter than the green sepals and the exerted stamens and style. The narrow seed capsules are 2 to 3 centimetres long and upward-arching.

VITAL STATISTICS

Maximum height: 100 centimetres
Flowering season: June to August

Top: Unlike those of most mustards, flixweed's petals are held erect. Bottom: The narrow leaves are bipinnate, finely dissected, and fern-like.

Disturbed

199

Mustard family / Brassicaceae

Wormseed mustard

Erysimum cheiranthoides

Wormseed wallflower, treacle mustard, treacle wallflower

VITAL STATISTICS

Maximum height: 100 centimetres
Flowering season: June to September

HABITAT: Wormseed mustard is a European introduction common in waste areas throughout Nova Scotia.

CHARACTERISTICS: Wormseed mustard is an upright annual or biennial with a single leafy stem or a few branches in the upper portion of the plant. Overwintering plants produce an evergreen rosette. The elliptical to lance-shaped leaves have slight teeth and often wavy edges and are alternately arranged along the stem. Both stems and leaves are finely pubescent. The stem is rough-textured and longitudinally ridged.

Flowers are produced in narrow racemes. Individual flowers are 0.6 to 0.8 centimetres wide with four bright yellow petals, four green sepals, six stamens, and one central style. The seed capsules are 1 to 2 centimetres long, narrow, and cylindrical.

Top: Flowers, with four wide-spreading yellow petals, are typical of the mustards. Bottom: Plants have simple lance-shaped to elliptical leaves and flowers in terminal racemes.

Disturbed

Native Species

Mustard family / Brassicaceae

Marsh yellowcress

Rorippa palustris
Bog yellowcress

HABITAT: Marsh yellowcress grows along wet shorelines and in damp waste areas, particularly in the St. Margaret's Bay region.

CHARACTERISTICS: Marsh yellowcress is a tap-rooted upright annual or biennial. If germination occurs late in the season, plants overwinter as an evergreen rosette. Stems are furrowed and may appear zigzagged. The alternate leaves are up to 15 centimetres long, becoming smaller as they ascend the stem. Smooth or hairy leaves are lance-shaped to spatulate and usually pinnately lobed with rounded teeth. One or two pairs of moderately deep lobes may be found near the base of each leaf; elsewhere, lobes are shallow. Some of the lowermost leaves may be pinnatifid. Lower leaves have petioles; upper leaves are mostly sessile.

Upper stems terminate in several 10- to 20-centimetre-long racemes of flowers. Racemes are at first globular, but elongate as the flowering season progresses. Each 0.3-centimetre-wide flower consists of four yellow petals, four greenish-yellow sepals, six stamens, and a single stout style. Seed capsules are 0.5 to 1 centimetre long, elliptical, and often curved.

Creeping yellowcress, *R. sylvestris*, a European introduction, is a perennial with wide-spreading or ascending stems that may reach 50 centimetres in length. Hairless lanceolate pinnatifid leaves have seven to 11 lobes; the terminal lobe is the largest. Branch ends have a raceme of bright yellow flowers up to 0.8 centimetres wide.

Top: Marsh yellowcress has globular racemes of flowers early in the season. Middle: Creeping yellowcress racemes are not as globular as those of marsh yellowcress. Bottom: Creeping yellowcress is bushy with deeply lobed pinnatifid leaves.

Wetlands

Disturbed

201

Mustard family / Brassicaceae

Tall tumble mustard

Introduced Species

Sisymbrium altissimum

Tumble mustard, tall hedge mustard, tall rocket, tall mustard

HABITAT: Tall tumble mustard has been naturalized in disturbed areas throughout Nova Scotia, particularly in the Annapolis Valley.

CHARACTERISTICS: Tall tumble mustard is a tall, slender branched annual. The lower stem and lower petioles are densely hairy; hairs are scattered higher up the plant. Alternate lance-shaped leaves are deeply pinnately lobed to pinnatifid, with toothed edges. The lower leaves have broad lobes; the upper are linear and threadlike.

Flowers are produced on slender branching racemes. Individual 1-centimetre-wide flowers have four pale yellow petals, six stamens (four long and two short), and a two-lobed stigma. Cylindrical slender seed capsules, up to 10 centimetres long, are held outward from the main stem and often curve.

Common tumble mustard, *S. officinale*, reaches 60 centimetres in height and is more hairy than tall tumble mustard. Its lance-shaped pinnatifid leaves are toothed; the terminal lobe is large and triangular. Upper leaves are often simply lanceolate or elliptical. Flowers are about 0.5 centimetres wide; seed capsules are just 1 to 2 centimetres long and held erect, parallel to the main stem.

Common dog mustard, *Erucastrum gallicum*, is usually confined to railway yards. Its toothed lance-shaped leaves are pinnatifid with round-lobed divisions. Stems are pubescent. Flowers are pale yellow and about 1 centimetre in diameter. Seed capsules are 2.5 to 3.5 centimetres long and angle away from the main stem.

Top: Tall tumble mustard produces flowers in narrow branched racemes. Middle: Common tumble mustard has simple lanceolate leaves near its flowers. Bottom: Dog mustard has pale yellow flowers and pinnatifid leaves with round-lobed divisions.

Native Species

Orpine family / Crassulaceae

Roseroot

Rhodiola rosea
Goldenroot, king's crown

HABITAT: Roseroot is primarily restricted to exposed coastal cliffs of the province.

CHARACTERISTICS: Roseroot forms a clump of several upright stems arising from a thickened root. Plants often grow between cracks, where there is minimal soil. The alternately arranged hairless leaves are obovate to oblong, fleshy, and pale grey-green. Leaves are crowded on the stems and often spirally arranged; edges may be smooth or finely toothed.

Plants are dioecious. Both sexes produce a flat-topped corymb of flowers. Male flowers have four or five narrow yellow petals and an equal number of stamens. Female flowers lack petals and are simply composed of four or five pistils which vary from green to orange, often with a purple tint. Seeds are produced in green or purple-tinted starlike capsules.

VITAL STATISTICS

Maximum height: 40 centimetres
Flowering season: June to July

Top: Male flowers have four or five narrow petals with a similar number of stamens. Middle: The petal-less female flowers are often tinted orange or purple. Bottom: Roseroot often grows in narrow rock cracks.

Barrens

Coastal

203

Evening primrose family / Onagraceae
Common evening primrose

Oenothera biennis
King's cure-all, yellow evening primrose

Native Species

Coastal

Disturbed

VITAL STATISTICS

Maximum height: 150 centimetres
Flowering season: June to October

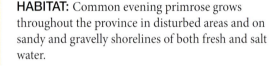

HABITAT: Common evening primrose grows throughout the province in disturbed areas and on sandy and gravelly shorelines of both fresh and salt water.

CHARACTERISTICS: Common evening primrose is a biennial. During the first season, plants form a flat rosette of leaves from a fleshy taproot. Each long tapered leaf is lance-shaped and up to 20 centimetres in length with finely hairy undersides and smooth or slightly toothed edges. Leaves are often tinted red, especially in winter. In the second year, plants produce a stout stem that may be unbranched or branched to become bush-like. The stem is green or tinted red and covered in white hairs. Densely arranged stem leaves are alternate and willow-like.

Flowers are in terminal leafy-bracted racemes. Each 2.5-centimetre-wide lightly fragrant flower has four shallow-notched lemon yellow petals, four backward-facing narrow green sepals, eight stamens and a distinct cross-shaped stigma. Flowers generally open in the evening and close by late morning.

Small-flowered evening primrose, *O. parviflora*, has non-branching, less upright stems, fleshier leaves, and slightly smaller narrow-petalled flowers than common evening primrose. Flowers are covered in sticky hairs when in bud. It is common along the Atlantic coast.

Perennial evening primrose, *O. perennis*, is widespread. Often less than 30 centimetres tall, it has several non-branching thin stems with small linear to lanceolate smooth-edged leaves and spikes of 1-centimetre-wide flowers.

Top: Common evening primrose flowers are held on leafy-bracted racemes. Middle: Small-flowered evening primrose's petals rarely overlap. Bottom: Perennial evening primrose has narrow leaves and a terminal spike of four-petalled flowers.

204

 **Native Species**

Buttercup family / Ranunculaceae

Marsh marigold

Caltha palustris
Yellow marsh marigold, kingcup

HABITAT: Marsh marigold grows in swamps, wet meadows, ditches, and wet woodlands. It is primarily confined to Inverness County with a few sites in Victoria and Pictou counties.

CHARACTERISTICS: Common marsh marigold forms a clump of several upright or partly sprawling stems. Stems are hollow and furrowed. Plants produce both basal and alternately arranged stem leaves. The long-stalked leaves are round, heart-, or kidney-shaped with a rounded tip and deeply cleft base. Leaves are glossy, fleshy, and hairless with smooth or finely toothed edges.

Flowers are produced in an open corymb. Individual flowers are composed of five (rarely to nine) rounded shiny yellow petal-like sepals. Three to 5 centimetres in diameter, the flowers have a dense cluster of stamens and pistils at their centres. Flowers are reminiscent of a large buttercup, to which marsh marigold is related. This plant is toxic if eaten raw.

VITAL STATISTICS

Maximum height: 60 centimetres
Flowering season: Late May to
early July

Wetlands

Top: The five-petalled flowers have a dense cluster of stamens and styles in their centre. Bottom: Plants form clumps with round leaves.

Buttercup family / Ranunculaceae

Kidney-leaved buttercup

Ranunculus abortivus
Small-flowered buttercup

Native Species

VITAL STATISTICS

Maximum height: 60 centimetres
Flowering season: May to June

HABITAT: Kidney-leaved buttercup is occasionally found in partly shaded rich deciduous or mixed forest hillsides and intervales throughout Nova Scotia.

CHARACTERISTICS: Kidney-leaved buttercup is a slender, forking biennial or short-lived perennial. Fleshy basal leaves are 4 to 9 centimetres wide, long petioled, and round to kidney-shaped with rounded teeth. Lower stem leaves are alternate and shorter petioled and are deeply divided into three rounded lobes. Upper stem leaves are sessile and lance-shaped to elliptical with smooth, rarely lobed or toothed, edges. Stems and leaves are hairless and slightly waxy.

Stems terminate into one to three flowers. Individual flowers, each about 0.6 centimetres wide, have five pale yellow triangular petals which are smaller than the five green sepals.

Hooked buttercup, *R. recurvatus*, grows in similar habitats and blooms at a similar time as kidney-leaved buttercup, but is less common. Its basal leaves have long hairy petioles and are tri-lobed or palmately cleft with five lobes, which are often divided again into smaller lobes and teeth. Main stems are softly hairy. Alternate stem leaves are smaller than the basal leaves, with shorter petioles and fewer, deeper lobes. Flowers are produced in a loose cyme. Individual flowers have five pale yellow petals, which are smaller than the green sepals. Seeds have a hooked beak.

All buttercups are toxic if ingested.

Top: Kidney-leaved buttercup leaves vary dramatically; the small pale yellow flowers have short triangular petals. Middle: Hooked buttercup leaves are often broad and tri-lobed; flowers have five tiny pointed petals.

 **Introduced Species**

Tall buttercup

Ranunculus acris
Common buttercup, meadow buttercup

HABITAT: Tall buttercup, a European species commonly found in pasturelands and gardens and along roadsides, especially in moist sites, is common throughout Nova Scotia.

CHARACTERISTICS: Tall buttercup is a clumping plant with upright branching stems. Plants have both basal and alternately arranged stem leaves. Basal leaves have long petioles; upper stem leaves are nearly sessile. Leaves are palmately lobed with five to seven divisions and coarsely toothed. Stems and leaves are covered in hairs and are a solid green; this colouring helps differentiate tall buttercup from creeping buttercup, which generally has pale mottling on its leaves.

Flowers are produced in a loose panicle. Individual flowers are 2.5 centimetres wide with five overlapping rounded petals. The centre of each flower has a globular mass of stamens and pistils; five small green sepals are covered in hairs.

All buttercups are toxic if ingested.

VITAL STATISTICS
Maximum height: 100 centimetres
Flowering season: June to August

Top: Flowers have five, often overlapping, petals.
Middle: Flowers are in loose panicles.
Bottom: Leaves are palmately lobed and green.

Disturbed

207

Buttercup family / Ranunculaceae

Lesser spearwort

Ranunculus flammula
Creeping spearwort

VITAL STATISTICS

Maximum height: 40 centimetres
Flowering season: July to September

HABITAT: Lesser spearwort is found along damp shores and in shallow water throughout Nova Scotia.

CHARACTERISTICS: Lesser spearwort is a creeping plant with stoloniferous stems that root as they grow over muddy surfaces. Elliptical basal leaves are up to 5 centimetres long with petioles that are up to 7 centimetres long. Leaves are fine-toothed or have smooth, undulate edges. Stem leaves are alternate, linear to lanceolate, toothless, and sessile or nearly so. Most plants are hairless.

Flower stems are erect or upward-arching and often purple-tinted, especially at their base. Flowers are produced in loose cymes with individual flowers that are about 1.5 centimetres wide with five yellow petals.

Ranunculus flammula var. *reptans* (formerly *R. reptans*) is more aquatic than lesser spearwort and prostrate, with linear grass-like foliage and solitary 0.5- to 1-centimetre-wide flowers in the leaf axils along the wiry stolons.

Seaside buttercup, *Halerpestes cymbalaria* (formerly *R. cymbalaria*), grows in saline marshes and muds. This species is tufted, with creeping stolons. The long petioled basal leaves are round to kidney-shaped, up to 3 centimetres wide, and fleshy, with rounded teeth. Flower stems are erect to 25 centimetres in height with a solitary flower or a loose cluster of 0.5- to 1-centimetre-wide five-petalled yellow flowers. The seed head is thimble-shaped rather than globose as typically found on *Ranunculus*.

All buttercups are toxic if ingested.

Top: Lesser spearwort has flowers in loose cymes. Middle: The variety *reptans* has solitary long-stemmed flowers. Bottom: Seaside buttercup appears tufted with round basal leaves and a few rounded teeth; flowers are often solitary.

Introduced Species

Creeping buttercup

Ranunculus repens
Creeping crowfoot

HABITAT: Creeping buttercup is a European introduction common in damp disturbed areas, lawns, and gardens throughout Nova Scotia. Considered invasive, this species has infiltrated wetlands and open woodlands.

CHARACTERISTICS: Creeping buttercup is a mat-forming plant with trailing hairy stems that root along their length. The long petioled leaves are basal but alternately arranged along any trailing stems. Leaves are up to 6 centimetres long, trifoliate, and dark green, often with pale mottling. The obovate to elliptical leaflets are deeply lobed and coarsely toothed and covered with stiff hairs, especially on their undersides. The lower pair of leaflets is often sessile; the middle leaflet has a distinct petiole.

Solitary or loose cymed flowers are produced from the axils of the leaves on the trailing stems. They are about 2 centimetres wide with five (rarely to nine) shiny rounded yellow petals that often overlap. The centre of each flower has a globular mass of stamens and pistils. The five small green sepals are covered in hairs.

All buttercups are toxic if ingested.

VITAL STATISTICS
Maximum height: 10 centimetres
Flowering season: May to September

Top: Flowers are held in loose cymes with petals that often overlap. Middle: Creeping buttercup can form large mats. Bottom: The trifoliate leaves have deeply lobed leaflets; lateral leaflets are nearly sessile and the terminal leaflet has a distinct stem.

Wetlands

Disturbed

Purslane family / Portulacaceae

Common purslane

Introduced Species

Portulaca oleracea

Purslane, little hogweed

VITAL STATISTICS

Maximum height: 50 centimetres
Flowering season: June to October

HABITAT: A European species, common purslane is becoming a weed in disturbed areas and gardens, primarily in central Nova Scotia.

CHARACTERISTICS: Common purslane is a low creeping many-branched annual with fleshy leaves and stems. Stems, which are often tinted red, radiate from a central taproot. The alternate or opposite leaves are up to 3 centimetres long, smooth-edged, and spatulate to oval with a short petiole. The entire plant is hairless.

Flowers are solitary at the ends of short branches. A whorl-like cluster of three to six leaves is at the base of each flower. Flowers are 0.5 to 0.8 centimetres wide with five yellow notched petals, six to 12 stamens, and three to six stigmas. Each flower lasts a single day and is open only for a few hours in the morning.

Top: The solitary flowers have five notched yellow petals. Bottom: The trailing stems have spoon-shaped fleshy leaves.

St. John's-wort family / Hypericaceae

Canada St. John's-wort

Hypericum canadense

Native Species

HABITAT: Canada St. John's-wort is found in damp to wet areas throughout Nova Scotia.

CHARACTERISTICS: Canada St. John's-wort is a slender upright annual plant with one to several smooth stems. The hairless opposite leaves are linear, stemless, and smooth-edged. Leaves have one to three main veins and taper toward their bases. Although plants can reach 70 centimetres in height, they are more commonly less than 20 centimetres high.

Flowers are produced in a few-flowered cyme. Individual flowers are about 0.5 centimetres wide with five yellow petals that are nearly the same length as the sepals. Flowers have fewer than 20 stamens each; their red seed capsules are pointed.

Dwarf St. John's-wort, *H. mutilum* (also known as *H. boreale*), is also found in wet areas. Its oblong to ovate-shaped leaves have five main veins and clasp the stem at its base, differentiating it from Canada St. John's-wort. Seed capsules are rounded at the tips.

Pale St. John's-wort, *H. ellipticum*, is present throughout the province, especially in the southwest. Unlike dwarf St. John's-wort, pale St. John's-wort has elliptical leaves and three to five flowers which have more than 20 stamens each. It is a perennial with creeping underground stolons.

VITAL STATISTICS

Maximum height: 70 centimetres
Flowering season: July to August

Top: Canada St. John's-wort has small narrow leaves and loose clusters of small flowers. Middle: Dwarf St. John's-wort has round leaves and more than five flowers per terminal cluster. Bottom: Pale St. John's-wort has terminal flowers in small clusters of only three to five flowers.

Wetlands

211

St. John's-wort family / Hypericaceae

Common St. John's-wort

Hypericum perforatum

Introduced Species

VITAL STATISTICS

Maximum height: 90 centimetres
Flowering season: July to August

HABITAT: Common St. John's-wort, a European introduction, is now widespread and common in disturbed habitats throughout Nova Scotia.

CHARACTERISTICS: Common St. John's-wort is an upright shrub-like plant with many branches. Plants form subterranean stolons that give rise to more plants, resulting in a colonial, invasive habit. The smooth stems are often red-tinted and the base of the plant is somewhat woody. The hairless opposite stemless leaves are elliptical to oblong with smooth edges. When the leaves are held up to the light, they show minute transparent dots.

Flowers are produced in flat-topped many-flowered cymes. Individual flowers are about 2.5 centimetres wide with five pointed yellow petals which occasionally have fine black dots along their edges. The flower has three pistils; numerous tufted stamens give the plant a starburst appearance. Developing seed capsules are red-brown and covered in fine sticky hairs.

Spotted St. John's-wort, *H. punctatum*, native to Nova Scotia, is often mistaken for common St. John's-wort. Its leaves have both transparent and fine black dots. The sepals are also black-spotted. Flowers have narrower petals and less tufted stamens and are paler yellow than common St. John's-wort.

Top: Individual common St. John's-wort flowers have five pointed petals and a starburst of central stamens. Middle: Flowers are in flat-topped cymes. Bottom: Spotted St. John's-wort has small petals and fewer stamens than common St. John's-wort; sepals have black dots.

Disturbed

 **Native Species**

Common silverweed

Potentilla anserina
Silverweed

HABITAT: Common silverweed is commonly found along gravelly and sandy shorelines around the entire coast of Nova Scotia. It is also found inland on disturbed areas such as roadsides.

CHARACTERISTICS: A rosetted plant, common silverweed forms dense mats and multiplies quickly through stolons that are often tinted red. All parts of the plant are densely covered in fine hairs. Ten- to 20-centimetre-long basal leaves are pinnately compound with up to 23 oblong sharply toothed leaflets. The lower leaflets are much smaller than those farther along the leaf. The top leaf surface is usually shiny, while the underside is silver-white with a dense coating of fine hairs. The variety *sericea* has silver hairs on both leaf surfaces.

Flowers, solitary at the ends of slender stems, are produced from the leaf axils of the stolons or basal rosettes. Individual flowers are 1.5 to 2.5 centimetres in diameter with five rounded yellow petals and a central cluster of many stamens and pistils.

VITAL STATISTICS

Maximum height: 20 centimetres
Flowering season: June to August

Top: Each flower has five rounded yellow petals and a central cluster of stamens and pistils. Middle: Pinnate leaves with sharply toothed leaflets. Bottom: Plants produce many red-stemmed stolons.

Coastal

Disturbed

213

Rose family / Rosaceae
Rough cinquefoil

Introduced Species

Potentilla norvegica
Norwegian cinquefoil

VITAL STATISTICS

Maximum height: 50 centimetres
Flowering season: July to August

HABITAT: Rough cinquefoil is scattered in disturbed habitats throughout Nova Scotia.

CHARACTERISTICS: Rough cinquefoil is an upright annual, biennial, or short-lived perennial. In the first season, plants produce a flat basal rosette of long petioled evergreen trifoliate leaves, similar to those of strawberries. Each leaflet is ovate, up to 5 centimetres long, and lightly hairy with coarsely toothed edges. The petiole is covered in long hairs. In subsequent seasons, plants produce upright hairy, often red-tinted, stems. The stem leaves are similar to basal leaves but are alternately arranged with shorter petioles. The uppermost leaves are often simple, not trifoliate.

Flowers are produced in open leafy cymes. Individual flowers are about 1.5 centimetres in diameter with five heart-shaped yellow petals which are a little shorter than the five green sepals. Below the sepals are five green bracts that give the flowers the appearance of having 10 sepals.

Downy cinquefoil, *P. intermedia*, is found occasionally in disturbed areas, primarily from Cumberland County east to Antigonish County. It resembles rough cinquefoil but has palmately divided leaves with five leaflets covered in fine grey hairs. Downy cinquefoil petals are more rounded than those of rough cinquefoil, and a little longer than the green sepals below them.

Top: Rough cinquefoil petals are shorter than the sepals. Middle: Rough cinquefoil has mostly trifoliate leaves; its flowers are in leafy cymes. Bottom: Downy cinquefoil has palmately compound leaves; petals are slightly longer than the sepals.

Rose family / Rosaceae

Sulphur cinquefoil

Potentilla recta
Sulphur five-fingers, rough-fruit cinquefoil

Introduced Species

HABITAT: Sulphur cinquefoil, a European introduction, is found on dry fields and other disturbed areas throughout Nova Scotia.

CHARACTERISTICS: An upright plant with non-branching stems, sulphur cinquefoil has long petioled basal leaves and alternate shorter petioled to sessile stem leaves. The palmately compound leaves have five to seven oblanceolate toothed leaflets, each up to 5 centimetres long. The base of each leaf has a pair of deeply cut stipules. Stems and leaves are covered in hairs. Leaflet undersides are paler than their upper surfaces.

Flowers are produced in a cyme. Individual flowers are up to 2.5 centimetres in diameter with five pale yellow, rarely deep yellow, slightly notched petals. The base of each petal is often a deeper yellow than the rest of the petal. At the centre of the flower is a mass of about 30 stamens and pistils. Petals are nearly twice as long as the hairy sepals below them.

VITAL STATISTICS

Maximum height: 60 centimetres
Flowering season: July

Top: Flowers are typically pale yellow with deeper yellow centres. Middle: Leaves are palmately compound with five or seven toothed leaflets. Bottom: Less commonly, flowers may be deep yellow.

Disturbed

Rose family / Rosaceae

Old field cinquefoil

Potentilla simplex
Common cinquefoil

Introduced Species

VITAL STATISTICS

Maximum height: 20 centimetres
Flowering season: June to July

HABITAT: Old field cinquefoil, a European introduction, is found on old meadows, barrens, and roadsides throughout Nova Scotia.

CHARACTERISTICS: Old field cinquefoil is a low spreading plant with trailing, often red-tinted stems and stolons. The leaves, up to 7.5 centimetres long, are alternate and palmately compound with five ovate to elliptical leaflets. The outer three-quarters of the leaflet edge is toothed; the lower quarter, smooth. Young leaves often have upwardly curled edges. The upper leaf surfaces are smooth; stems and undersides may have hairs. Lower leaves have long petioles; the upper are nearly sessile.

The long-stemmed flowers are solitary in the upper leaf axils; they are about 2 centimetres wide with five rounded yellow petals. The five green sepals are shorter than the petals.

Silvery cinquefoil, *P. argentea*, another trailing cinquefoil occasionally found in disturbed areas, has palmately compound leaves with five narrow leaflets. Leaf undersides are white and hairy; upper surfaces have scattered hairs and are deep green. Leaves have a few sharp teeth at their tips. The 1- to 1.5-centimetre-wide flowers, in open cymes, have five yellow petals and five near-equal-length green sepals. Lower leaves are long petioled; the upper, nearly sessile.

English cinquefoil, *P. anglica*, is a trailing plant with trifoliate or palmately compound leaves with five leaflets. Leaflets may have scattered hairs. The axillary solitary long-stalked flowers usually have four rather than five petals.

Top: Old field cinquefoil has palmately compound leaves and solitary flowers. Middle: Silvery cinquefoil's palmately compound dark green leaves have narrow, deeply toothed leaflets. Bottom: English cinquefoil has solitary flowers, each with four petals.

Myrsine family / Myrsinaceae

 **Native Species** # Swamp yellow loosestrife

Lysimachia terrestris

Bog loosestrife, swamp loosestrife, bog candles

HABITAT: Swamp yellow loosestrife is common in wet habitats such as ditches, wet thickets, marshes, and stream and lake shorelines throughout Nova Scotia.

CHARACTERISTICS: Swamp yellow loosestrife produces slender upright sparsely branching smooth stems that arise from a creeping stoloniferous root. Opposite lance-shaped leaves reach 10 centimetres in length; they are hairless and smooth-edged, often with minute dots. Leaves taper to the base but have no petiole. Late in the season, reddish bulblets, resembling caterpillars, can form in the leaf axils. These drop to produce new plants.

Starlike flowers, produced in long narrow terminal spike-like racemes, are 1.5 to 2 centimetres wide; the five yellow petals have red dots at their bases and fine red veins in their centres.

Tufted yellow loosestrife, *L. thyrsiflora*, is generally restricted to wet habitats in central Nova Scotia and Cape Breton. It has non-branching smooth stems and narrow lance-shaped to elliptical smooth-edged leaves. Leaves, nearly hairless, increase in size up the stem. Dense 2.5- to 4-centimetre-long racemes are produced from the leaf axils of the middle stem leaves. Flowers are about 0.8 centimetres wide with narrow yellow petals.

Fringed yellow loosestrife, *L. ciliata*, is scattered but locally common. Smooth-edged elliptical to egg-shaped leaves have finely hairy petioles. The 1.5- to 3-centimetre-wide yellow flowers are solitary or in loose clusters among the upper leaf axils. It is not restricted to wet soils.

Top: Swamp yellow loosestrife has terminal racemes of starlike flowers. Middle: Tufted yellow loosestrife has axillary flowers in dense conical racemes. Bottom: Fringed yellow loosestrife has fewer but larger flowers than other native loosestrifes.

Maximum height: 80 centimetres
Flowering season: July

Wetlands

Saxifrage family / Saxifragaceae

Yellow mountain saxifrage

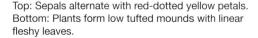

Saxifraga aizoides

Golden saxifrage

VITAL STATISTICS

Maximum height: 10 centimetres
Flowering season: June to September

HABITAT: Yellow mountain saxifrage, a very rare calciphile in Nova Scotia, is confined to the wet limestone cliffs of northern Inverness County.

CHARACTERISTICS: Yellow mountain saxifrage is a tufted or mat-forming evergreen plant with alternate fleshy linear hairless leaves, which are generally 1 to 2 centimetres long. The tip of each leaf is white with lime encrustation.

Flowers are produced in small loose racemes at stem ends. Each flower is about 1 centimetre in diameter and composed of five golden yellow petals often dotted orange or red, five green sepals that alternate with the petals, 10 stamens, and two styles. The sepals are about half the size of the petals. The seed capsule is globular with two beaks.

Top: Sepals alternate with red-dotted yellow petals.
Bottom: Plants form low tufted mounds with linear fleshy leaves.

Barrens

Native
Species

Rose family / Rosaceae

Woodland agrimony

Agrimonia striata

Grooved agrimony, roadside agrimony

HABITAT: Woodland agrimony usually grows along the borders of woodlands and thickets and, less commonly, in disturbed areas. It is found throughout most of Nova Scotia except along the Atlantic coast, where it is rare.

CHARACTERISTICS: Woodland agrimony is a clumping plant with multiple arching leafy stems. The alternately arranged leaves are pinnately compound with five to nine large coarsely toothed veiny lance-shaped leaflets. Smaller leaflets are scattered between the larger leaflets. Uppermost leaves are often trifoliate. A pair of small deeply cleft leafy stipules are at the base of each leaf. Leaf undersides are finely hairy and slightly sticky, and stems are covered in hairs.

Flowers are produced in terminal and axillary narrow wand-like racemes. The main flower stem is covered in fine glandular hairs. Individual flowers are about 0.6 centimetres wide with five, rarely six, ovate yellow petals. Below the sepals is a flange of ascending hooked bristles. The minute fruit are bell-shaped and burr-like, which enables them to stick to fur and clothing.

Hooked or common agrimony, *A. gryposepala*, is uncommon throughout the province. It resembles woodland agrimony but its leaves have a thinner texture and are less veiny. Hairs on the undersides of leaves are restricted to the veins. Stems have scattered hairs and the flower stem has scattered long, but non-glandular, hairs. The flange of hooked bristles are wide-spreading rather than ascending.

VITAL STATISTICS

Maximum height: 150 centimetres
Flowering season: July to August

Top: Flowers are in narrow wand-like racemes; the hooked bristles at their base point upward. Middle: The pinnate leaves have large leaflets interspersed with the smaller. Bottom: The bases of hooked agrimony flowers have wide-spreading hooked bristles.

Rose family / Rosaceae

Large-leaved avens

Native Species

Geum macrophyllum

Big-leaved avens

VITAL STATISTICS

Maximum height: 50 centimetres
Flowering season: June

HABITAT: Large-leaved avens grows in damp sites such as streamsides, wet thickets, swamps, and damp meadows. Found throughout Nova Scotia, it is rare along the Atlantic coast.

CHARACTERISTICS: Large-leaved avens is a leafy clumping plant with short thick rhizomes. Basal leaves have long petioles; alternate stem leaves are nearly sessile. The basal leaves, up to 30 centimetres in length, are pinnately compound with five to nine toothed leaflets. The rounded terminal leaflet is much larger than the ovate to elliptical lateral leaflets. Upper stem leaves are often tri-lobed and pointy with leafy stipules at their bases. All parts of the plant are hairy.

Flowers, produced in loose cymes, are 1 to 1.5 centimetres in diameter with five widely spaced rounded yellow petals and five broadly triangular sepals. Spiky seed heads are slightly sticky.

Yellow avens, *G. aleppicum*, grows in damp habitats, particularly in the central regions and Cape Breton. It may reach 100 centimetres in height. Its large terminal leaflet is wedge-shaped and often deeply tri-lobed; flowers are 1.5 to 2 centimetres in diameter; spiky seed heads are not sticky.

Eastern mountain avens, *G. peckii*, is rare on the sphagnum hummocks of Brier Island. Glossy leaves have a large rounded terminal leaflet and two pairs of small lateral leaflets. One to five 1.5- to 3-centimetre-diameter yellow flowers do not form spiky seed heads. It reaches 20 to 40 centimetres in height.

Top: Large-leaved avens has small flowers with widely spaced petals in open cymes. Middle: Yellow avens has larger flowers than large-leaved avens. Bottom: Eastern mountain avens has five overlapping petals.

Introduced Species

Shamrock family / Oxalidaceae
European wood-sorrel
Oxalis stricta
Common yellow wood sorrel

HABITAT: European wood-sorrel, an introduced species, is locally naturalized in disturbed areas, primarily near settlements, throughout Nova Scotia.

CHARACTERISTICS: European wood-sorrel is a tufted plant with upright or reclining stems. Leaves are often in whorls of three or four but may also be alternately arranged. Each leaf is trifoliate with three folded heart-shaped leaflets. Each leaflet is 1 to 2 centimetres wide and smooth-edged. The main stems have fine scattered hairs.

Flowers are solitary or produced in umbels of up to four flowers from the leaf axils. Each flower has 10 stamens and five styles. Flower stems usually overtop the leaves. The sepals are finely hairy. Flowers are about 1 centimetre wide with five yellow petals; flower stems become reflexed as seeds develop. Cylindrical ridged seed capsules, which are 1.5 to 2.5 centimetres in length, explode when ripe to shoot seeds from the parent plant.

Fairly similar in appearance to European wood-sorrel is creeping wood-sorrel, *O. corniculata*, but it is much less common, found mostly near plant nurseries. It is creeping in habit, often rooting at the leaf nodes, and usually red-tinted. Leaves are alternately arranged and petioles are slightly hairy. Flowers are in axillary umbels but they are just 0.4 to 0.8 centimetres wide. Flower stems are generally shorter than the petioles. Cylindrical seed capsules explode when ripe.

VITAL STATISTICS

Maximum height: 40 centimetres
Flowering season: May to October

Top: Each five-petalled flower has 10 stamens and five styles. Middle: The green trifoliate leaves have folded heart-shaped leaflets. Bottom: Creeping wood-sorrel often has red-tinted foliage.

Disturbed

221

Parsley family / Apiaceae
Wild parsnip
Pastinaca sativa

Introduced Species

VITAL STATISTICS

Maximum height: 150 centimetres
Flowering season: July

HABITAT: Wild parsnip, a European introduction, is occasionally found in disturbed areas such as roadsides, old meadows, and waste areas, particularly in the Annapolis Valley.

CHARACTERISTICS: Wild parsnip is a biennial plant with a stout taproot, a rosette of leaves in the first season, and sparsely branching stems with alternately arranged leaves in the second season. Plants are hairless with furrowed stems. Long petioled basal and lower stem leaves, each up to 45 centimetres long, are pinnately compound with seven to 11 leaflets. Leaflets are elliptical to ovate, with cleft lobes and sharp teeth.

Flowers are produced in terminal flat-topped umbels. Each umbel is composed of 15 to 25 umbellets; each umbellet, 12 to 35 flowers. Individual flowers are about 0.7 centimetres in diameter with five tiny yellow inwardly curling petals. Flowers later develop into flattened winged seeds.

Golden alexanders, *Zizia aurea*, is a native perennial occasionally encountered along damp roadsides and in old meadows and damp thickets of central Nova Scotia. Its smooth shiny stems can reach 80 centimetres in length. Long petioled leaves are trifoliate to biternately compound. Leaflets are thin, hairless, and toothed; the lowest leaflets often have one or two cleft lobes. Each flat-topped umbel is composed of up to 12 umbellets; each umbellet, 20 0.7-centimetre-wide five-petalled yellow flowers. Petals curve inward. Their flattened seeds are not winged.

Top: Wild parsnip flowers have inwardly curling petals. Middle: Flowers are in multiple flat topped umbels, and their large leaves are pinnate. Bottom: Golden alexanders' trifoliate or biternately compound leaves have sharply toothed edges.

Introduced
Species

Common mullein

Verbascum thapsus

Great mullein, flannel mullein, flannel plant

HABITAT: Common mullein, a European species, is naturalized in disturbed habitats throughout Nova Scotia.

CHARACTERISTICS: Common mullein is a tap-rooted biennial. In the first year, plants produce a large rosette of white woolly felted leaves. These finely toothed leaves are oblong to lance-shaped and may reach 50 centimetres in length. In the second year, plants produce a leafy stout white woolly stem that can reach 2 metres in length. Leaves are alternately arranged and reduce in size up the stem. Plants are generally non-branching but may have several smaller flower spikes at the base of the main flower spike.

The stem terminates in a dense cylindrical spike of nearly stemless yellow flowers. Flowers are 1.5 to 3 centimetres in diameter and consist of five petals which are fused at their base. Flowers are slightly unequal in outline, with two petals on top and three on the bottom. They have five stamens: three smaller and shorter ones on the top and two larger and longer ones on the bottom. Sepals are white and woolly.

The old stems are woody and often persist through the winter to release seeds over the fall and winter.

VITAL STATISTICS
Maximum height: 2 metres
Flowering season: Late June to September

Top: Petals are slightly unequal. Middle: Flowers are in dense spikes. Bottom: First-year plants produce a basal rosette of elliptical felted leaves.

Disturbed

223

Waterlily family / Nymphaceae

Yellow pond-lily

Nuphar variegata

Bullhead lily, spatterdock, variegated pond-lily

VITAL STATISTICS

Maximum height: 2 metres
(water depth)

Flowering season: July to August

Wetlands

HABITAT: Yellow pond-lily grows in shallow ponds or slow-moving streams throughout Nova Scotia.

CHARACTERISTICS: An aquatic plant, yellow pond-lily has a thick rhizome that embeds in the mud and gravel of ponds, usually in water less than 2 metres deep. Leaves float on the water's surface and are essentially basal, arising individually from the rhizome. Ten- to 25-centimetre-long leaves are ovate to heart-shaped with a rounded tip and deeply cleft base; they are deep green, waxy, hairless, and smooth-edged.

Solitary globular flowers are held on a thick stalk above the water's surface. Each 5-centimetre-wide blossom consists of six thick waxy yellow sepals (three outside, three inside). The outside base of the sepals may be green; the inside base, red. Petals are small and indistinct. At the flower's centre is a round disc surrounded by a dense ring of stamens. Seeds are produced in a flat-topped globular ribbed capsule.

Small yellow pond-lily, *N. microphylla*, is smaller than yellow pond-lily, with 10-centimetre-long leaves and 1.5- to 3-centimetre-wide flowers with five yellow sepals. Rare to uncommon, this species is most likely to be seen in alkaline soil in central Nova Scotia regions. A natural hybrid of the two species, *N. X rubrodisca*, also exists.

Yellow pond-lily often cohabits with white water-lily, *Nymphaea odorata*. When not in bloom, the latter can be distinguished by its purple-red leaf undersides.

Top: The centres of the solitary flowers have a rounded disc of stamens. Bottom: Plants produce round floating leaves with a deeply cleft base.

Native Species

Lily family / Liliaceae

Corn lily

Clintonia borealis
Bluebead lily, yellow clintonia

HABITAT: Corn lily is a woodland plant common across the province in shady forests and, less commonly, on open barrens.

CHARACTERISTICS: A low plant, corn lily forms colonies through thin underground rhizomes. Each plant produces two to four elliptical to narrow egg-shaped basal leaves. These leaves are light green and glossy and have smooth but finely hairy edges.

A loose umbel of two to eight flowers is produced at the end of a leafless stem. The 2.5-centimetre-diameter flowers are outward-facing or pendant. They have six yellow to yellow-green tepals—three sepals and three petals that look alike. The six stamens are slightly longer than the tepals. By August, each flowering stem may produce one to a few berries on stiff erect stalks. Berries are mildly poisonous, about 1 centimetre in diameter, bright to deep blue, and often shiny. Berry flesh is firm and white, with many seeds.

European lily-of-the-valley, *Convallaria majalis*, is a European garden plant which is occasionally naturalized in moist woods, thickets, and waste places, primarily in the southern half of the province. Its flowers are held on leafless racemes. The white sweetly fragrant flowers are nodding with recurved petal tips. Plants produce red berries in late summer.

Corn lily and European lily-of-the-valley are both toxic if ingested.

Top: The yellow flowers are lily-like with six narrow tepals; the basal leaves have smooth edges. Middle: Flowers develop into blue berries. Bottom: European lily-of-the-valley produces racemes of nodding white bell-shaped flowers.

VITAL STATISTICS

Maximum height: 30 centimetres
Flowering season: June

225

Lily family / Liliaceae

Yellow trout lily

Erythronium americanum

American trout lily, yellow dog's-tooth violet, yellow adder's-tongue

Native Species

VITAL STATISTICS

Maximum height: 20 centimetres
Flowering season: May

HABITAT: In Nova Scotia, yellow trout lily is generally restricted to the upland hardwood forests and intervales of the north-central region.

CHARACTERISTICS: Yellow trout lily is a small stature plant that arises from a tooth-shaped bulb. The plant is ephemeral, arising early in spring but going dormant and then disappearing by late June to early July. Non-flowering plants produce a single basal elliptical to lance-shaped leaf. Flowering plants produce a pair of basal leaves, which are smooth-edged, fleshy, hairless, grey-green, and usually mottled purple-brown. Leaves are 7 to 20 centimetres long.

A single nodding flower is produced on a 10- to 15-centimetre-long leafless stalk that arises between the pair of basal leaves. The flower is 2 to 4 centimetres in diameter with six reflexed tepals; the three petals and three sepals look alike. Tepals are yellow, often with fine brown spots at their bases, and have six stamens with brown anthers and a single pistil. The globular seed capsule matures as the plants go dormant.

Top: The solitary nodding flowers have six yellow tepals.
Bottom: Leaves are mottled purple-brown.

 **Native Species**

Lily family / Liliaceae

Canada lily

Lilium canadense

Yellow Canada lily, meadow lily

HABITAT: Canada lily is localized in the northern half of Nova Scotia, where it grows in riverside meadows and moist open deciduous forests.

CHARACTERISTICS: Canada lily is a tall slender non-branching plant that arises from a scaly bulb. Plants produce whorls of three to eight sessile, lance-shaped, smooth-edged leaves with parallel veins. The upper leaf surface is hairless and waxy; veins on the leaf underside have fine hairs.

Stems terminate in a single flower or an umbel-like cluster of several flowers. Flower stems are long and curve at the ends so that the flowers are nodding. Individual flowers are 6 to 7 centimetres wide with six tip-reflexed tepals; the three petals and three sepals look alike. Tepals are thick-textured and yellow to orange, with copious brown spots on the inside surface. The seed capsule is up to 5 centimetres long, cylindrical, and longitudinally ribbed.

VITAL STATISTICS

Maximum height: 150 centimetres
Flowering season: July

Top: The nodding flower's six tepals are reflexed at their tips. Middle: Flowers are in umbels. Bottom: The sessile lance-shaped leaves are in whorls.

Deciduous Forest

Wetlands

Autumn-crocus family / Colchicaceae

Sessile-leaved bellwort

Native Species

Uvularia sessilifolia

Sessile bellwort, straw-lily, wild-oats

VITAL STATISTICS

Maximum height: 30 centimetres
Flowering season: May

HABITAT: Sessile-leaved bellwort occurs in lightly shaded locations in rich hardwood forests and intervales. It is common in the north-central regions of Nova Scotia and rare or absent in the southwest.

CHARACTERISTICS: Sessile-leaved bellwort produces loose colonies of plants that spread by thin underground rhizomes. Their smooth stems commonly fork at their upper ends. Bright green elliptical leaves are alternately arranged and sessile. Leaves, which may reach 7.5 centimetres in length, are hairless, waxy on both surfaces, and smooth-edged.

The 2.5-centimetre-long narrow bell-shaped flowers are strongly pendent on a thin stalk. They bloom before leaves are fully expanded. Individual flowers have six pale yellow to cream-coloured tepals which curve slightly outward at their tips. Hidden inside the flower are six stamens and a single three-lobed stigma. Most plants produce just a single flower but, less commonly, they produce a pair; flowers are often hidden under the leaves. The 2.5-centimetre-diameter globular seed capsule has three distinct winged edges.

Top: Less commonly, plants produce a pair of narrow bell-shaped straw yellow flowers. Bottom: The sessile elliptical leaves alternate along the stem.

Native Species

Aster family / Asteraceae
Long-leaved arnica
Arnica lonchophylla (formerly *A. chionopappa*)
Northern arnica

HABITAT: Long-leaved arnica is a rare calciphile restricted in Nova Scotia to a few sites on Cape Breton Island, where it grows on limestone cliffs and gravels.

CHARACTERISTICS: Long-leaved arnica is a clumping plant with several upright non-branching stems. Opposite leaves vary from lance-shaped to ovate and have coarsely toothed edges. Stems have two to seven pairs of leaves. Lower stem leaves have a petiole; upper stem leaves are nearly sessile. Both leaves and stems have scattered long hairs. Basal leaves are present early in the season but wither by the time plants flower.

Stems terminate in a solitary flower head or small corymb of up to seven flower heads. Individual flowers are 4 to 6 centimetres wide and have six to 15 yellow ray florets and a central cluster of yellow disc florets. Seed heads are like small dandelions: each seed has a plume of white hair that allows it to be carried by the wind.

VITAL STATISTICS

Maximum height: 40 centimetres
Flowering season: June to July

Top: Flowers may be in small clusters. Bottom: Some plants are slender with only two pairs of leaves and a solitary flower.

Barrens

229

Aster family / Asteraceae

Nodding beggarticks

Native Species

Bidens cernua

Pitchfork, sticktight, nodding burr marigold

VITAL STATISTICS

Maximum height: 100 centimetres
Flowering season: July to September

HABITAT: Nodding beggarticks grows in swamps and wet thickets and along streams. It is scattered throughout the province but rare in the southwest.

CHARACTERISTICS: Nodding beggarticks is a colonial annual plant whose lower stems root if they come in contact with soil. Opposite linear to lance-shaped leaves are finely toothed and hairless and may reach 12 centimetres in length. Leaf bases usually clasp the stem. Leaves often become purple-tinted in the autumn.

Long-stalked flowers are solitary or in small clusters from the upper leaf axils. Individual flowers are 2 to 4 centimetres wide and usually have eight yellow ray florets, if present, and numerous yellow disc florets. The base of each flower has six to 10 narrow leaf-like bracts which curl backward. Flower heads nod as seeds develop. Four barbed awns allow seeds to stick to fur and clothing.

Purple-stemmed beggarticks, *B. connata*, is uncommon and most likely found along the Atlantic coast. Stout bushy plants grow to 150 centimetres in height and typically have purple stems. Narrow leaves have petioles and coarse teeth. Loosely clustered flowers usually lack ray florets; large green bracts at the flower base are held horizontal. Flower heads remain erect as seeds mature.

Water beggarticks, *B. beckii*, is occasionally found in slow-moving streams or ponds. Submersed leaves are dissected and threadlike. Emergent leaves are lance-shaped and finely toothed. Solitary 2- to 3-centimetre-wide flowers have eight ray florets.

Top: The flower heads of nodding beggarticks typically have eight ray florets. Middle: Purple-stemmed beggarticks flowers lack ray florets. Bottom: Water beggarticks has solitary flowers.

Aster family / Asteraceae

Jerusalem artichoke

Helianthus tuberosus

**Introduced
Species**

HABITAT: A North American species native to areas south and west of Nova Scotia, Jerusalem artichoke was introduced as a garden ornamental. Now becoming naturalized, it is most frequently found from Kings County north to northern Cape Breton along roadsides, trails, and waste areas near settlements.

CHARACTERISTICS: A tall colonial plant, Jerusalem artichoke is generally unbranched with rough and hairy stems and leaves. Leaves are opposite on the lower portion of the plant but alternate on the upper. The slightly toothed leaves are elliptical to ovate; lower leaves have petioles, the upper are sessile. Lower leaves may reach 25 centimetres in length; they become smaller toward the flowers. Plants produce an irregularly shaped edible tuber.

Flowers are produced in open corymbs. Individual flower heads are 5 to 10 centimetres wide with 10 to 20 bright yellow ray florets and numerous yellow disc florets.

Another introduced species also widely scattered is beautiful sunflower, *H. X laetiflorus*, a hybrid of *H. tuberosus* and *H. pauciflorus*. This naturalized ornamental plant looks like a smaller version of Jerusalem artichoke but does not produce swollen tubers. It may reach a height of 2 metres but is usually 100 to 150 centimetres high. Most leaves are elliptical and opposite, except those close to the flowers.

Top: Jerusalem artichoke flowers have 10 to 20 yellow ray florets surrounding a mass of yellow disc florets. Middle: Stems are rough-hairy and the upper leaves alternate on the stem. Bottom: Beautiful sunflower is similar to Jerusalem artichoke but has smaller flowers.

Disturbed

231

Aster family / Asteraceae

Narrow-leaved hawkweed

Hieracium umbellatum

Northern hawkweed, narrowleaf hawkweed, umbellate hawkweed, Canada hawkweed

VITAL STATISTICS

Maximum height: 100 centimetres
Flowering season: July to August

HABITAT: Narrow-leaved hawkweed occurs along roadsides and in clearings, waste places, thickets, and open woods throughout Nova Scotia.

CHARACTERISTICS: Narrow-leaved hawkweed is a slender often clumping plant with leafy non-branching stems. Alternate leaves, up to 12 centimetres in length, are lanceolate, sessile, and pointed at their tips; they have scattered large teeth or toothlike projections. Leaves and stems are covered in fine stiff hairs, which impart a rough texture. All parts of the plant ooze a milky sap when cut.

Loose nearly flat-topped panicles are composed of up to 25 flower heads. Individual flower heads, 2 to 2.5 centimetres wide, have many yellow ray florets but no disc florets. The phyllaries below the flower are green and curl back—this feature distinguishes this species from the introduced hawkweeds. Developing seed heads look like small dandelion seed heads.

The species *H. canadense*, *H. scabriusculum*, and *H. kalmii*, sometimes listed in older wildflower reference books, are now all included under *H. umbellatum*.

Rough hawkweed, *H. scabrum*, another native hawkweed found on sandy soils, has leafy stems but dull-tipped, oval to elliptical, hairy leaves with smooth or slightly toothed edges. Leaves near the base have short petioles and are larger than the sessile upper leaves. Stems are hairy and glandular near the flowers. Flowers are in a loose panicle but their phyllaries are covered in sticky hairs.

Top: The narrow leaves have scattered teeth; the phyllaries curl back. Middle: Rough hawkweed phyllaries are covered in sticky hairs. Bottom: Rough hawkweed has broad leaves with smooth edges; the lower leaves are much larger than the upper.

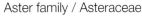

Introduced Species

Aster family / Asteraceae

Common hawkweed

Hieracium vulgatum

English hawkweed, showy hawkweed

HABITAT: Common hawkweed is a European species commonly found throughout Nova Scotia on old disturbed sites such as roadsides, thickets, and pasturelands and also in open woodlands.

VITAL STATISTICS

Maximum height: 100 centimetres
Flowering season: July to August

CHARACTERISTICS: Common hawkweed, an upright non-branching plant, often forms colonies. Plants have both basal and alternately arranged stem leaves; the elliptical to lance-shaped leaves are up to 15 centimetres long with tapered bases. The shallow teeth along leaf edges may be larger toward the base of the leaf. Leaves may be mottled purple or bronze. Both stems and leaves are covered in hairs. All parts of the plant exude a milky sap when cut.

Flowers are produced in a loose panicle. Flower stems have two to 12 scattered leaves. Individual flower heads are dandelion-like and up to 4 centimetres wide with bright yellow ray florets but no disc florets. Ray florets are rectangular in outline with comb-like tips. Phyllaries are hairy, with glandular dark tips. Seed heads are like those of dandelion, but smaller. *Hieracium lachenalii*, listed in older wildflower reference literature, is now considered the same species as *H. vulgatum*.

Wall hawkweed, *H. murorum*, is scattered in the province. It is similar in appearance to common hawkweed but distinguished by its heart-shaped to rounded leaf bases; it may have no, or up to two, leaves on the flower stems.

Top: The dandelion-like flowers, composed of all ray florets, are in loose panicles. Middle: Common hawkweed stems are leafy and their toothed leaves taper at the base. Bottom: Wall hawkweed leaves are often mottled and its leaf bases lobed; flower stems may be leafless or have one or two leaves.

Aster family / Asteraceae

Elecampane

Inula helenium

Inula

Introduced Species

VITAL STATISTICS

Maximum height: 150 centimetres
Flowering season: August

HABITAT: Elecampane, a European species introduced to Nova Scotia as a garden ornamental, is occasionally found in fields or along damp roadsides or shorelines, especially on the Fundy side.

CHARACTERISTICS: Elecampane, a stout leafy plant arising from a thick rootstock, produces stout non-branching stems. Large alternate leaves, which are up to 50 centimetres long, are ovate with finely toothed edges; the hairs are rough on the upper surface and soft on the underside. Lower leaves have petioles; upper leaves clasp the stem. Young plants produce basal leaves only until they are old enough to bloom.

The 5-centimetre-diameter flower heads are solitary or in a loose terminal cluster. Individual flower heads have numerous narrow yellow ray florets surrounding orange-yellow disc florets. Green bract-like phyllaries are usually wide-spreading. Seeds have a tuft of hairs at one end.

Top: The ray florets are narrow. Bottom: Plants have large broad leaves and loose terminal clusters of flowers.

Coastal

Disturbed

 **Introduced Species**

Aster family / Asteraceae

Tansy ragwort

Jacobaea vulgaris (formerly *Senecio jacobaea*)

Stinking Willie

HABITAT: Tansy ragwort is a European introduction common in disturbed habitats and waste places throughout Nova Scotia.

CHARACTERISTICS: Tansy ragwort is a bush-like biennial or, rarely, short-lived perennial. In the first year, plants produce a low but leafy rosette of evergreen bi- to tripinnatifid oblanceolate leaves. Lobes and teeth are rounded. These petioled basal leaves reach 20 centimetres in length and have a ruffled appearance; upper leaf surfaces are hairless, and leaf undersides are whitened with dense fine hairs. Alternately arranged stem leaves are sessile and smaller and more finely lobed than the basal leaves. The stout stems can also be white-haired when young, but the hair often wears away later in the growing season. The plant has a rank smell when bruised.

Flowers are produced in large flat-topped compound corymbs. Individual flower heads are 2 to 2.5 centimetres wide with 10 to 15 yellow ray florets and numerous yellow disc florets. Seed heads resemble miniature dandelions; each seed has a parachute of hairs that helps it blow for miles in the wind.

This plant is toxic if ingested.

VITAL STATISTICS
Maximum height: 120 centimetres
Flowering season: July to September

Top: Flowers are in flat-topped clusters. Middle: Plants are busy when in bloom. Bottom: The fern-like leaves have rounded lobes and teeth.

Disturbed

235

Aster family / Asteraceae

Canada lettuce

Lactuca canadensis
Arrow-leaved lettuce

Native Species

VITAL STATISTICS

Maximum height: 2.5 metres
Flowering season: July to August

HABITAT: Canada lettuce grows in disturbed habitats but also in open woodlands, thickets, and clearings throughout the province.

CHARACTERISTICS: Canada lettuce is a biennial. In the first season, it produces a rosette of low evergreen leaves; in the second, a tall non-branched stem with alternate leaves. The hairless waxy stem may be tinted red or purple. Leaves are pinnatifid and lance-shaped to elliptical with variable-sized deep lobes and sharp teeth; they may have hairs on the lower midvein. Upper stem leaves may be lance-shaped with smooth edges. This plant oozes a milky sap when cut.

Flowers are produced in narrow panicles. Flower heads are about 0.8 centimetres in diameter and composed of 12 to 20 light yellow ray florets. Phyllaries are 1 to 1.4 centimetres long. Seed heads look like miniature dandelions.

Hairy lettuce, *L. hirsuta*, is uncommon but native to the southern half of Nova Scotia. It usually has long hairs along the lower portion of its stem. Its leaves, stems, and flower buds are purple-tinted; its phyllaries are 1.6 to 2.2 centimetres long.

Prickly lettuce, *L. serriola*, a European species found in Kings and Cape Breton counties, has bristly edged clasping leaves and scattered stiff prickles along the midvein of the leaf undersides. The lower main stem has scattered bristles. Its panicle of pale yellow flowers is conical. Each flower head has five to 12 ray florets and four sets of overlapping phyllaries.

Top: The small flowers have 12 to 20 small light yellow ray florets. Middle: The pinnatifid leaves have a mixture of large and small lobes, all with sharp teeth.
Bottom: Prickly lettuce has clasping leaves and bristle-tipped teeth.

Common nipplewort

Lapsana communis
Nipplewort

Introduced Species

HABITAT: Common nipplewort, a European species occasionally seen in waste areas and gardens, is widely scattered throughout Nova Scotia.

CHARACTERISTICS: Common nipplewort is a slender annual or biennial which only branches near the flowers. The shallowly ridged stem, often red- or purple-tinted, has glandular hairs, especially near the base. Overwintering plants have a basal rosette; flowering plants, alternate stem leaves. The lower elliptical to ovate leaves may reach 15 centimetres in length. Each leaf has a large arrowhead-shaped terminal lobe and two smaller nipple-like lateral lobes which are widely separated from the terminal lobes. Leaf edges have hairs and large shallow teeth. The leaf surface is wrinkly with scattered hairs; hairs on the lower surface are confined to the veins. The petiole is fringed with hair and slightly winged. Upper stem leaves, smaller than the lower stem leaves, are unlobed and lanceolate to elliptical. Plants exude a white sap when cut.

Flowers are produced in an open panicle. Flower stems are hairless. Individual flower heads are 1.5 to 2 centimetres wide and composed of about 20 light yellow ray florets. Ray petals end in five fine teeth. Unlike many of the yellow composites found in Nova Scotia, this species does not have a tuft of hair at the tip of its seeds.

Top: The ray florets end in five fine teeth. Bottom: Lower leaves are often ovate, with large teeth; the stems are often purple.

Disturbed

237

Aster family / Asteraceae
Fall dandelion
Leontodon autumnalis
Autumn hawkbit

Introduced
Species

VITAL STATISTICS

Maximum height: 30 centimetres
Flowering season: July to September

HABITAT: Fall dandelion, a European introduction, is well established in waste places, lawns, and gardens throughout the province.

CHARACTERISTICS: Fall dandelion is a rosette-producing plant with all basal leaves. Leaves, lance-shaped in outline, are either pinnatifid or have long thin well-spaced teeth often perpendicular to the leaf edge. Leaves and flower stems have scattered fine hairs. All parts of the plant ooze a milky sap when cut.

Flower stems, which are commonly branching, are leafless but have small scale-like bracts. Flower heads are in loose cymes. Stems thicken just below each flower head, which is 2.5 to 3.5 centimetres wide with yellow ray florets. Ray florets end in comb-like tips. Seed heads are like those of a dandelion but smaller and tawny rather than white.

Hairy cat's-ear, *Hypochaeris radicata*, is similar in appearance but less common than fall dandelion. It occurs in waste places primarily in Yarmouth, Shelburne, and Cape Breton counties. It also has pinnatifid basal leaves, but they are densely hairy and broader than those of fall dandelion. The naked flower stem is stouter than that of fall dandelion and it does not thicken immediately below the flower head.

Top: The flower stems are conspicuously thickened immediately below the flower. Middle: Fall dandelion produces a rosette of narrow pinnatifid leaves. Bottom: Hairy cat's-ear has hairy pinnatifid leaves.

Balsam groundsel

Packera paupercula (formerly *Senecio pauperculus*)

Balsam ragwort, showy butterweed

Native Species

HABITAT: Balsam groundsel is primarily confined to calcareous gravels, ledges, and slopes from Hants County to northern Cape Breton.

CHARACTERISTICS: Balsam groundsel, a clumping plant, has several non-branching stems. Most leaves are basal, but flowering stems have a few alternate leaves. Long petioled basal leaves are oblanceolate, oblong to spatulate, and taper at the base, with sharp teeth. Lower stem leaves, smaller than basal leaves, are sessile or short petioled, lance-shaped, and pinnatifid. Upper flower stems have a few bracts. Leaves and stems have scattered woolly tufts, especially at leaf axils and on leaf undersides. Young leaves may have cobwebby hairs.

Flowers are produced in a loose corymb, resulting in a flat-topped appearance. Individual flower heads are about 2 centimetres wide with eight to 13 golden yellow ray florets surrounded by many disc florets. Seed heads look like a small dandelion.

Scattered throughout the province, golden groundsel, *P. aurea* (*S. aureus*), prefers moist shaded woodland conditions. Plants reach 80 centimetres in height; woolly tufts are present only when leaves first expand. Basal leaves are round to egg- and heart-shaped at the base; alternate stems leaves are pinnatifid.

Swamp ragwort, *P. schweinitziana* (*S. robbinsii*), is found in peaty meadows and fields of the province, although it is rare in the southwest. It is distinguished by its narrow oval to triangular basal leaves, which have heart-shaped to rounded bases and sharp teeth.

Top: Flowers are in loose flat-topped corymbs. Middle: Balsam groundsel's basal leaves are often spoon-shaped. Bottom: Golden groundsel has longer ray florets than balsam groundsel and is often more densely flowered.

VITAL STATISTICS
Maximum height: 50 centimetres
Flowering season: July

Barrens

239

Aster family / Asteraceae

Orange hawkweed

Pilosella aurantiaca (formerly *Hieracium aurantiacum*)
Devil's paintbrush

VITAL STATISTICS

Maximum height: 60 centimetres
Flowering season: June to August

HABITAT: Orange hawkweed is a European introduction found along roadsides, old meadows, and other previously disturbed areas throughout Nova Scotia. It is not common on recently disturbed sites.

CHARACTERISTICS: A matted plant, orange hawkweed can form large colonies by producing leafy rooting stolons. Leaves, which are up to 12 centimetres long, are primarily basal and partly evergreen. Elliptical to obovate in outline, leaves are smooth-edged and covered in long hairs. The plant oozes a milky sap when cut.

Flowers are produced in a dense corymb at the end of generally leafless stems, which may occasionally have one or two alternately arranged leaves. The flower stem is also covered in long hairs. Individual flower heads are dandelion-like, about 2 centimetres in diameter, and deep orange with numerous ray florets but no disc florets. Ray florets are rectangular with comb-like tips. Phyllaries are covered in black glandular hairs. Seed heads are a smaller version of a dandelion's; dark-coloured seeds have an attached parachute that can carry them for many kilometres on the wind.

Top: The distinctive orange dandelion-like flowers.
Bottom: The basal leaves are elliptical and long-haired with smooth edges; flower stems also have long hairs.

 **Introduced Species**

Meadow hawkweed

Pilosella caespitosa (formerly *Hieracium pratense/caespitosum*)

King devil

HABITAT: A European species, meadow hawkweed is scattered on old pasturelands and meadows throughout Nova Scotia. It is generally not found on recently disturbed sites.

CHARACTERISTICS: Meadow hawkweed forms mat-like colonies that increase rapidly through leafy rooting stolons. Leaves are basal and partly evergreen, elliptical to lance-shaped, up to 20 centimetres long, with either smooth or slightly toothed edges. Leaves are finely hairy with longer hairs along the edges and the midrib of the undersides. Flower stems are densely hairy and may have one to three alternately arranged leaves on its lower portion. All parts of the plant ooze a milky sap when cut.

Flowers are produced in a dense flattened corymb of five to 25 flowers. Individual flower heads are dandelion-like and 2 centimetres wide and composed of only ray florets, which are bright yellow and rectangular with comb-like tips. Phyllaries are covered in black glandular hairs. Fluffy seed heads resemble small dandelions.

Pale hawkweed, *P. floribunda* (*H. floribundum*), is similar to meadow hawkweed, but its leaves are usually hairless on their upper surfaces. Hairs are restricted to leaf edges and undersides.

Tall hawkweed, *P. piloselloides* (*H. florentinum* or *H. praealtum*), another look-alike, lacks long leafy stolons and has more leaves along its flowering stems.

VITAL STATISTICS

Maximum height: 50 centimetres
Flowering season: Late June to July

Top: Flowers are in a dense corymb. Middle: Plants produce leafy stolons and narrow long-haired basal leaves. Bottom: Pale hawkweed also has flowers in dense corymbs.

Disturbed

Aster family / Asteraceae

Mouse-ear hawkweed

Introduced Species

Pilosella officinarum (formerly *Hieracium pilosella*)

VITAL STATISTICS

Maximum height: 25 centimetres
Flowering season: Mid-June to
August

HABITAT: Mouse-ear hawkweed, a European species, is common in clearings, pastures, and fields throughout Nova Scotia. It is generally not found on recently disturbed sites.

CHARACTERISTICS: Mouse-ear hawkweed is a mat-forming plant which can form large colonies through leafy rooting stolons. Leaves are basal, up to 8 centimetres long, oblong to spatulate, and smooth-edged with copious stiff hairs. Leaf undersides, especially those of young leaves, are whitened with a dense covering of fine tomentose hair. The entire plant oozes a milky sap when cut.

Flowers are solitary at the tips of wiry densely hairy stems. Individual flower heads are 2.5 to 3 centimetres wide with numerous ray florets but no disc florets. Pale lemon yellow ray florets are rectangular with comb-like tips. The undersides of the outermost ray florets are often striped in pale red. Phyllaries are covered in black glandular hairs. Seed heads are dandelion-like, but smaller: the dark seeds have an attached parachute that can carry them for several kilometres on the wind.

Whiplash hawkweed, *P. flagellaris* (*Hieracium flagellare*), is less common than mouse-ear hawkweed but occurs in similar habitats. It is distinguished by its green (not whitened) leaf undersides. Leaves may be longer, up to 15 centimetres, and the flower stem stouter, reaching 45 centimetres in length. Plants typically have two flowers per stem, but occasionally one or up to four flowers. Flowers are deep yellow.

Top: The solitary flowers have lemon yellow ray florets. Middle: Plants produce a mat-like growth with solitary flowers on leafless stems. Bottom: Whiplash hawkweed leaf undersides are hairy, but not whitened; plants typically produce two or three flowers per stem rather than being solitary.

Disturbed

242

Native Species

Black-eyed Susan

Rudbeckia hirta

Hairy coneflower

HABITAT: Black-eyed Susan is often seen along roadsides and in old meadows and thickets throughout Nova Scotia.

CHARACTERISTICS: Black-eyed Susan is a clumping plant with one to several upright stems. Plants have basal and alternately arranged stem leaves. All leaves are ovate to lance-shaped and coarsely toothed or smooth-edged, but basal leaves are long petioled and stem leaves mostly sessile. The largest leaves may reach 15 centimetres in length. Stems and all leaves are rough and hairy.

Long-stemmed flowers are produced in loose cymes or, rarely, are solitary. Individual flower heads are composed of both yellow ray florets and central dark brown disc florets. Flower heads are 6 to 7.5 centimetres wide. At the base of each flower is a ring of hairy green phyllaries of irregular lengths that bend backward.

Cut-leaved coneflower, *R. laciniata*, is uncommon along the swales and swamp edges of central Nova Scotia. Plants grow to 2 metres high. Leaves have three to seven large lobes, with or without additional teeth. Lower leaves have petioles; the upper are sessile. Hairy or smooth, they can reach 30 centimetres in length. Stems end in a loose 6- to 7.5-centimetre-wide cluster of yellow flowers. Ray florets arch downward; yellow-green disc florets form a cone-like centre as the flowers mature. Five green hairless leafy phyllaries grow beneath each flower head.

Top: Black-eyed Susan flowers have large golden yellow ray florets and a dense central cluster of dark brown disc florets. Middle: Leaves are covered in rough hairs; the base of the flower has a ring of green leafy phyllaries. Bottom: Cut-leaved coneflower leaves have three to seven large lobes.

VITAL STATISTICS

Maximum height: 100 centimetres
Flowering season: July and August

Disturbed

243

Aster family / Asteraceae

Seaside ragwort

Senecio pseudoarnica
False arnica, beach groundsel

VITAL STATISTICS

Maximum height: 100 centimetres
Flowering season: Mid-July to August

HABITAT: Although seaside ragwort is restricted to sandy or gravelly coastal beaches, it is widely scattered around the province.

CHARACTERISTICS: Seaside ragwort is a clumping plant with stout unbranched stems. Plants form colonies by their spreading rhizomes. Early leaves are densely arranged on short stems, appearing like a basal rosette. As stems elongate, they reveal alternate leaves which have short petioles at the base of the plants but are nearly sessile farther up. Leaves are fleshy, toothed, and elliptical to oblanceolate and covered in web-like hairs when they emerge. If the hairs on the upper surface wear away, the leaves become glossy. However, leaf undersides remain white with a dense coating of woolly hairs.

Flower heads are produced in a leafy corymb made up of a few flowers. Flower stems and buds are covered in white hairs. Individual flower heads are 5 to 8 centimetres wide with 10 to 20 yellow ray florets and numerous yellow disc florets. Tawny brown seed heads are much like those of a dandelion, except smaller. Seeds have a crown of hairs that enables them to drift many kilometres on the wind.

Top: The daisy-like flowers have long ray florets surrounding a central cluster of yellow disc florets.
Middle: Plants produce densely overlapping leaves; new leaves are covered in cobwebby hairs.
Bottom: Flowers are in leafy corymbs.

Coastal

244

**Introduced
Species**

Aster family / Asteraceae

Woodland ragwort

Senecio sylvaticus
Woodland groundsel

HABITAT: Woodland ragwort is a naturalized European species commonly found in moist disturbed habitats throughout Nova Scotia. Common along the coast, it is also occasionally found in woodlands.

CHARACTERISTICS: Woodland ragwort is a low bushy annual or winter annual with sparsely branching stems. The plant is covered in soft slightly sticky hairs. Alternate leaves are soft, fleshy, oblong to lanceolate, pinnatifid or variously pinnately lobed and toothed. Lower leaves have petioles; upper leaves are sessile or clasp the stem. The plant emits a strong oily smell when bruised.

Flowers are produced in loose corymbs. Individual flowers are less than 1 centimetre wide with primarily yellow disc florets. Ray florets, when present, are small and curl backward. Seed heads are small puffballs that look like miniature dandelions.

Common ragwort, *S. vulgaris*, is similar to woodland ragwort but has fewer hairs, most of which are confined to the base of new leaves. It is also shorter (to 60 centimetres) and bushier, with a hollow stem and rayless flowers. The distinguishing feature of this species is black-tipped phyllaries on the outside base of the flower.

Sticky ragwort, *S. viscosus*, another look-alike, is covered in sticky hairs, which impart a grey-green appearance. It has distinct ray florets.

Top: Woodland ragwort flowers are in loose corymbs and the small ray florets often curl backward.
Middle: Common ragwort flowers have black-tipped phyllaries and rayless flowers. Bottom: Sticky ragwort has grey-green foliage and flowers with distinct ray florets.

VITAL STATISTICS

Maximum height: 100 centimetres
Flowering season: June to September

Disturbed

245

Aster family / Asteraceae

Large-leaved goldenrod

Solidago macrophylla

Native Species

VITAL STATISTICS

Maximum height: 100 centimetres
Flowering season: August to
                   September

HABITAT: Large-leaved goldenrod, found in open shady woodlands and shaded ravines, is confined mostly to Cape Breton and Colchester and Cumberland counties.

CHARACTERISTICS: Large-leaved goldenrod has a single stout upright stem with basal and stem leaves. Basal leaves, which reach 12 centimetres in length, are ovate, spatulate, or elliptical with rounded bases and elongate petioles; they are sharply toothed and are hairless except along the main underside veins. Stem leaves are alternate; upper leaves are more lanceolate than the lower and have short winged petioles or are sessile. Stem leaves may be smooth-edged or slightly toothed and are hairless or have scattered hairs.

Terminal and axillary flowers produced in a loose leafy raceme or panicle create a wand-like effect. Individual flower heads are about 0.5 centimetres wide with eight to 10 ray florets and a similar number of central disc florets. Unlike the flowers of many other goldenrods, those of large-leaved goldenrod are held outward.

Zigzag goldenrod, *S. flexicaulis*, grows in rich woodlands in the province's north-central regions and on Cape Breton Island. It is distinguished by zigzagged stems, especially on the upper half of the plant, and long soft hairs on the upper portion of the main stem. Both the upper and lower leaves are ovate; the upper leaves often have longer teeth than the lower ones. Individual flowers have three to four ray florets.

Top: Large-leaved goldenrod has wand-like clusters of outward facing flowers. Middle: The basal leaves are egg-shaped, toothed, and long petioled. Bottom: Zigzag goldenrod has all ovate leaves and an often kinked upper stem.

Multi-rayed goldenrod

Solidago multiradiata

Alpine goldenrod, Rocky Mountain goldenrod, northern goldenrod

Native Species

HABITAT: A rare calciphile, multi-rayed goldenrod is restricted in the province to Cape Breton, where it occurs on limestone gravels and cliffs.

CHARACTERISTICS: Multi-rayed goldenrod is a tufted leafy plant. Basal leaves, which are up to 12 centimetres long, are oblanceolate with rounded teeth and hairless except along the edges of the winged petioles. Stem leaves are alternate, sessile, and usually smooth-edged. Stems are hairless at the base but may have white hairs closer to the summit.

Flowers are produced in dense hemispherical corymbs. Stems are hairy close to the flowers. Individual flower heads are about 1.5 centimetres in diameter with 12 to 18 golden yellow ray florets and up to 30 disc florets. Seeds have a tuft of golden brown hair at their tips.

VITAL STATISTICS

Maximum height: 30 centimetres
Flowering season: July to August

Barrens

Top: Flowers are in dense hemispherical corymbs.
Bottom: Plants are tufted with hairless round-toothed basal leaves.

247

Aster family / Asteraceae

Grey-stemmed goldenrod

Native
Species

Solidago nemoralis

Grey goldenrod, field goldenrod, old field goldenrod

VITAL STATISTICS

Maximum height: 75 centimetres
Flowering season: August to
September

HABITAT: Grey-stemmed goldenrod is found in old meadows and along dry sandy roadsides throughout Nova Scotia but more commonly in the Annapolis Valley.

CHARACTERISTICS: Grey-stemmed goldenrod, a slender plant with unbranched stems, is covered in short grey hairs which impart a grey-green look. Plants have both basal and alternate stem leaves. Lower stem leaves and basal leaves are oblanceolate to spatulate with a petiole and slightly toothed edges; upper stem leaves are smaller than the lower leaves, sessile, and smooth-edged. Small leafy tufts often appear in the middle and upper leaf axils. The main stem may be red-tinted.

Lemon yellow flowers are in narrow wand-like panicles with short lateral branches. The flower heads of the side-branches are one-sided and upward-facing. The panicle tends to nod at the tip. Individual flower heads, which are about 0.6 centimetres in diameter, have three to six disc florets and five to 10 ray florets.

Downy goldenrod, *S. puberula*, is common in sterile dry soils of the province. This species has pubescent stems but its lanceolate leaves are primarily smooth. The wand-like golden yellow flower clusters are erect; the flower heads of the short side-branches are not one-sided. Flower heads have 10 ray florets that are, overall, larger than the previous species.

Top: Grey-stemmed goldenrod flowers are held in narrow wand-like panicles with one-sided short lateral branches. Bottom: Downy goldenrod flowers are also wand-like but its short side-branches are not one-sided and its ray florets are more noticeable than those of grey-stemmed goldenrod.

Rough-stemmed goldenrod

Solidago rugosa

Rough goldenrod, wrinkle-leaved goldenrod

Native Species

HABITAT: Rough-stemmed goldenrod occurs in damp woods, thickets, roadsides, old meadows, and other disturbed sites throughout Nova Scotia.

CHARACTERISTICS: Rough-stemmed goldenrod is a clumping colonial plant with numerous un-branched stems. Alternate leaves are lanceolate, elliptical to narrowly ovate, nearly sessile, and sharply toothed. Leaves are crowded on the stems. Each leaf, which is up to 10 centimetres long, has a single central vein. Stems and leaves are covered in rough hairs.

Flowers are in terminal panicles which vary from wand-like to broadly pyramidal. Upward-pointing flower heads are on arching one-sided lateral branches. Each flower head is about 0.3 centimetres wide and composed of five to eight yellow ray florets and a similar number of yellow disc florets.

Elliot's goldenrod, *S. latissimifolia* (formerly *S. elliotii*), an Atlantic Coastal Plain species restricted to swamps in southwestern Nova Scotia, is distinguished by its smooth stems and relatively smooth leaves.

Canada goldenrod, *S. canadensis*, another look-alike, has two side veins that run parallel to the central vein. Its stem is finely hairy toward the flowers but smooth toward the base. It is common throughout the province except in the southwest.

Giant goldenrod, *S. gigantea*, looks like Canada goldenrod but its smooth stems often have a waxy whitened bloom. It is most often found from north-central Nova Scotia to Cape Breton.

Top: Rough-stemmed goldenrod often has pyramidal panicles of many one-sided lateral branches.
Middle: Canada goldenrod leaves have two lateral veins that run parallel to the midvein. Bottom: Giant goldenrod has smooth stems and leaves.

VITAL STATISTICS
Maximum height: 2 metres
Flowering season: August to September

Disturbed

Aster family / Asteraceae
Seaside goldenrod
Solidago sempervirens
Evergreen goldenrod, salt-marsh goldenrod

Native Species

HABITAT: Seaside goldenrod is restricted to brackish shorelines, marshes, and coastal dunes around Nova Scotia's coastline.

CHARACTERISTICS: Seaside goldenrod is a clumping plant with several upright non-branching stems. The thick leaves are fleshy. Basal leaves, which are up to 30 centimetres long, are evergreen, elliptical, oblanceolate or spatulate, smooth-edged, and long petioled. Stem leaves are alternate and sessile, partly clasping the stem. Upper stem leaves are smaller, more lanceolate than the lower; upper leaves are sessile, partly clasping the stem.

Flowers are produced in dense pyramidal panicles. Flowers are held upright along side-branches. Individual flower heads are up to 0.8 centimetres wide with seven to 10 ray florets and a similar number of disc florets. Its seeds have the dense plume of hairs characteristic of all goldenrods.

Top: Flowers are in dense pyramidal clusters with upward-facing flower heads. Middle: Seaside goldenrod often forms dense clumps. Bottom: The hairless narrow leaves have smooth edges.

Coastal

 **Native Species**

Bog goldenrod

Solidago uliginosa
Northern bog goldenrod

HABITAT: Bog goldenrod commonly occurs in peatlands, damp barrens, meadows, and woodlands throughout Nova Scotia.

CHARACTERISTICS: An upright plant, bog goldenrod has one or a few unbranched stems. Plants have both basal and stem leaves, which are firm and lanceolate, oblanceolate, or elliptical. Basal leaves may reach 20 centimetres in length and are smooth-edged or slightly toothed and long petioled and partly clasp the stem. Stem leaves are alternate, smaller than basal leaves, smooth-edged, and sessile. Leaves and stems are usually hairless. The stems may be purple-tinted.

Flowers are produced in a dense panicle which varies from wand-like to broadly pyramidal. Flowering branches are generally held at a narrow angle close to the main stem but are occasionally one-sided. Individual flower heads are 0.3 centimetres wide with one to eight (usually six to eight) golden yellow ray florets. Seed heads are tiny and fluffy; seed plumes help them travel on the wind.

Early goldenrod, *S. juncea*, is found throughout the province, except in the southwest. Early goldenrod may have ciliate hairs along its leaf edges. In addition to its preference for dry sites, early goldenrod is distinguished by small leafy tufts in its upper leaf axils and a wide-spreading panicle of flowers that imparts a fireworks effect. Individual flower heads have up to 12 ray florets.

Top: Bog goldenrod may have narrow or broad flower clusters. Middle: Some bog goldenrod have narrow flower clusters; its leaves are often narrow and hairless. Bottom: Early goldenrod has wide-spreading panicles of flowers; the narrow foliage is similar to that of bog goldenrod.

Wetlands

Barrens

Aster family / Asteraceae
Field sow-thistle
Sonchus arvensis
Perennial sow-thistle, corn sow-thistle

Maximum height: 120 centimetres
Flowering season: July to September

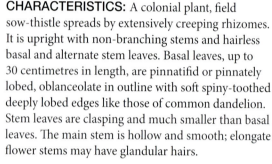

HABITAT: Field sow-thistle is a European introduction found in waste places and occasionally along gravelly coastal beaches throughout Nova Scotia.

CHARACTERISTICS: A colonial plant, field sow-thistle spreads by extensively creeping rhizomes. It is upright with non-branching stems and hairless basal and alternate stem leaves. Basal leaves, up to 30 centimetres in length, are pinnatifid or pinnately lobed, oblanceolate in outline with soft spiny-toothed deeply lobed edges like those of common dandelion. Stem leaves are clasping and much smaller than basal leaves. The main stem is hollow and smooth; elongate flower stems may have glandular hairs.

Flower heads are produced in loose terminal corymbs. Individual flower heads are 3 to 5 centimetres wide with numerous golden yellow ray florets and no disc florets. Seed heads look like those of a dandelion, but smaller.

Common sow-thistle, *S. oleraceus*, is an introduced slender annual scattered along the coast. It reaches 100 centimetres in height. Its thin pinnatifid leaves have a terminal lobe that is larger than its lateral lobes. Stem leaves clasp the stem and have pointed auricles. Lemon yellow flower heads are 1.5 to 2.5 centimetres wide.

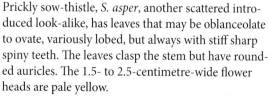

Prickly sow-thistle, *S. asper*, another scattered introduced look-alike, has leaves that may be oblanceolate to ovate, variously lobed, but always with stiff sharp spiny teeth. The leaves clasp the stem but have rounded auricles. The 1.5- to 2.5-centimetre-wide flower heads are pale yellow.

Top: Field sow-thistle flowers are in loose corymbs; flower and seed heads resemble those of small dandelions. Middle: Common sow-thistle has pinnatifid leaves with a large terminal lobe. Bottom: The leaf edges of prickly sow-thistle have sharp spiny teeth.

Introduced Species

Common dandelion

Taraxacum officinale

Dumble-dor, blowballs, piss-n-the-beds

HABITAT: Common dandelion grows in disturbed habitats and waste places, including lawns and gardens. It is abundant throughout Nova Scotia.

CHARACTERISTICS: Common dandelion is a low rosetted plant with a deep taproot and only basal leaves. Leaves, which are up to 45 centimetres long, are oblanceolate and mostly pinnatifid with deep, coarse lobes and teeth. Sometimes the leaves are only sharply toothed. Leaves taper into a long narrow-winged petiole and are sparsely covered in fine white hairs, especially along the central vein. The entire plant oozes a milky sap when cut.

The many solitary flower heads are at the ends of hollow pubescent stems. Flowers are up to 5 centimetres in diameter and composed of numerous ray florets but no disc florets. Seed heads are large and distinct: a globular mass of seeds with long-stalked plumes. The main flowering season is May and June, but plants flower sporadically through September.

VITAL STATISTICS
Maximum height: 40 centimetres
Flowering season: April to September

Top: The many solitary flowers have numerous ray florets. Middle: Common dandelion are low-rosetted plants with only basal leaves. Bottom: Large plumed seed heads.

Disturbed

253

Aster family / Asteraceae

Meadow goatsbeard

Introduced Species

Tragopogon pratensis

Meadow salsify

VITAL STATISTICS

Maximum height: 100 centimetres

Flowering season: June to August

HABITAT: Meadow goatsbeard, a European species, is found in disturbed habitats. It is scattered throughout Nova Scotia.

CHARACTERISTICS: Meadow goatsbeard is a slender biennial plant arising from a taproot. In the first season, plants produce a rosette of narrow lance-shaped to linear smooth-edged hairless leaves. Leaves may be up to 30 centimetres in length and have parallel veins. In the second season, one or a few stems arise with alternate lance-shaped to linear leaves which are sessile and clasp the stem. All parts of the plant exude a milky sap when cut.

Flowers are solitary on long stems from the axils of the upper leaves. Flower buds are long and tapered with a rounded base. Flower stems widen at the base of each flower head; flower heads are about 5 centimetres wide with numerous ray florets. Outer florets have larger rays than the inner florets; no disc florets are present. The base of each flower head has eight narrow green phyllaries that are almost as long as the outer ray florets. These heads close at night or during wet weather. The seed head resembles that of a dandelion.

Top: The outer set of ray florets on the solitary flowers is much larger than the inner sets. Middle: Hairless linear leaves clasp the stem. Bottom: Flower buds are tapered with a rounded base; seed heads are similar to those of dandelion.

Introduced
Species

Coniferous Forest

Mixed Forest

Deciduous Forest

Wetlands

Coastal

Disturbed

Aster family / Asteraceae
Coltsfoot
Tussilago farfara
Coughwort

Maximum height: 45 centimetres
Flowering season: April to May

HABITAT: Coltsfoot, of European origin, is found in damp waste areas throughout Nova Scotia. It also invades open woodlands, swamps, and coastal rocky beaches, especially in limestone-rich areas.

CHARACTERISTICS: Coltsfoot is a ground-cover-like plant that forms large patches as it rapidly spreads by underground rhizomes. Leaves are primarily basal. Each leaf is toothed and palmately lobed, with five to 12 shallow lobes. New leaves are covered in white downy hairs which disappear from the upper surfaces as the season progresses; leaf undersides remain white with tomentose hairs. Leaves are up to 20 centimetres wide. Stems are white and woolly; alternate stem leaves are reduced to green bracts.

Plants produce numerous flower stems, each terminated by a single flower head. Individual flower heads are about 2.5 centimetres in diameter and composed of several overlapping rings of numerous narrow yellow ray florets, which surround numerous yellow disc florets.

Plants flower before they produce leaves; this makes them among the earliest wildflowers to bloom in Nova Scotia. Flowers close on wet days or at night. The flower stem nods as the seeds develop but becomes erect as seeds are released from the small dandelion-like puffball. Seeds are released as leaves emerge.

Top: Individual flower heads have several overlapping rings of narrow ray florets. Middle: Solitary flowers before the plant sends up leaves. Bottom: Palmately lobed leaves with many shallow lobes.

255

Aster family / Asteraceae

Common burdock

Arctium minus

Lesser burdock, stickly-buds

Introduced Species

VITAL STATISTICS

Maximum height: 150 centimetres
Flowering season: June to September

HABITAT: A European species, common burdock is found in waste places, around buildings, and along roadsides, especially in shady areas throughout Nova Scotia.

CHARACTERISTICS: Common burdock is a robust large-leaved biennial. In their first season, plants produce a rosette of large basal leaves, which are up to 60 centimetres long and look like rhubarb. Leaves are ovate to heart-shaped with long furrowed hollow petioles and smooth, often undulating, edges. The upper sides of the leaves are usually hairless; undersides are whitened with fine pubescent hairs. In the second year, plants produce a stout stalk with alternate stem leaves that are smaller than those produced in the first year and ovate in outline. Plants produce many flowering stems; these stems are whitened with finely pubescent hairs.

Upper stems end in dense raceme-like clusters of flower heads on short stalks. The globular flower heads are 1.5 to 2.5 centimetres wide with purple-pink disc florets but no ray florets. White styles, which extend beyond the pink corolla, create a pincushion effect. The phyllaries below the flower heads are strongly hooked, resulting in burrs that, when seeds are ripe, stick to animal fur or woolly clothing.

Top: The petal-less flowers are in dense racemes; the phyllaries have hooked tips. Bottom: Leaves are large and heart-shaped with undulating edges.

Introduced Species

Black knapweed

Centaurea nigra

Lesser knapweed, black starthistle

HABITAT: A European species, black knapweed is naturalized throughout Nova Scotia along roadsides and in old pastures and other waste places.

CHARACTERISTICS: Black knapweed is a bushy clumping plant with numerous upright and branching stems. Plants have both basal and alternate stem leaves which vary from elliptical to lanceolate. Leaves are generally smooth but wavy-edged; occasionally they may be slightly toothed or lobed. Basal leaves have petioles; stem leaves are usually sessile. Veins on the undersides of leaves are raised and ribbed. Hairs on the entire plant give it a grey-green appearance.

The rose-purple flower heads are held on long stems in an open corymb. Individual flower heads are about 3 centimetres wide with a globular base covered in dark brown fringed phyllaries. Flower heads are composed of only disc florets; close examination reveals five petals on each, although, from a distance, the flowers look like pincushions.

VITAL STATISTICS

Maximum height: 80 centimetres
Flowering season: July to September

Top: The petal-less flowers have a globular base covered in brown fringed phyllaries. Bottom: The basal leaves are occasionally lobed and toothed.

Disturbed

257

Aster family / Asteraceae

Canada thistle

Cirsium arvense
Field thistle, creeping thistle

Introduced Species

VITAL STATISTICS

Maximum height: 150 centimetres
Flowering season: July to August

HABITAT: Canada thistle is a European species found in disturbed habitats throughout Nova Scotia.

CHARACTERISTICS: Canada thistle, a clumping plant, forms large colonies as it spreads through underground rhizomes. Plants have both basal and alternate stem leaves. Leaves are rigid, lanceolate to oblong, and pinnately lobed or pinnatifid with wavy, stiff, and spiny toothed edges. The upper sides of the leaves may be smooth, but undersides have white woolly hairs. The uppermost leaves often clasp the stem. Stems have longitudinal ridges and scattered long white hairs. Upper stems are often purple-tinted.

Plants are dioecious, but male and female flowers look similar. Flower heads are produced in an open corymb. Each 1.5- to 2-centimetre-wide flower head is composed only of florets; close examination reveals that each floret has five distinct narrow petals. From a distance, however, the flowers look like pincushions. The base of each flower head is globular with spine-tipped purple-green phyllaries. Seeds have feathery plumes, reminiscent of small dandelion seed heads.

Marsh thistle, *C. palustre*, is occasional in both damp waste places and wetlands. Plants are biennial with solitary stems. Leaves are similar to those of Canada thistle but have spiny winged stems. Tightly clustered flower heads are terminal and nearly sessile.

Top: The pincushion-like petal-less flowers are in corymbs. Middle: Canada thistle leaves have wavy spiny-toothed edges. Bottom: Marsh thistle has spiny-winged edges along its stems; flowers are densely arranged.

258

<small>Introduced
Species</small>

Aster family / Asteraceae

Bull thistle

Cirsium vulgare
Common thistle, Scotch thistle

VITAL STATISTICS

Maximum height: 150 centimetres
Flowering season: Late July to
September

HABITAT: Bull thistle, a European species, is found in waste places throughout Nova Scotia.

CHARACTERISTICS: Bull thistle is a biennial plant with a solitary stout stem. First-year plants have evergreen basal leaves; second-year plants have alternate stem leaves. Pinnatifid leaves are lanceolate to elliptical with sharp spine-tipped lobes and teeth. Leaves have scattered hairs on their top surfaces but undersides are white and woolly. Stems have spiny wings.

The 3- to 5-centimetre-wide flower heads are in small corymbs. Flower bases are globular with 1- to 2-centimetre-long spiny phyllaries. Flowers, composed of only rose-purple disc florets, have a pincushion appearance. Seeds have plumed hairs and, when released, the seed heads resemble those of dandelion.

A slender biennial scattered in wet open woodlands, streamsides, swamps, and marshes, swamp thistle, *C. muticum*, is Nova Scotia's only native species of thistle. Leaves are pinnatifid, more deeply lobed than those of bull thistle, and have fewer spines. Stems are smooth with scattered long hairs. The base of the 3-centimetre-wide flower heads is globular, but the phyllaries have sharp, rather than spiny, tips—more thorn-like than needle-like.

Top: The globular petal-less flower heads have long-spined phyllaries. Middle: First-season bull thistle produces a basal rosette of pinnatifid spiny-edged leaves. Bottom: Swamp thistle phyllaries have sharp spines but its stems are smooth.

Disturbed

259

Aster family / Asteraceae
Spotted Joe-Pye weed

Native
Species

Eutrochium maculatum (formerly *Eupatorium maculatum*)

VITAL STATISTICS

Maximum height: 2 metres
Flowering season: July to September

HABITAT: Spotted Joe-Pye weed occurs along streamsides, wet ditches, swamps, and marshes throughout Nova Scotia.

CHARACTERISTICS: Spotted Joe-Pye weed is a robust clumping plant with multiple upright non-branching stems. Lance-shaped to ovate leaves are dark green, sharply toothed, slightly hairy, and in whorls of four or five, rarely three. Leaves taper gradually to the base of the short petiole. Stems are often purple-tinted.

Flower heads are produced in flat-topped dense corymbs that are up to 20 centimetres wide. Individual dusty rose to purple flower heads are 0.5 to 1 centimetre long and composed of eight to 20 disc florets. Overall, flower clusters look fluffy. The seeds have attached hairs that allow them to blow for many kilometres in the wind.

Coastal plain Joe-Pye weed, *E. dubium*, is a rare Atlantic Coastal Plain species confined primarily to southwestern Nova Scotia. It is smaller in stature than spotted Joe-Pye weed; leaves are generally in whorls of three or four. Leaves taper abruptly to the petiole, which is generally longer than that of spotted Joe-Pye weed. The stem is sticky with glandular hairs near the flowers. Flower clusters are 6 to 8 centimetres wide with five to 12 disc florets per flower head.

Top: Spotted Joe-Pye weed's fluffy flowers are in flat-topped clusters. Middle: Leaves are in whorls. Bottom: Coastal plain Joe-Pye weed has rugose leaves in whorls of three.

 **Introduced Species**

Common fumitory

Fumaria officinalis
Fumitory, earth-smoke

HABITAT: Common fumitory, a European species, is occasionally found in recently disturbed areas of Nova Scotia.

CHARACTERISTICS: Common fumitory is a weakly ascending annual with multiple thin branches. Alternate leaves are bipinnately compound. Each leaflet is also deeply lobed. The result is a delicate fern-like leaf. The entire plant is hairless, waxy, and grey-green.

Flowers are produced in axillary racemes which are up to 7 centimetres long. Individual flowers are tubular and 0.7 to 0.9 centimetres long. The main floral tube is light purple, but its tip is dark purple. The flower has four petals: two central petals are partly fused and house the six stamens and single style; the other two form an upper and lower lip. The upper petal has a pouch-like spur.

Pink corydalis, *Capnoides sempervirens* (formerly *Corydalis sempervirens*), a slender native annual or biennial, can reach 60 centimetres in height. Similar to common fumitory, it has delicate grey-green fern-like foliage. Flowers are held in narrow panicles. Individual tubular flowers are about 1.5 centimetres long and pink with a yellow tip. Plants favour disturbed areas and are scattered throughout much of the province.

VITAL STATISTICS
Maximum height: 30 centimetres
Flowering season: July to September

Top: The tubular dark purple-tipped flowers of common fumitory are in racemes. Middle: The smooth grey-green leaves are delicate and fern-like. Bottom: Pink corydalis has tubular flowers with yellow tips.

Disturbed

Pea family / Fabaceae

American groundnut

Apios americana

American potato-bean, groundbean

Native Species

VITAL STATISTICS

Maximum height: 3 metres
Flowering season: Late July to August

HABITAT: American groundnut is found in moist soils along rivers, thickets, and bottomlands, primarily in southwestern Nova Scotia, but also scattered in the central region.

CHARACTERISTICS: American groundnut is a leafy twining vine arising from strings of edible tuberous roots. Alternate leaves are pinnately compound with three to seven elliptical to ovate smooth-edged leaflets. Leaves may reach 15 centimetres in length; stems and leaves are almost hairless.

Plants produce a dense raceme of axillary flowers. Each broad pea-like flower is maroon-purple to mauve, with a sweet fragrance, and is about 1 centimetre long. Flowers develop slender 6- to 12-centimetre-long seed pods.

American hog-peanut, *Amphicarpaea bracteata*, is an annual twining pea-family vine that may reach 250 centimetres in length. Long petioled leaves are trifoliate with ovate smooth-edged leaflets. The terminal leaflet has a distinct stalk; lateral leaflets are nearly sessile. Stems and leaves are finely pubescent. Plants have two types of flowers. The 1-centimetre-long upper flowers are pea-like, pale lilac to white, narrow, and produced in dense axillary racemes. Flowers develop scimitar-shaped seed pods that reach 7 centimetres in length. Lower flowers are petal-less and often push developing seed pods into the soil, similar to the seed pods of peanuts. American hog-peanut is found along shady thickets and riverbanks throughout mainland Nova Scotia; it is rare on Cape Breton Island.

Top: The pea-like flowers of American groundnut are in dense racemes. Middle: American groundnut has pinnate leaves with three to seven smooth-edged leaflets. Bottom: American hog-peanut is a twining vine with trifoliate leaves and small axillary clusters of pale lilac pea-like flowers.

Canada tick-trefoil

Desmodium canadense
Showy tick-trefoil, Canada tick-clover

Native Species

HABITAT: Canada tick-trefoil, found along open riverbanks and in open woodlands and alluvial thickets, is rare and scattered in Hants, Kings, and Queens counties.

CHARACTERISTICS: Canada tick-trefoil is a slender upright plant. Stems are covered in fine white to brown hairs. Alternate short petioled leaves are trifoliate. Leaflets, which have short stems and rounded tips, are oblong to lanceolate and up to 8 centimetres long. Leaflets are smooth-edged but hairy, giving them a grey-green appearance.

Rose pink flowers grow in a panicle of elongate narrow racemes both in the upper leaf axils and at the ends of the stems. Individual pea-like flowers are up to 1.25 centimetres in length. The dorsal petal base has two pale spots outlined in deep purple. Flat elongate seed pods have three to five rounded segments and are covered in hooked hairs.

Large tick-trefoil, *D. glutinosum*, also rare, is found in rich shady deciduous woods and inter-vales within Hants, Kings, and Queens counties. It is a bushy plant with long petioled trifoliate leaves. Ovate pointed leaflets, covered in fine hairs, have smooth edges. The terminal leaflet is larger than the two lateral ones and has a longer stem. Leaves are alternate to whorled. Stems have glandular hairs. Light pink pea-like flowers are produced in narrow branching terminal racemes. Their flattened seed pod has one to four triangular segments.

Top: The pea-like flowers of Canada tick-trefoil are in a panicle of racemes. Middle: Canada tick-trefoil's short petioled trifoliate leaves have narrow leaflets; the stems are covered in fine hairs. Bottom: Large tick-trefoil flowers are in elongate narrow racemes; the terminal leaflet of the trifoliate leaves is much larger than the lateral leaflets.

VITAL STATISTICS

Maximum height: 80 centimetres
Flowering season: Late July to August

Deciduous Forest

Wetlands

Pea family / Fabaceae

Red clover

Trifolium pratense
Purple clover

Introduced
Species

VITAL STATISTICS

Maximum height: 40 centimetres
Flowering season: June to September

HABITAT: Red clover, a European introduction, grows in disturbed habitats and waste places throughout Nova Scotia.

CHARACTERISTICS: Red clover is a clumping plant with many loosely ascending stems arising from a stout taproot. Plants have basal and alternate stem leaves that are trifoliate with ovate smooth-edged 1- to 3-centimetre-long sessile leaflets. Basal and lower leaves have long petioles; upper leaves are nearly sessile. The middle of each leaflet has a pale V-shaped chevron. Each leaf has a pair of ovate stipules at its base. Stems and leaves may be smooth or covered in fine pubescent hairs.

Flowers are produced in dense globular heads, which are 1.5 to 3 centimetres in diameter. A pair of sessile leaves grows below each head. The tiny narrow pea-like flowers are rose pink.

Rabbit's-foot clover, *T. arvense*, a low bushy annual, has stems which reach 40 centimetres in length. Hairy-edged trifoliate leaves have narrow sessile leaflets. The entire plant is covered in fine hairs. Flowers, in dense grey-pink fuzzy cylindrical 1- to 4-centimetre-long heads, bloom from July to September.

Crown vetch, *Securigera (Coronilla) varia*, has pinnately compound leaves with 11 to 25 tiny oblong leaflets. Axillary flowers, produced in July, are in 3.5-centimetre-wide globular umbels of 10 to 25 two-tone pink pea-like blossoms. It is widely scattered in the province.

Top: Red clover flowers are in dense globular heads; the trifoliate leaves have a pale V-shaped chevron.
Middle: Rabbit's-foot clover has grey-pink fuzzy heads; the trifoliate leaves have narrow leaflets. Bottom: Crown vetch has pinnate leaves and flowers in globular umbels.

264

Blood milkwort

Polygala sanguinea

Purple milkwort, rose milkwort, field milkwort, common polygala

Native Species

HABITAT: Blood milkwort is rarely found in widely scattered locations in Nova Scotia; it grows in acidic fields, open woodlands, and recent burn sites.

CHARACTERISTICS: Blood milkwort is a slender but leafy annual plant. Stems are angled and hairless. Sessile hairless smooth-edged linear leaves reach 3.5 centimetres in length and may be opposite or alternate.

Pink to purple flowers are produced in 2.5-centimetre-long cone-like racemes at the ends of branches. Each flower is composed primarily of two large overlapping petal-like sepals located on the bottom of the flower. Set atop these sepals are three small petals that form a tube. One of these has a yellow crest.

Racemed milkwort, *P. polygama*, is restricted to Annapolis and Digby counties, where it occurs in dry open locations. Its raceme is more open and elongate than that of blood milkwort; its flowers pink-purple; and its round sepals wide-spreading and ear-like. The lowermost of the three petals has long fringes. Plants also produce one-sided racemes of inconspicuous flowers at the base of the plant; these flowers develop into globular off-white capsules.

VITAL STATISTICS
Maximum height: 40 centimetres
Flowering season: Late June to October

Top: Blood milkwort flowers are in cone-like racemes. Middle: Each racemed milkwort flower has two ear-like sepals; the lower petal is long-fringed. Bottom: Inconspicuous racemes at the base of racemed milkwort plants produce globular off-white seed capsules.

Balsam family / Balsamaceae

Purple jewelweed

Impatiens glandulifera

Policeman's helmet, Himalayan balsam

Introduced Species

VITAL STATISTICS

Maximum height: 2 metres

Flowering season: August to September

HABITAT: Purple jewelweed, a Himalayan species, likely introduced in the province as a garden ornamental, is occasionally encountered in damp waste areas and roadside thickets and along streamsides. It is scattered primarily in the southern half of Nova Scotia.

CHARACTERISTICS: Purple jewelweed is a tall coarse annual with succulent stems that are square in cross-section, hairless, and often tinted purple. Lanceolate to elliptical leaves are opposite or in whorls of three; leaves are hairless with finely toothed edges and measure up to 18 centimetres in length.

Axillary flowers are produced in racemes of two to 14 flowers. Individual flowers, each 3 to 4 centimetres long, have three sepals and three petals. The lower sepal forms a pouch with a backward-pointing spur; the two upper sepals are small and insignificant. The upper petal forms a hood-like (the "helmet") structure; the lower pair of petals forms a landing pad for pollinating insects. Each of the lower petals has an upward-curling lobe near its base. Sepals and petals are coloured in shades of pink or purple-pink. Nodding and ridged elliptical seed capsules are up to 3.5 centimetres long and literally explode when touched.

Top: Flowers have three petals: the upper forms a hood, the lower pair hangs downward. Bottom: The opposite or whorled leaves are narrow and finely toothed.

Mint family / Lamiaceae
Wild basil

Clinopodium vulgare (formerly *Satureja vulgaris*)
Dogmint

Introduced Species

HABITAT: Wild basil is found in old pastures, open woods, damp rocky ravines, and waste places primarily in the northern half of Nova Scotia.

CHARACTERISTICS: Wild basil is a clumping plant with numerous upright stems. Leaves are elliptical to ovate, opposite, shallowly toothed, and nearly sessile. Veins on leaf undersides are prominent and raised. Stems are square in cross-section. All parts of the plant are covered in soft hairs and emit a basil fragrance when bruised.

Pink to violet flowers are in dense terminal and axillary cymes and have densely hairy and bristle-tipped sepals. Tubular flowers, each about 0.8 to 1.5 centimetres long, end in five petals: two form an upper lip; three, a lower lip.

VITAL STATISTICS	
Maximum height:	60 centimetres
Flowering season:	June to September

Top: The two-lipped flowers are in sessile axillary whorls; flowers may be violet. Middle: The opposite nearly sessile leaves have rounded teeth; flowers may be pale pink. Bottom: Flowers are also in dense terminal clusters; flowers may be pink.

267

Mint family / Lamiaceae
Common hemp-nettle

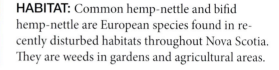

Galeopsis tetrahit
Dog nettle, brittle-stemmed hemp-nettle

VITAL STATISTICS

Maximum height: 75 centimetres
Flowering season: June to September

HABITAT: Common hemp-nettle and bifid hemp-nettle are European species found in recently disturbed habitats throughout Nova Scotia. They are weeds in gardens and agricultural areas.

CHARACTERISTICS: Common hemp-nettle is an upright leafy annual with a single stem and many branches. Stems and leaves are covered in bristly hairs. Stems are swollen below the joint of each opposite leaf pair and appear square in cross-section. Ovate to elliptical leaves are sharply toothed and have distinct petioles.

Flowers are held in dense axillary cymes. The five sepals are fused into a short tube and have conspicuous spiny tips that are 0.8 to 1.1 centimetres long. Petals, hairy on the outside, are fused into an elongate tube which is about 2 centimetres long. The upper two petals form a hood-like structure over the anthers and pistil; the lower three petals, a three-lobed lip. The central lobe of the lip is square. Flowers are white to deep pink, often with a darker blotch on each of the lateral lower lobes. The middle of the central lower lobe has a yellow blotch surrounded by a deeper pink.

Bifid hemp-nettle, *G. bifida*, is nearly identical in appearance to common hemp-nettle. Sepal spines are shorter, just 0.5 to 0.8 centimetres long; the lower central lobe of the lip is distinctly notched.

Top: The two-lipped flowers are in dense axillary whorls; the sepals are spine-tipped. Bottom: Bifid hemp-nettle has a distinctly notched lower lip.

Purple dead-nettle

Lamium purpureum
Red dead-nettle, red henbit

Introduced Species

HABITAT: Purple dead-nettle, a European species, is often encountered in newly disturbed areas, primarily in the central regions of Nova Scotia.

CHARACTERISTICS: Purple dead-nettle is a mounding annual which freely branches from the base. The green or purple-tinted stem is square in cross-section and hollow. The 1- to 2.5-centimetre-long opposite leaves are ovate, covered in soft hairs, and have shallow-toothed edges. The veins on the undersides of the leaves are prominent and raised. Lower leaves have distinct petioles and are widely spaced; leaves closer to the flowers are nearly sessile and overlap. Upper leaves are often tinted purple, especially early and late in the growing season. The plant has a rank smell when bruised.

Nearly stemless flowers are in axillary whorls at the tips of the many branches. Sepals are fused and hairy with bristly tips. Petals fuse to form a 0.8- to 1.5-centimetre-long tube which ends in a mouth-like arrangement of fused petals. Two upper petals form a curved hood, which is hairy on the outer surface; the lower three, a lip which is pinched in appearance. The central lobe on the bottom itself has two lobes. Flowers are purple-red with darker spots on the lip.

Common dead-nettle or henbit, *L. amplexicaule*, is localized from Kings to Colchester counties. It often grows alongside purple dead-nettle and is distinguished by its round to kidney-shaped leaves, which have large rounded teeth.

Top: The fuzzy leaves are often purple-tinted, especially early and late in the season. Middle: The lower lip of purple hemp-nettle has a pinched look. Bottom: Common dead-nettle has round leaves with large teeth.

VITAL STATISTICS

Maximum height: 20 centimetres
Flowering season: July to October

Disturbed

269

Mint family / Lamiaceae

Marsh hedge-nettle

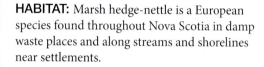

Stachys palustris

Woundwort, marsh woundwort

VITAL STATISTICS

Maximum height: 100 centimetres
Flowering season: July to September

HABITAT: Marsh hedge-nettle is a European species found throughout Nova Scotia in damp waste places and along streams and shorelines near settlements.

CHARACTERISTICS: Marsh hedge-nettle is a clumping upright sparingly branched plant that increases through subterranean white tuber-like rhizomes. The stem, square in cross-section, is often tinted purple, especially near the top. Opposite leaves are lanceolate to elliptical, finely toothed, generally sessile, and up to 10 centimetres in length. The entire plant is covered in fine hairs; it has a rank smell when bruised.

Flowers are produced in terminal spikes which are 10 to 20 centimetres long. Each spike is composed of four to 12 whorls of stemless 1.5-centimetre-long rose-purple flowers. Individual flowers have a two-lipped appearance: the upper two petals are fused to form a hood or upper lip; the lower three, to form a three-lobed lip. The central lower lobe is much larger than the two lateral lobes, and usually mottled with paler and darker tones. The five hairy sepals are often purple-tinted and have pointed, but not sharp, tips.

Canada germander, *Teucrium canadense*, is a look-alike to marsh hedge-nettle and is occasionally found along gravelly coastlines; it is distinguished by its split upper lip.

Top: Whorls of stemless flowers are arranged in a raceme. Middle: The narrow leaves are sessile with rounded teeth. Bottom: Canada germander is distinguished from marsh hedge-nettle by its split upper lip.

Mint family / Lamiaceae
Lemon thyme

 **Introduced Species**

Thymus pulegioides (formerly *T. serpyllum* subsp. *chamaedrys*)
Wild thyme, creeping thyme

HABITAT: Lemon thyme, a European species originally grown as a garden ornamental in Nova Scotia, is occasionally naturalized along roadsides, pasturelands, and waste places from Cumberland to Pictou counties.

CHARACTERISTICS: Lemon thyme is a creeping matted evergreen that roots at the nodes as it creeps over the soil surface. Ascending stems are unbranched. Stems are square in cross-section and often purple-tinted and have hairs along their edges. Small opposite leaves, which are up to 1 centimetre in length, are ovate to elliptical, short petioled, smooth-edged, and hairless. The plant emits a lemony fragrance when bruised.

Flowers are produced in axillary clusters as well as densely arranged raceme-like terminal whorls. Individual flowers are about 0.6 centimetres long and tubular with a two-lipped appearance. The upper two petals form the upper lip; the lower three petals form a three-lobed lower lip. The inside of the flower is hairy and has four stamens. Flowers are generally purple-pink but can vary from pale pink to lavender to reddish-purple.

VITAL STATISTICS

Maximum height: 20 centimetres
Flowering season: July to August

Top: The two-lipped flowers are in whorls arranged in racemes. Bottom: Lemon thyme forms mats with opposite elliptical smooth-edged leaves.

Disturbed

271

Broomrape family / Orobanchaceae

Red bartsia

Odontites vulgaris (formerly *O. serotina*)

Introduced Species

VITAL STATISTICS

Maximum height: 30 centimetres
Flowering season: July to September

HABITAT: Red bartsia is a European species occasionally found in disturbed areas of Nova Scotia.

CHARACTERISTICS: Red bartsia is a slender multi-stemmed annual. Finely pubescent stems are square in cross-section. Plants are initially unbranched but, later in the season, produce both basal and upper branches. The stem and leaves are often purple-tinted; opposite leaves are narrow and lanceolate and sessile with short stiff hairs and sparse shallow teeth.

Flowers are produced in terminal one-sided racemes. A leaf-like bract, often tinted purple, is located at the base of each flower. Individual rose-red flowers are tubular and about 1 centimetre in length. The end of the floral tube has a two-lipped opening. The upper lip is notched; the lower is deeply three-lobed with a darker throat. Fine hairs fringe the edges of the petals. There are four stamens, and a single style extends beyond the end of the flower. Four green or purple-tinted sepals are finely pubescent.

Red bartsia, a hemiparasitic plant, obtains some of its nutrients from nearby plants.

Top: A leaf-like bract is located at the base of each flower on the one-sided racemes. Bottom: Stems and leaves are often purple-tinted.

Disturbed

272

Broomrape family / Orobanchaceae

Marsh lousewort

Pedicularis palustris

Purple lousewort, swamp lousewort

Introduced
Species

HABITAT: Marsh lousewort, a European species, is rare and localized in northern Cape Breton, where it grows in wet marshes and meadows.

CHARACTERISTICS: Marsh lousewort is an erect branching annual or biennial plant. Alternate leaves are pinnately compound with narrow, pinnately lobed leaflets. Dark green, often purple-tinted, leaves are up to 5 centimetres long and look like a miniature fern frond. Stems are longitudinally ridged and commonly dark purple. The plant is hairless except for the sepals, which have long white hairs.

Flowers are produced on leafy racemes. Sepals, which are often purple-tinted, are fused into a slightly ribbed tube with two crested lobes. Rose-purple petals are fused into a tube which is 1.8 to 2.5 centimetres long. The upper two petals are fused to form a hook-shaped hood; the lower three, a three-lobed lip.

Wetlands

Top: The upper petals are modified into a hook-shaped hood; the lower petals form a three-lobed lip.
Bottom: Flowers are held in terminal racemes; stems are usually purple-tinted.

Disturbed

Orchid family / Orchidaceae

Dragon's-mouth

Arethusa bulbosa

Arethusa, swamp pink

Native Species

VITAL STATISTICS

Maximum height: 30 centimetres
Flowering season: Mid-June to mid-July

Wetlands

HABITAT: Dragon's-mouth, which prefers sphagnum bogs and fens, is found primarily along the Atlantic coast and on Cape Breton Island.

CHARACTERISTICS: Dragon's-mouth is slender and not easily seen when out of flower. A single linear grass-like leaf arises from a bulb-like tuber. The hairless leaf elongates after flowering is complete.

The flower is solitary atop a leafless hairless stalk. The pink, rarely white, flower is 2.5 to 5 centimetres long; its length is greater than its width. Three narrow blunt-tipped sepals are erect or slightly outward-arching. Two narrow lateral petals arch forward and form a hood over the column and base of the lip; the base of the lip is erect but abruptly arches downward, causing it to appear tongue-like. The base of the lip is often paler than the rest of the flower, spotted, and streaked dark purple with three to five yellow or white-fringed crests running down the centre. The tip of the lip is fringed. Flowers have a sweet fragrance.

Top: Flowers are solitary on leafless stalks.
Bottom: The narrow grass-like leaves appear just as the flowers open.

Native Species

Orchid family / Orchidaceae
Grass pink
Calopogon tuberosus
Tuberous grass pink, swamp pink

HABITAT: Grass pink, common in sphagnum bogs and fens, is occasionally found in swamps or along lakeshores. It is well distributed in Nova Scotia.

CHARACTERISTICS: Grass pink is slender and not easily seen when out of bloom. The plant produces a single, rarely paired, linear to lanceolate hairless leaf which looks like a blade of grass. It arises from a bulb-like tuber.

A raceme of two to 10 flowers is produced atop a slender leafless hairless stalk. The 2.5- to 4.5-centimetre-wide flowers are pink, or, rarely, white. Broad sepals have pointed tips, are held on the same plane, and may arch slightly backward. Broad petals arch slightly forward. The lip is uppermost—an unusual feature in Nova Scotia's native orchids—and hinged at the base, allowing it to drop down to hit the outwardly arching column located in front of the lowermost sepal. The lip is narrow at the base but widens at the tip. A beard of white (lower) and yellow (upper) hairs occurs where the lip widens. These hairs look like anthers but are called pseudo-anthers as their only sexual function is to attract a pollinator.

VITAL STATISTICS
Maximum height: 30 centimetres
Flowering season: July

Wetlands

Top: The lip is uppermost and has a cluster of hair-like pseudo-anthers. Bottom: Flowers are held in loose racemes on leafless stems.

Orchid family / Orchidaceae

Pink lady's-slipper

Cypripedium acaule

Moccasin flower, pink moccasin flower

Native Species

VITAL STATISTICS

Maximum height: 30 centimetres
Flowering season: June to July

HABITAT: Pink lady's-slipper, found in open peaty barrens and acidic coniferous and mixed forests throughout Nova Scotia, is its most common lady's-slipper.

CHARACTERISTICS: Pink lady's-slipper, a low clumping plant, has a pair of oblong to elliptical basal leaves. These leaves may reach 30 centimetres in length and have distinct folded parallel ribs and smooth edges. Leaves are finely pubescent.

Six-centimetre-long flowers are solitary on leafless finely pubescent stems. The dorsal sepal arches forward; the other two sepals unite to form one broad sepal behind the pouch. The two lateral petals arch downward, sometimes backward, and may be twisted. They have long hairs at their base. The downward-hanging lip is rose pink or, rarely, white and resembles an inflated sack. The opening of the pouch is groove-like. Sepals and petals are brownish- to greenish-purple. A single green leafy bract arches over the top of the flower parallel to the dorsal sepals.

Ram's-head lady's-slipper, *C. arietinum*, is very rare in the gypsum-rich areas of Hants County. It has three to five alternate lance-shaped leaves that clasp the 20- to 30-centimetre-long stem. Leaves are smooth-edged with parallel ribs. The flower is solitary and only 1.5 to 2 centimetres long. The bronzy green to purplish-brown sepals and petals arch forward. The funnel-shaped pouch is white with raspberry pink veins. The top of the pouch has no veins and the opening has white hairs.

Top: The characteristic pink slipper-like pouch. Middle: Plants produce a pair of basal leaves and solitary flowers on leafless stems. Bottom: Ram's-head lady's-slipper has solitary flowers with a funnel-shaped pouch.

Orchid family / Orchidaceae

Native Species

Small purple-fringed orchid

Platanthera psycodes
Lesser purple-fringed orchid

HABITAT: Small purple-fringed orchid occurs in wetland areas such as fens, marshes, shorelines, and wet meadows throughout Nova Scotia.

CHARACTERISTICS: Small purple-fringed orchid is a slender plant with one or several non-branching stems. The alternate elliptical leaves are smooth-edged and hairless, have parallel veins, and clasp the stem. Each stem has two to five leaves. Lower leaves may be up to 20 centimetres long; upper leaves are shorter.

Plants produce a raceme of many 1.5- to 2-centimetre-wide lavender to rose-purple flowers. A narrow leafy bract is located at the base of each flower. Two broad lateral wide-spreading sepals often arch backward. The dorsal sepal and lateral petals arch forward to form a hood over the column. The lip is three-lobed and heavily fringed. Lateral lobes are smaller than the terminal lobe and often arch backward. A narrow spur extends behind the lip; the opening to the spur is rectangular.

Large purple-fringed orchid, *P. grandiflora*, occurs in similar habitats as, and often grows with, small purple-fringed orchid, but it is less common, found mostly in north and central regions of the province. Plants are robust, reaching to 100 centimetres in height, and the flowers are twice the size of the small purple-fringed orchid. The lateral lobes of the lip arch forward rather than backward. The opening to the nectar spur is rounded.

Wetlands

Top: The heavily fringed lip of small purple-fringed orchid is deeply three-lobed; these lobes often arch backward. Middle: Flowers are held in a dense cylindrical raceme. Bottom: On large purple-fringed orchid the lateral lobes of the fringed lip arch forward and the nectary opening is rounded.

Orchid family / Orchidaceae
Rose pogonia
Pogonia ophioglossoides

Native
Species

VITAL STATISTICS

Maximum height: 30 centimetres
Flowering season: July to early
August

Wetlands

HABITAT: Rose pogonia is common in peat bogs and, less frequently, along wet shorelines or wet meadows. It is found primarily along the Atlantic coast and on Cape Breton Island.

CHARACTERISTICS: A small plant, rose pogonia can form loose colonies as it spreads by slender subterranean rhizomes. Each non-flowering plant produces a single basal lanceolate to narrow ovate fleshy leaf that has a short petiole. The slender flowering stem has one elliptical clasping leaf partway up the stem and a single smaller leafy bract immediately below the flower. The entire plant is hairless.

Pink flowers, each 2 to 3 centimetres wide, are mostly solitary, rarely paired. Three narrow blunt sepals are wide-spreading. Two lateral petals arch forward to form a hood over the column and the base of the lip. The lip is fringed and bearded, with three rows of centrally located yellow hairs.

Top: The lip is heavily fringed and bearded; a leafy bract is located immediately behind the flower.
Bottom: Rose pogonia is often hidden among other peatland plants.

Native Species

Red trillium
Trillium erectum
Wakerobin, purple trillium, stinking Benjamin

HABITAT: Red trillium inhabits rich deciduous forests, especially on slopes. It is most likely to be seen along the Bay of Fundy, especially along the North Mountain.

CHARACTERISTICS: Red trillium, a clumping plant, has non-branching stems and a whorl of three ovate sessile leaves which are up to 18 centimetres long. Leaf edges are smooth but often wavy. The entire plant is hairless.

A stem, which is up to 10 centimetres long, arises from the junction of the leaf whorl and holds a solitary flower. The blossom is often outward-facing or slightly nodding. Three narrow pointed sepals vary from green to brownish-purple. Three reddish-purple petals are the same length as the sepals but much broader; six large anthers and three recurved styles are present. Flower width varies from 4 to 9 centimetres. Flowers become small dark red poisonous berries when mature.

VITAL STATISTICS
Maximum height: 40 centimetres
Flowering season: Late May to early June

Deciduous Forest

Top: Solitary flowers have three red petals alternating with three green sepals. Bottom: Each plant produces a whorl of three ovate sessile leaves.

American sea rocket

Native
Species

Cakile edentula

Sea rocket

VITAL STATISTICS

Maximum height: 50 centimetres
Flowering season: July to September

HABITAT: American sea rocket is common on coastal sandy to fine gravelly beaches and dunes around the entire coast of Nova Scotia.

CHARACTERISTICS: American sea rocket is a bushy fleshy many-branched annual. Stems are prostrate or weakly ascending. Alternate leaves, averaging about 5 centimetres in length, are obovate to oblanceolate with rounded teeth, lobes, or smooth edges. The entire plant is hairless.

Flowers are produced in narrow 5- to 25-centimetre-long racemes. Individual flowers are 0.6 centimetres wide and composed of four lavender-pink or white petals, four green sepals, six stamens, and a single style. Only a few flowers are open on any raceme at a time.

Seed pods, which are up to 2 centimetres in length, are composed of two sections with a slight constriction between them. The lower section is globular and cylindrical; the upper, more lance-shaped and tapered. The upper section contains one seed; the lower, one or more seeds. When mature, the upper section breaks away and floats on the waves to wash up on another beach. The lower section remains attached to the parent plant and drops its seeds around the parent.

Top: The four-petalled lilac-pink flowers are held in a raceme. Middle: The seed capsule's two sections have a slight constriction between them; some plants have nearly white petals. Bottom: The spoon-shaped leaves have rounded teeth or lobes.

Coastal

Mustard family / Brassicaceae

 **Introduced Species**

Meadow bittercress

Cardamine pratensis

Cuckooflower, lady's smock, European field bittercress

HABITAT: Meadow bittercress, a European species found in damp meadows and along wet shorelines, is distributed throughout Nova Scotia.

CHARACTERISTICS: Meadow bittercress is a slender but clumping plant with several upright non-branching stems. Plants have basal and alternate stem leaves, both of which are glossy. Basal leaves are pinnately compound with numerous rounded short-stemmed leaflets. The terminal leaflet is the largest and often has a few obscure teeth. Stem leaves are also pinnately compound but the leaflets are linear. The entire plant is hairless.

Flowers are initially produced in a compact raceme but, as the season advances, the raceme elongates. Fragrant flowers are 1 to 1.5 centimetres wide with four lavender-pink petals, six stamens, and a single style. The four sepals are often yellow-green or tinted purple. The seed capsule is thin, erect, and up to 3 centimetres long.

Toothed bittercress, *C. dentata*, is similar to meadow bittercress but its flowers are white and 1.6 to 2.4 centimetres wide. Its terminal leaflet is not toothed. This species is native to damp calcareous meadows on Cape Breton Island.

VITAL STATISTICS
Maximum height: 50 centimetres
Flowering season: Late May to mid-June

Wetlands

Top: The lavender-pink flowers are in a dense raceme, which elongates with time. Middle: Meadow bittercress often grows with other wet meadow grasses and sedges. Bottom: Toothed bittercress has flowers similar to those of meadow bittercress but are white.

Mustard family / Brassicaceae
Dame's rocket

Introduced Species

Hesperis matronalis
Sweet rocket, dame's violet, mother-of-the-evening

VITAL STATISTICS

Maximum height: 150 centimetres
Flowering season: June to July

HABITAT: Dame's rocket, a European species introduced to Nova Scotia as a garden ornamental, is occasionally found in waste places and along roadsides, especially near settlements.

CHARACTERISTICS: Dame's rocket is a tall clumping biennial or short-lived perennial with multiple erect stems. In the first season, plants produce a rosette of evergreen lance-shaped leaves which are up to 12 centimetres long. Leaf edges are finely toothed and tips are long and narrow. Leaves are typically wider at the base. In the second and subsequent years, leaves are alternate along the stem and may either have a short petiole or be sessile. The entire plant is covered in coarse hairs.

Each stem is unbranched at the base but produces multiple upper branches that terminate in a raceme of purple, lavender-pink, or white flowers. Flowers are crowded at first but become more widely spaced as the raceme elongates later in the season. Flowers are fragrant, especially in the evening. Each blossom is about 2 centimetres in diameter with four petals; six stamens and a single style are often hidden within the petals. The seed capsule is narrow and up to 14 centimetres long.

Top. Flowers range from pale lilac-pink to deeper purple-pink; blossoms are in racemes. Bottom: Plants form large clumps with multiple stems and masses of flowers.

Evening primrose family / Onagraceae

Fireweed

Chamerion angustifolium (formerly *Epilobium angustifolium*)

Great willowherb, rosebay willowherb

Native Species

HABITAT: A conspicuous plant after forest fires, fireweed also occurs along roadsides and in thickets, open woodlands, and disturbed areas throughout Nova Scotia.

CHARACTERISTICS: Fireweed is a tall slender leafy non-branching plant that forms large colonies. Alternate smooth-edged leaves are lanceolate, up to 20 centimetres long, and nearly sessile. Stems, especially their upper half, are often purple. The entire plant is nearly hairless.

Flowers are produced in long terminal racemes. Buds are reclined but become outward-facing when open. Individual flowers, each 3 to 4 centimetres wide, are rose-purple, including stems and sepals. Rarely, they may be white. Four narrow sepals are shorter than the four rounded petals; there are eight stamens and a single elongate style that ends in four recurved stigmas. The base of the pistil is hairy. Seed capsules are finely pubescent, slender, and 5 to 8 centimetres long, and, when ripe, split to release white silky-haired seeds.

VITAL STATISTICS	
Maximum height:	2 metres
Flowering season:	Mid-July to August

Top: The single elongate style has four recurved stigmas. Middle: Fireweed flowers are rarely white. Bottom: Flowers are in narrow racemes; stems are slender and non-branching.

283

Coniferous Forest

Mixed Forest

Deciduous Forest

Wetlands

Coastal

Disturbed

Evening primrose family / Onagraceae

Northern willowherb

Epilobium ciliatum

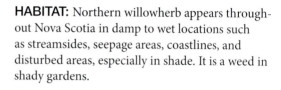

Native Species

VITAL STATISTICS

Maximum height: 100 centimetres
Flowering season: July to September

HABITAT: Northern willowherb appears throughout Nova Scotia in damp to wet locations such as streamsides, seepage areas, coastlines, and disturbed areas, especially in shade. It is a weed in shady gardens.

CHARACTERISTICS: Northern willowherb is an upright leafy, often branched, plant. Stems are square in cross-section and often purple-tinted. Two subspecies are found in Nova Scotia: stems of *ciliatum* are short-haired near the flowers; *glandulosum* has sticky hairs near the flowers.

Leaves vary from lanceolate to ovate and are toothed, sessile, or short petioled with hairs along the lower veins. Leaves, mostly opposite but become alternate among the flowers, may reach 15 centimetres in length. Plants overwinter as a tight reddish-purple bulb-like rosette.

Flowers are crowded in terminal leafy racemes with axillary lowermost flowers. Individual flowers are 0.5 to 1 centimetre wide and held at the ends of long stalks. Each flower has four smaller green or purple-tinted sepals; four larger, deeply notched, white to rose-purple petals; eight stamens; and a single style with a knob-like stigma. Slender seed capsules are 4 to 8 centimetres long and finely pubescent and split when ripe to release white silky-haired seeds.

Top: Each flower has four notched petals and a central style with a knob-like stigma. Middle: The upper, toothed leaves are alternate; flowers may be white with darker veins. Bottom: Seed capsules are slender; flowers may be rose-purple.

Native Species

Evening primrose family / Onagraceae

Marsh willowherb

Epilobium palustre
Swamp willowherb

HABITAT: Scattered in the province, marsh willowherb grows in bogs, ditches, seepage areas, and damp peaty barrens, especially along the Atlantic coast.

CHARACTERISTICS: Marsh willowherb is a slender plant with a few erect non-branching or sparingly branched stems. Stems and flower stalks are finely pubescent; upper leaf surfaces may or may not be pubescent. Sessile, linear to lanceolate, and smooth but revolute-edged leaves are mostly opposite but may be alternate toward the flowers. Plants often produce thin stolons after flowering.

Flowers are terminal, in loose racemes. Unopened buds are often nodding. Individual flowers are 0.4 to 0.8 centimetres wide with four deeply notched lilac, pink, or violet petals, eight stamens, and a single style with a knob-like stigma. The narrow erect seed capsule is finely pubescent and up to 9 centimetres long. It splits to release silky-haired seeds.

Although bog willowherb, *E. leptophyllum*, resembles marsh willowherb, it is often more branched; its linear leaves are longer, pubescent on the upper surface, and mostly alternate. Unopened flowers are held erect. Flowers are pale pink to almost white. Plants have no, or short, stolons. This species is found in wetlands throughout the province.

Top: Each marsh willowherb flower has four notched pink petals and a knob-like stigma; its leaves are linear.
Middle: The lance-shaped leaves of this marsh willowherb have smooth edges and hairless upper surfaces.
Bottom: Bog willowherb has linear leaves and its unopened flowers are held erect.

Wetlands

Barrens

Melanstome family / Melastomataceae

Virginia meadow beauty

Rhexia virginica

Meadow beauty, handsome Harry

VITAL STATISTICS

Maximum height: 75 centimetres
Flowering season: July to August

HABITAT: Virginia meadow beauty is rare and only encountered along wet shorelines and marshes in southwestern Nova Scotia. It is considered an Atlantic Coastal Plain species.

CHARACTERISTICS: Virginia meadow beauty is a narrow mostly non-branching plant with erect or sprawling stems. Stems are square in cross-section and usually purple-tinted and have glandular hairs. Opposite leaves are ovate to oblong, sessile, and up to 7.5 centimetres long. Slightly hairy or smooth leaves have sharply toothed and hairy edges.

Flowers are produced in short cymes with glandular stems. Individual flowers are 2.5 to 3.5 centimetres wide with four wide-spreading pink to rose-purple petals, eight bright yellow sickle-shaped stamens, and a single style. The fused sepals produce a vase-like structure, constricted at the upper end, which is covered in scattered long bristly hairs.

Top: Flowers have eight sickle-shaped anthers.
Bottom: The opposite leaves are sessile and the stems square.

Wetlands

Purslane family / Portulacaceae

 **Native Species**

Carolina spring beauty

Claytonia caroliniana

Northern spring beauty, wide-leaved spring beauty

HABITAT: Carolina spring beauty is found in rich open woodlands and slopes throughout most of Nova Scotia.

CHARACTERISTICS: Carolina spring beauty is a dainty spring ephemeral that disappears by early summer. Plants arise from a rounded tuber. About halfway along the length of the stem is a pair of opposite and elliptical, oblong or broadly ovate leaves, which are up to 7.5 centimetres long. Leaves are fleshy with smooth edges and an obvious petiole. The entire plant is hairless.

Flowers are produced on a terminal raceme with two to 11 1.5- to 2-centimetre-wide five-petalled flowers. Buds are nodding but become erect when they open. Flowers are white or pale pink with dark pink veins and a small yellow patch at their bases. Each blossom has five stamens and a single style with a three-cleft stigma. Flowers close at night and during cloudy weather.

VITAL STATISTICS

Maximum height: 12 centimetres
Flowering season: May to early June

Top: Flowers are pale pink with darker veins; each petal has a yellow patch at its base. Bottom: Each plant has a single pair of hairless leaves.

287

Pink family / Caryophyllaceae

Deptford pink

Dianthus armeria

Field pink

Introduced
Species

VITAL STATISTICS

Maximum height: 60 centimetres
Flowering season: May to July

HABITAT: Deptford pink is occasionally found in dry fields and along roadsides in Nova Scotia. It was introduced from Europe as a garden plant but has become naturalized.

CHARACTERISTICS: Deptford pink is a slender annual or biennial plant with several erect branching stems. Plants have opposite leaves that are linear, sessile, smooth-edged, and usually lightly pubescent. Leaves may reach 7 centimetres in length. A tuft of white hairs is found on the stem below each pair of leaves. The stem has a swelling at the node of each leaf pair.

Flowers are produced in small dense clusters with narrow pointed bracts at their base. The bracts, the tubular fused sepals, and the flower stems are all pubescent. Individual flowers are about 1 centimetre in diameter. The five petals are pink with white spots and have toothed edges. Flowers have 10 stamens with pink anthers and two styles.

Top: Petals have toothed edges and fine white spots.
Bottom: The edges of the plant's opposite linear sessile leaves are smooth.

Disturbed

Bouncing-bet

Saponaria officinalis
Soapwort

**Introduced
Species**

HABITAT: Bouncing-bet, a European plant, was introduced to Nova Scotia as a garden ornamental. It is occasionally encountered in waste places and along roadsides and trails near communities.

CHARACTERISTICS: Bouncing-bet, a stout clumping plant with multiple unbranched stems, is entirely hairless. Sessile leaves, which are 4 to 12 centimetres long, are opposite, lanceolate, and smooth-edged and often have three parallel veins. Stems are often purple-tinted.

Flowers are produced in dense terminal panicles. Individual flowers are 2.5 centimetres wide with five pink petals, 10 stamens, and two diverging styles. The base of each petal has two scale-like crests. Sepals are fused to form a narrow tube, which is often purple-tinted at the tip. Flowers are sweetly scented, especially in the evening. A double-flowered form is occasionally seen.

VITAL STATISTICS

Maximum height: 70 centimetres
Flowering season: July to September

Top: Flowers are in dense terminal panicles.
Middle: Sometimes a double-flowered form is encountered. Bottom: The opposite narrow leaves are sessile with smooth edges; stems are often purple-tinted.

Disturbed

289

Pink family / Caryophyllaceae

Red campion

Silene dioica (formerly *Lychnis dioica*)
Red catchfly, red cockle

HABITAT: Red campion, a European plant, was introduced to Nova Scotia as a garden ornamental. It is occasionally found along roadsides and trails around and near settlements, mostly along the Fundy coast.

CHARACTERISTICS: Red campion is a clumping biennial or short-lived perennial with multiple branching hairy stems. Opposite elliptical to ovate leaves have smooth edges and are covered in hairs. Some hairs are glandular, imparting a slight stickiness to the leaves and stems. Lower stem leaves and basal leaves, which are up to 12 centimetres long, have petioles; upper stem leaves, often 4 to 6 centimetres long, are sessile.

Plants are dioecious with the flowers produced in small cymes, terminally and from the upper leaf axils. Individual flowers are 2 to 2.5 centimetres in diameter with five deeply notched petals. The hairy calyx has 10 purple-tinted ribs. Male flowers have 10 stamens; female flowers have five styles. The seed capsule is globular.

Ragged robin, *Silene (Lychnis) flos-cuculi*, another garden ornamental, is scattered and localized near settlements. It has spatulate basal leaves and lance-shaped stem leaves. The plant is hairy and glandular. Cymes are looser than those of red campion, and the flower's five rose pink petals have four deep wide-spreading lobes, giving it a distinct ragged appearance.

Top: Each red campion flower has five deeply notched petals. Bottom: Each ragged robin flower has five petals, each with four deep wide-spreading lobes.

Disturbed

 Native Species

Saltmarsh sand-spurrey

Spergularia salina (formerly *S. marina*)
Marine sand-spurrey, lesser sand-spurrey

HABITAT: A coastal plant, saltmarsh sand-spurrey is found on brackish shorelines and the upper tide line along the entire coast of Nova Scotia.

CHARACTERISTICS: Saltmarsh sand-spurrey is a mat-forming annual. Leaves, which reach 4 centimetres in length, are opposite, fleshy, linear, and pointed. Stems are usually prostrate and often purple-tinted, especially toward their base. Plants may be hairless or covered in sticky glandular hairs.

The flowers, which are 0.3 to 0.5 centimetres in diameter, are produced in cymes. They have five lilac-pink or, less commonly, white petals, five often sticky green sepals, two to five stamens, and three pistils.

Canada sand-spurrey, *S. canadensis*, often grows with saltmarsh sand-spurrey. The two are virtually identical except Canada sand-spurrey leaves have blunt tips and usually white flowers, which may be solitary or in loose cymes.

Red sand-spurrey, *S. rubra*, is a European introduction occasionally found on disturbed sites throughout Nova Scotia. It has non-fleshy linear pointed leaves that are often in a whorl of four. It is generally covered in glandular hairs. The flowers are pink, usually with 10 stamens.

VITAL STATISTICS
Maximum height: 25 centimetres
Flowering season: July to September

Top: The paired linear leaves have pointed tips. Middle: Canada sand-spurrey often has solitary flowers and blunt-tipped linear leaves. Bottom: Red sand-spurrey has matted growth and appears on gravelly disturbed areas.

Coastal

Knotweed family / Polygoniaceae

Water smartweed

Native Species

Persicaria amphibia (formerly *Polygonum amphibium*)
Water knotweed, amphibious bistort

VITAL STATISTICS

Maximum height: 150 centimetres
(floating stems)
Flowering season: June to September

HABITAT: Water smartweed is terrestrial and found along muddy or sandy shorelines, or aquatic and found in shallow ponds and slow-moving streams. It grows throughout Nova Scotia but it is rare along the Atlantic coast.

CHARACTERISTICS: Water smartweed, a low spreading plant, is weakly erect or floating aquatic. If terrestrial, leaves are lance-shaped, pointed, pubescent, and short petioled or sessile; stems root where they touch the soil. Aquatic forms have long petioled elliptical hairless leaves with rounded tips; petioles and stems are often pink-tinted. Both forms have alternate leaves up to 15 centimetres in length.

Flowers are in solitary dense terminal racemes which are 1 to 2 centimetres long. Individual flowers are 0.35 centimetres long with five deep pink petaloid sepals, five exerted stamens, and two styles.

Dotted knotweed, *P. punctata*, also found along shorelines and in marshes, has upright stems which reach 75 centimetres in height. Scarcely hairy leaves are narrow, lanceolate to elliptical, short petioled, and 3 to 9 centimetres long. Stems terminate in several 5- to 20-centimetre-long narrow racemes with a sparse arrangement of tiny white, rarely pale pink, flowers. Leaves have a peppery taste.

False waterpepper, *P. hydropiperoides*, an Atlantic Coastal Plain species, is found primarily in southern Nova Scotia. Similar to dotted knotweed, it has narrow linear to lanceolate leaves, which are 6 to 15 centimetres long, and narrow racemes of rose pink flowers.

Top: Water smartweed has floating leaves and dense spikes of pink flowers. Middle: Dotted knotweed has narrow racemes with widely scattered small white flowers. Bottom: False waterpepper produces narrow spikes of pink flowers.

Buckwheat family / Polygonaceae

Spotted lady's-thumb

 **Introduced Species**

Persicaria maculosa (formerly *Polygonum persicaria*)

Lady's-thumb, heart's-ease, redshank

HABITAT: Spotted lady's-thumb, a European species found in moist waste places and disturbed areas throughout Nova Scotia, can be a weed in vegetable gardens. It also occurs along gravelly riversides and shorelines.

CHARACTERISTICS: Spotted lady's-thumb is a bushy annual with both erect and wide-spreading stems. Alternate leaves are lanceolate with smooth edges, commonly 8 to 10 centimetres long, and short petioled; a dark purple blotch is usually seen on the middle, upper surface of the leaf. Smooth stems are often red-tinted. At the junction of the leaf and stem is a thin sheath, which is fringed in hairs. Stems have a jointed appearance.

Flowers are produced in dense cylindrical spike-like terminal and axillary racemes. Individual flowers are about 0.35 centimetres wide with five pink to white petaloid sepals, four to eight stamens, and two to three styles.

Pale smartweed, *P. lapthifolia*, is scattered in the province but it occurs in similar habitats to spotted lady's-thumb. It can reach 2 metres in height, but it may also be low and creeping. Leaves reach 20 centimetres in length and have pubescent or hairless undersides; they may have a purple blotch. Taller forms often have pendulous flowers. The distinguishing feature is a sheath at the base of the leaves, which lacks hairs; individual flowers usually have only four sepals.

Wetlands

Top: Spotted lady's-thumb has dense cylindrical racemes of small pink five-sepalled flowers. Middle: Spotted lady's-thumb leaves have a central dark purple blotch. Bottom: Pale smartweed is distinguished from spotted lady's-thumb by its four-sepalled flowers.

Disturbed

Buckwheat family / Polygonaceae

Pennsylvanian smartweed

Persicaria pensylvanica (formerly *Polygonum pensylvanicum*)

Pinkweed, pink knotweed

Native Species

VITAL STATISTICS

Maximum height: 120 centimetres
Flowering season: June to October

HABITAT: Pennsylvanian smartweed occurs in moist cultivated areas and ditches and along shorelines throughout Nova Scotia; it is rare in the southwest.

CHARACTERISTICS: Pennsylvanian smartweed is a bushy branching annual; the stem is often pink-tinted. Alternate leaves are lanceolate to elliptical with smooth edges and a short petiole. The sheath at the base of the leaf lacks hairs. Leaves may be smooth or have stiff hairs. Stems often have a jointed appearance.

This species is distinguished by its flower stems, which are covered in sticky glandular hairs. Flowers are produced in dense cylindrical spike-like racemes, both terminally and axillary. Individual flowers, about 0.3 centimetres wide, have five pink petaloid sepals, six to eight stamens, and two styles.

Marshpepper or common smartweed, *P. hydropiper*, is a European species found in high-fertility waste places such as cultivated fields or, less commonly, along shorelines. It rarely exceeds 50 centimetres in height. Its lanceolate wavy-edged leaves are up to 9 centimetres long and have a sharp peppery taste. The sheath at the leaf base may be hairless or have short hairs. The leaf node is often a darker red than the remainder of the stem. Flower racemes are narrow and often arching; flowers are more widely spaced along the raceme than on Pennsylvanian smartweed. Individual flowers commonly have four sepals; they are green with a pink tint and scattered minute dark spots.

Top: Flowers are in dense cylindrical racemes. Middle: The pink-tinted stems have a jointed appearance. Bottom: Marshpepper has wavy-edged leaves and arching narrow racemes of widely spaced green pink-tipped flowers.

Native Species

St. John's-wort family / Hypericaceae

Fraser's St. John's-wort

Hypericum fraseri
Marsh St. John's-wort

HABITAT: Fraser's St. John's-wort is scattered along muddy and boggy shores and beaches throughout Nova Scotia.

CHARACTERISTICS: Fraser's St. John's-wort is a slender mostly non-branching plant, usually erect but sometimes leaning. Stems are often red-tinted. Oblong to ovate leaves are opposite, smooth-edged, and sessile to partly clasping the stem. Reaching 7.5 centimetres in length, leaves are dull and waxy and often have a blue-green or purple tint. Leaf undersides have minute dark spots. The entire plant is hairless.

Flowers, each 1 to 2 centimetres wide, are produced in small cymes at the ends of the stems and among the upper leaf axils. Blunt-tipped sepals, each 0.25 to 0.5 centimetres long, are half the length of the petals and form a green or purple-tinted cup at the base of the flower. The flower has five flesh pink petals, nine to 12 stamens, and a single 0.5- to 1.3-millimetre-long style. Flowers rarely open fully. Seed capsules are ovate-shaped and dark wine-red.

Virginia marsh St. John's-wort, *H. virginicum*, is found in muddy and boggy habitats, particularly in southwestern regions. It is considered an Atlantic Coastal Plain species. It is difficult to distinguish from Fraser's St. John's-wort unless flowers are present; flowers have 0.5- to 0.7-centimetre-long pointed sepals and 0.2- to 0.3-centimetre-long styles.

VITAL STATISTICS

Maximum height: 80 centimetres
Flowering season: July to August

Wetlands

Top: Plants have pairs of sessile round leaves with smooth edges; the flesh pink five-petalled flowers are in small clusters. Bottom: Foliage is often waxy and purple-tinted; the dark wine-red seed capsules are teardrop-shaped.

Mallow family / Malvaceae

Musk mallow
Malva moschata

Introduced Species

Maximum height: 70 centimetres
Flowering season: July

HABITAT: Musk mallow is a garden escape occasionally seen along roadsides and in waste areas and old abandoned gardens throughout Nova Scotia.

CHARACTERISTICS: Musk mallow is a bushy plant with several sparsely branched stiffly haired stems. Plants have both basal and stem leaves. Basal leaves are evergreen and overwintering, rounded in outline with five shallow lobes and rounded teeth. Stem leaves are alternate and round in outline but pinnatifid with deep lobes. Each individual lobe is bipinnately lobed. The overall effect is a finely dissected but round leaf. There are two small stipules at the base of each leaf. Leaves have fine hairs along the edges. The entire plant emits a musky fragrance when bruised.

Tissue-like flowers are produced in terminal racemes. Individual flowers have five pink or white widely notched petals similar in shape to a trout's tail. Flowers are about 5 centimetres in diameter. Five green sepals, which have scattered stiff hairs, enfold the developing seeds.

Vervain mallow, *M. alcea*, is occasionally encountered along roadsides. Plants reach 125 centimetres in height. While palmately lobed, the individual lobes are less dissected than those of musk mallow. Flowers are often among the upper leaf axils but, overall, are in a raceme arrangement. Flowers are commonly pink with darker pink, rarely white, veins and are virtually identical in shape to those of musk mallow although the petal edges may be more ragged.

Top: The tissue-like flowers have five petals whose tips are broadly notched like a trout's tail. Middle: Less commonly, musk mallow flowers are white; flowers are in terminal racemes. Bottom: Vervain mallow petals often have a ragged-edged look.

Mallow family / Malvaceae

Dwarf mallow

Malva neglecta

Running mallow, cheese plant, common mallow

Native Species

HABITAT: Dwarf mallow is a European introduction occasionally seen in waste areas and gardens throughout the province, but more commonly in the Annapolis Valley.

CHARACTERISTICS: Dwarf mallow is a mat-forming annual or biennial plant with trailing stems that reach to 60 centimetres in length. The round to heart-shaped 1.5- to 4-centimetre-long leaves have five to seven obscure lobes and sharp-toothed edges. Alternately arranged, leaves have a wrinkled appearance and long petioles. The entire plant is covered in short stiff hairs.

The flowers, which are pink with darker pink veins or white, are solitary or in groups of up to three flowers among the upper leaf axils. The centre of each flower has a knob-like cluster of stamens and stigma. Individual flowers are about 1.5 centimetres wide with five notched satiny petals. The petals are twice as long as the sepals. Sepals enfold the developing seeds.

Round-leaved mallow, *M. pusilla*, is uncommon in the province. It is similar to dwarf mallow, but the white petals are only about 1.5 times longer than the sepals and the flowers are less than 1 centimetre wide. Their sepals have long hairs. Leaves also differ from dwarf mallow slightly: they have five to nine shallow lobes and rounded teeth.

VITAL STATISTICS

Maximum height: 60 centimetres
Flowering season: June to October

Top: Dwarf mallow flowers have pink notched petals with darker veins and a central "knob" created by the stamens and stigma. Middle: Dwarf mallow's wrinkled leaves are round with five to seven shallow lobes and sharp teeth. Bottom: Round-leaved mallow has white flowers in small axillary clusters and long hairs on its sepals.

Disturbed

297

Pitcher plant family / Sarraceniaceae

Northern pitcher plant

Native Species

Sarracenia purpurea
Common pitcher plant

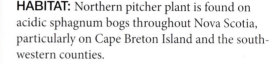

VITAL STATISTICS

Maximum height: 60 centimetres
Flowering season: June to July

HABITAT: Northern pitcher plant is found on acidic sphagnum bogs throughout Nova Scotia, particularly on Cape Breton Island and the south-western counties.

CHARACTERISTICS: Northern pitcher plant is a low clumping plant with rosettes of evergreen foliage. Leaves are hollow and pitcher-shaped, ranging from 10 to 30 centimetres in length. The outside leaf surfaces are leathery, hairless, green or purple-tinted and often red-veined. The "hood" or "lip" of the leaf has brown-red veins and downward-pointing stiff hairs. The inside of the leaf (the "pitcher") is smooth and contains water used to trap and drown insects. A "wing" extends down the length of the leaf's upper side. Leaves often turn completely wine-red in winter.

Plants produce several solitary globular 5-centi-metre-wide nodding flowers at the ends of leafless stems. Five persistent leathery shiny purple-red sepals are petal-like and remain into the autumn months. Five wine-red petals are larger than the sepals, drooping, and relatively short-lived. The ovary is large and globular, surrounded by a ring of numerous stamens. The single style is capped by a five-angled umbrella-like body that houses the stigmas.

Northern pitcher plant is the provincial floral emblem for Newfoundland and Labrador.

Top: The nodding flowers have red-tinted petal-like sepals and larger red petals. Middle: Plants form clumps of basal leaves and produce several leafless flower stems with solitary nodding flowers. Bottom: The pitcher-shaped leaves often have distinct red veins.

Wetlands

298

Native Species

Heath family / Ericaceae

Common pipsissewa

Chimaphila umbellata

Common prince's pine, pipsissewa

HABITAT: Common pipsissewa grows in dry mossy coniferous or mixed forests. It is uncommon and scattered throughout the province.

CHARACTERISTICS: This low colonial evergreen sub-shrub has unbranched stems. Common pipsissewa leaves are spatulate, dark green, and glossy with a leathery texture and toothed edges. They are 3 to 7 centimetres long and produced in whorls of three or four.

Plants produce a single flower stem that arises at the tip of the leafy stem. Five-petalled nodding white or pink blooms appear in an umbel of three to eight flowers. Each flower has 10 stamens and a single style. Petals often bend backward. The fruit is a globular capsule that often persists through winter.

VITAL STATISTICS

Maximum height: 30 centimetres
Flowering season: July

Top: Each flower has ten stamens, a single style, and five backward-arching petals. Middle: Flowers are in a small umbel atop a leafless stem. Bottom: The whorled leaves have sharp teeth along their edges.

Heath family / Ericaceae

Trailing arbutus

Epigaea repens

Mayflower

Native Species

HABITAT: Trailing arbutus, a common forest-floor species, occurs on open barrens throughout the province. It is the provincial floral emblem for Nova Scotia.

CHARACTERISTICS: A prostrate broad-leaved evergreen sub-shrub, trailing arbutus branches are green to reddish-brown and hairy. Alternate leaves are reticulated, oval, and 2.5 to 7 centimetres in length. Stiff hairs cover leaf edges, top surfaces, and undersides, especially on younger leaves. Leaf edges are untoothed; leaf bases are cordate. Rich green leaves become an increasingly lighter yellow-green with exposure to the sun.

Clusters of 1.5-centimetre-diameter flowers grow at the ends of trailing stems as well as from the upper leaf axils. Each blossom's five petals fuse at the base to form a tube; this floral tube is hairy. Within the tube are 10 stamens and a single style. Spicily fragrant, flowers are white or pink.

Top: Each five-petalled flower has a tubular base. Middle: Terminal and axillary flowers are in tight clusters. Bottom: The leathery leaves have a heart-shaped outline.

 **Native Species**

Heath family / Ericaceae
Pink pyrola
Pyrola asarifolia
Pink-flowered wintergreen, pink wintergreen

HABITAT: Pink pyrola grows in rich calcareous mixed or coniferous woodlands and barrens. It is widely scattered in the province, primarily in northern Cape Breton and Digby, Hants, and Cumberland counties.

CHARACTERISTICS: Pink pyrola is a low rosetted plant that may produce small mats as it spreads through subterranean stolons. All leaves are basal, round to kidney-shaped, leathery, evergreen, shiny, and slightly toothed with rounded teeth. Long petioled leaves are up to 6 centimetres long. The entire plant is hairless.

Four to 20 flowers are produced in a cylindrical raceme at the end of a leafless, often pink-tinted, stem that may reach 30 centimetres in length. Individual flowers, each 0.8 to 1.2 centimetres wide, are bell-shaped and often nodding. The five petals are crimson to pale pink; 10 stamens arch upward; the single thick 0.5- to 1-centimetre-long style arches downward at the base and may arch upward at the tip, appearing similar in shape to an elephant trunk. The style projects beyond the petals. The stigma appears slightly five-lobed.

Lesser pyrola, *P. minor*, prefers old-growth coniferous forests, particularly on Cape Breton. Its round evergreen leaves are dull, short petioled, and up to 4 centimetres long. The cylindrical raceme grows on a pink-tinted stem which may reach 25 centimetres in height. Globular, nodding flowers have five waxy white to light pink petals. The single style is about 0.1 centimetres long, and straight, and hidden within the recurved petals.

Top: The style extends beyond the petals and its bent shape is like that of an elephant's trunk. Middle: The nodding flowers are in racemes atop leafless stems. Bottom: Lesser pyrola has globular pink-tinted flowers, and its stigma does not extend beyond the petals.

VITAL STATISTICS
Maximum height: 30 centimetres
Flowering season: Late June to August

Myrsine family / Myrsinaceae

Sea milkwort

Lysimachia maritima (formerly *Glaux maritima*)

Saltwort, black saltwort, sea milkweed

VITAL STATISTICS

Maximum height: 20 centimetres
Flowering season: Mid-June to July

HABITAT: Sea milkwort is commonly found in coastal salt marshes around the entire coast of Nova Scotia.

CHARACTERISTICS: Sea milkwort is a low clumping plant with semi-upright stems from a creeping rootstock. Opposite leaves are fleshy, linear to oblong, sessile, and smooth-edged. Leaves are small, usually 1 centimetre in length, and densely arranged along the stem. The entire plant is hairless and exudes a milky sap when cut.

Small stemless 0.4- to 0.6-centimetre-wide flowers are cup-shaped and solitary among the upper leaf axils. They have no petals but five petaloid sepals which vary from white through shades of pink, lavender, and crimson. They have five stamens and a single style.

Top: Each flower has five stamens and a single style that extend beyond the five petaloid sepals. Middle: Flowers are solitary among the upper leaf axils. Bottom: The opposite fleshy leaves are densely arranged along the stems.

302

Wetlands

Coastal

Native Species

Laurentian primrose

Primula laurentiana
Bird's-eye primrose, mealy primrose

HABITAT: A calciphile, Laurentian primrose is restricted to calcareous ledges, cliffs, meadows, and shorelines primarily along the Bay of Fundy.

CHARACTERISTICS: Laurentian primrose is a small tufted plant. All leaves are basal, oblanceolate to spatulate with toothed edges, and 2 to 6 centimetres in length. Leaves are covered in white powdery scales called farina, especially on the undersides. The relatively stout flower stem is also covered in farina.

Flowers are produced in an umbel atop a leafless stem which is 5 to 10 centimetres high. Sepals are covered in white farina. Five lilac-pink notched petals are fused into a tube at their base. The five anthers and single style are hidden within this floral tube. Flowers are about 1 centimetre in diameter and have a distinct yellow eye.

Mistassini primrose, *P. mistassinica*, is also found in calcareous habitats. It is usually confined to northern Cape Breton and Colchester County. It is smaller than Laurentian primrose, with more slender flower stems and a fewer-flowered umbel. Plants are usually farina-free. Flowers look similar to those of Laurentian primrose.

VITAL STATISTICS
Maximum height: 30 centimetres
Flowering season: June to July

Barrens

Coastal

Top: Laurentian primrose produces small umbels of flowers atop stems covered in white powder-like farina; the spoon-shaped leaves are in basal rosettes.
Middle: Mistassini primrose has more slender stems and fewer flowers per umbel than Laurentian primrose.
Bottom: White-flowered Mistassini primroses are rare; the stems lack farina.

303

Orpine family / Crassulaceae

Garden stonecrop

Hylotelephium telephium (formerly *Sedum telephium*)
Live-forever, live-longs

Introduced Species

VITAL STATISTICS

Maximum height: 60 centimetres
Flowering season: July to September

HABITAT: Garden stonecrop, a European plant originally introduced in Nova Scotia as a garden ornamental, is scattered throughout the province and is occasionally encountered in damp shady waste places or along roadsides near settlements.

CHARACTERISTICS: Garden stonecrop is a clumping plant with many unbranched stems. Stems and leaves are thick, succulent, and hairless. Alternate, opposite, or occasionally whorled leaves are oblong, elliptical, or spatulate with toothed edges. The largest leaves may reach 10 centimetres in length.

Flowers are produced in compact panicles, terminally as well as in the upper leaf axils. Individual starlike flowers are about 1 centimetre in diameter with five pointed pink petals, 10 stamens, and five pointy styles. Rarely, the flowers may be creamy white. Seed capsules are five-pointed and starlike.

Top: Flowers are held in dense panicles at the ends of the stems and from the upper leaf axils. Bottom: Each flower is star-shaped with five pointed pink petals and five pointed styles.

Disturbed

Rose family / Rosaceae

Marsh cinquefoil

Native Species

Comarum palustre (formerly *Potentilla palustris*)

Marsh five-fingers, purple cinquefoil

HABITAT: Marsh cinquefoil is found occasionally in fresh- and saltwater marshes throughout Nova Scotia, particularly in the northern portions of the province.

CHARACTERISTICS: Marsh cinquefoil is a clumping or mat-forming plant with stout sprawling stems that often root along their length; flowering stems, however, are held relatively upright. Alternate leaves are pinnate with five to seven lanceolate to elliptical sharply toothed leaflets. Leaflets, which are up to 10 centimetres in length, are covered in fine hairs and often blue-green or purple-tinted. Stems are commonly pink or purple-tinted and have fine hairs, which may be glandular, on their upper sides.

Flowers are produced in a loose cyme. Individual flowers, each about 2 centimetres wide, have five pointed sepals which are hairy on the outside and strongly tinted purple-red and appear almost petaloid. The five petals are much shorter than the sepals, rendering them almost inconspicuous, and are rich purple-wine. The centre of the flower is a mass of purple-red stamens and styles. A small leafy bract is located between each sepal.

Wetlands

Top: Each flower has five small wine-red petals and five much larger purple-red-tinted sepals.
Bottom: Leaves are pinnate with five or seven narrow toothed leaflets.

Rose family / Rosaceae

Water avens

Geum rivale

Purple avens, chocolate root

 **Native Species**

VITAL STATISTICS

Maximum height: 50 centimetres
Flowering season: June

HABITAT: Water avens grows in swamps, wet meadows, and seepages throughout Nova Scotia.

CHARACTERISTICS: Water avens is a clumping leafy plant arising from a thick rhizome. It has several upright non-branching flower stems with a few alternately arranged leaves; most leaves, however, are basal. Basal leaves are pinnately compound with five to nine coarsely toothed leaflets. The terminal leaflet, which is often tri-lobed, is larger than the others. Smaller leaflets are often interspersed among the larger. Stem leaves are usually trifoliate and have a pair of stipules at their base. The entire plant is covered in hairs.

Flowers are nodding and produced in loose cymes. Flowering stems are usually dark purple. Individual flowers are about 2 centimetres wide with five conspicuously veined dull red to pale pink-purple petals with numerous yellow anthers and pistils. The five hairy sepals are the same length as the petals. A small linear bract is located between each sepal. As seeds develop, flowers become erect. The seeds are produced in a spiky globular head; each seed has an elongate hooked spine that enables it to stick to animal fur.

Top: The nodding flowers' sepals and petals are of equal length. Bottom: Basal leaves are pinnate with alternating large and small leaflets.

 **Native Species**

Lythrum family / Lythraceae
Swamp loosestrife
Decodon verticillatus
Water-willow

HABITAT: Swamp loosestrife, an Atlantic Coastal Plain species, grows in shallow bog pools and along lakeshores. Rare in Nova Scotia, it is found mainly in Digby, Shelburne, and Queens counties.

CHARACTERISTICS: Swamp loosestrife resembles an herbaceous perennial with a partially woody base. It usually roots in water or saturated soil. Bark at the plant base feels spongy.

Herbaceous upper stems die back in winter. Summer stems are smooth with longitudinal ridges; they are green with a red tint in early summer and redden as the season progresses. The flexible stems often arch to touch the soil, where they root into a new plant. Leaves are paired or in a whorl of three or four. Lance-shaped leaves are 5 to 15 centimetres in length with smooth edges and nearly sessile. In fall, they turn bright pink-red.

Pink five-petalled flowers are produced in clusters among the upper leaf axils. Stamens and pistils are longer than the petals, giving the flower a pincushion appearance. Flowers later produce globular pink-tinted capsules with a starlike crown (calyx remnants).

Top: Flowers are in axillary clusters among the upper stem leaves. Bottom: The narrow leaves are paired; plants are often partially aquatic.

Wetlands

Lythrum family / Lythraceae

Purple loosestrife

Lythrum salicaria

Spiked loosestrife

Introduced
Species

VITAL STATISTICS

Maximum height: 150 centimetres
Flowering season: July to September

HABITAT: Purple loosestrife, a European species introduced in Nova Scotia as a garden ornamental, is found along roadside ditches, streams, and lakeshores and in swamps and marshes throughout the province. It is spreading rapidly and considered an invasive species.

CHARACTERISTICS: Purple loosestrife is a tall slender clumping plant with non-branching stems, which are commonly tinted red or purple and square in cross-section. Sessile opposite or whorled leaves are lanceolate and up to 10 centimetres in length. The entire plant is usually downy, but the degree of hairiness varies. Leaf edges are smooth and leaf bases are rounded.

Stemless flowers are produced in narrow wand-like racemes. Individual flowers are 1 to 2 centimetres wide with six, less commonly five, narrow magenta petals. Sepals are often purple-tinted and hairy. The length of the 10 or 12 stamens and single style varies among the three types of flowers.

Top: Each flower has five narrow petals; flower stems are downy with short hairs. Middle: Flowers are held in wand-like racemes. Bottom: Purple loosestrife can form large colonies.

 **Native Species**

Shamrock family / Oxalidaceae
Common wood-sorrel
Oxalis montana
Mountain wood-sorrel, white wood-sorrel

HABITAT: Common wood-sorrel is primarily restricted to shady mossy old-growth forests throughout Nova Scotia.

CHARACTERISTICS: Common wood-sorrel grows as patches which are connected by subterranean rhizomes. All leaves are basal and trifoliate and composed of three heart-shaped leaflets. Each leaflet is 1.5 to 3 centimetres wide, hairless, and smooth-edged. Leaflets fold and unfold depending on light conditions.

Early flowers are solitary on leafless stems that arise to 10 centimetres. These 2-centimetre-diameter flowers have slightly notched, white to pink petals with darker purple-pink veins. Near the base of each petal is a purple band, imparting a purple ring in the centre of the flower. Below this purple ring, each petal has a yellow patch. Flowers have 10 stamens and five styles. Later season flowers lack petals, and self-pollinate.

VITAL STATISTICS
Maximum height: 10 centimetres
Flowering season: June to July

Top: Each flower is white with pink veins and has a yellow blotch at the base of each petal. Middle: The veins on the petals create a ring within the flower. Bottom: The trifoliate leaves have heart-shaped leaflets.

Geranium family / Geraniaceae

Herb-Robert

Geranium robertianum

Robert geranium, red robin

VITAL STATISTICS

Maximum height: 40 centimetres
Flowering season: May to September

HABITAT: Herb-Robert is found in shady ravines, rocky woods, and gravelly shorelines throughout most of Nova Scotia.

CHARACTERISTICS: Herb-Robert is a creeping annual or biennial. Thin branching stems are wide-spreading or weakly ascending. Basal and opposite stem leaves are palmately compound with three to five pinnatifid leaflets. The terminal leaflet has a stalk; others are sessile. The entire plant is sparsely hairy. Stems and leaves are often red-tinted.

Long-stalked flowers grow in pairs from the leaf axils. One-centimetre-wide flowers have five green or purple-tinted hairy pointed sepals; five rose-red, rarely white, slightly notched petals; 10 stamens; and a single style with five recurved stigmas. Seeds are produced at the bottom of a bill-like structure; when the seeds are ripe, part of the bill curls back, catapulting them.

Bicknell's geranium, *G. bicknelii*, uncommon on recently burned or cleared sites, is generally confined to central and southern Nova Scotia. Plants are sprawling; all leaflets on the sparsely hairy leaves are sessile. One-centimetre-wide pale pink flowers are either solitary or in pairs and grow from the upper leaf axils.

Common storksbill, *Erodium cicutarium*, a European species, grows in dry open areas. It has sticky sparsely hairy pinnately compound fern-like leaves. One-centimetre-wide rose pink flowers grow in few-flowered axillary umbels. Flowers have five anthers.

Top: Herb-Robert has palmately compound leaves with pinnatifid leaflets and axillary pink flowers. Middle: Bicknell's geranium has pale pink flowers; all leaflets of the palmately compound leaves are sessile. Bottom: Common storksbill has pinnately compound leaves with deeply lobed leaflets; flowers are in umbels.

Native Species

Dogbane family / Apocynaceae

Spreading dogbane

Apocynum androsaemifolium
Creeping dogbane

HABITAT: Spreading dogbane, found in open sandy barrens and dry meadows and along roadsides, is scattered throughout Nova Scotia but common in the Annapolis Valley.

CHARACTERISTICS: Spreading dogbane is a colonial plant that spreads by subterranean rhizomes. Stems are branching, smooth, and purple-tinted. Ovate to elliptical opposite leaves are up to 7 centimetres long and smooth-edged; short petioles make the leaves appear sessile. The top surfaces of leaves are hairless; undersides may be pubescent. Leaves often have a droopy appearance. The plant exudes a milky sap when cut.

Fragrant flowers are produced in small cymes, both terminally and axillary. Individual flowers, each up to 1 centimetre wide, are nodding and bell-shaped. They have five light pink recurved petals with darker veins on the inside. Stamens are fused to form a pointed structure. There is no visible style. The length of the sepals is half that of the petals. The pendant two-pronged seed capsules, up to 15 centimetres long, are narrow and cylindrical and split to release tawny-haired seeds.

Indian hemp, *A. cannabinum*, is found in open gravelly sites primarily in the northern half of the province. Its long ascending leaves with distinct petioles distinguish it from spreading dogbane. The greenish-white bell-like flowers are 0.5 centimetres wide, more numerous than those of spreading dogbane, always terminal, and point upward. Sepals are as long as the petals.

Top: The nodding bell-shaped flowers of spreading dogbane are pink with darker veins. Middle: Spreading dogbane's two-pronged narrow seed capsules are fang-like. Bottom: Indian hemp flowers are in larger clusters, always terminal, and upward-pointing.

VITAL STATISTICS
Maximum height: 50 centimetres
Flowering season: July to September

Barrens

Disturbed

Milkweed family / Asclepiaceae

Common milkweed

Asclepias syriaca

Silkweed, silky milkweed

VITAL STATISTICS

Maximum height: 120 centimetres
Flowering season: July

HABITAT: Scattered in the province, common milkweed is encountered on sandy meadows and in thickets and waste places.

CHARACTERISTICS: Common milkweed is a tall slender plant with several unbranched stems. Opposite oblong to ovate leaves are up to 20 centimetres long, smooth-edged, hairless on the upper surface, and velvet hairy on the lower. Stems and flower stalks are finely pubescent. All parts of the plant exude a milky sap when cut.

Flowers are produced in long-stemmed dense spherical umbels, both terminally and axillary. Pale flesh pink to dull purple flowers are highly fragrant. Each flower, which is nearly 1 centimetre wide, has five strongly reflexed petals. The reproductive parts are fused and appear thickened and starlike, resembling a flower atop a flower. The reproductive portion of the flower has five horn-like projections. Softly prickled seed capsules, which may reach 10 centimetres in length, are cylindrical but swollen on a sharply elbowed stem. They split to release silky-haired seeds.

Swamp milkweed, *A. incarnata*, is rare and widely scattered in Nova Scotia. It prefers damp to wet shorelines and thickets; leaves are more lance-shaped than those of common milkweed, and usually hairless. The umbels of purple-pink flowers are terminal and bloom in August. Cylindrical seed capsules are on erect stems.

Top: Petals arch backward from the flower's starlike reproductive parts. Middle: Common milkweed flowers are in spherical umbels among the upper leaves. Bottom: Swamp milkweed has terminal umbels of bright pink flowers.

Honeysuckle family / Caprifoliaceae

Twinflower

Linnaea borealis
Northern twinflower, pink-bells

Native
Species

HABITAT: Twinflower is a predominant wildflower in coniferous and mixed forests and open areas throughout Nova Scotia.

CHARACTERISTICS: A low trailing broad-leaved evergreen sub-shrub, twinflower's paired short petioled round leaves are about 1 centimetre long with a few rounded teeth and scattered hairs on both surfaces.

As its name suggests, twinflower produces a pair of nodding bell-like flowers atop a thin wiry 5- to 8-centimetre-long stalk. Highly fragrant blossoms are light pink with dark pink stripes and hairy inner surfaces. Flowers consist of five petals, which are fused to form the distinct bell-like shape, four stamens—two on short stems, two on longer—and a single style.

VITAL STATISTICS

Maximum height: 8 centimetres
Flowering season: Late June to July

Top: The nodding pink bell-shaped flowers are in pairs.
Middle: Twinflower forms a low mat on the forest floor.
Bottom: The trailing stems produce opposite round leaves.

313

Valerian family / Valerianaceae

Common valerian

Introduced
Species

Valeriana officinalis

Garden valerian, garden heliotrope

VITAL STATISTICS

Maximum height: 150 centimetres
Flowering season: Mid-July to
mid-August

HABITAT: Common valerian is a European plant introduced as a garden ornamental. It has escaped and is scattered in the province, occasionally found in waste areas and along roadsides and trails near settlements.

CHARACTERISTICS: Common valerian is a coarse but slender plant with unbranched grooved stems. Plants have both basal and opposite stem leaves, all of which are pinnate with five to 12 pairs of irregularly toothed or smooth-edged sessile leaflets. Leaflet undersides, leaflet edges, and leaf stems are hairy. Basal leaves have wider lanceolate leaflets; upper stem leaves have more linear leaflets.

Fragrant flowers are terminal and produced in several corymbs, which, when combined, become a rounded panicle. Individual flowers are about 0.4 centimetres wide with five roseate petals fused at their base. Flowers also have three stamens that extend beyond the petals and a single style with a two-lobed stigma.

Top: Pale pink flowers in multiple corymbs create a rounded panicle. Bottom: Plants produce opposite pinnate leaves with narrow leaflets.

Native Species

Watershield

Brasenia schreberi
Purple wendock

HABITAT: Found in shallow nutrient-rich pools, watershield is scattered primarily in the southern half of the province.

CHARACTERISTICS: Watershield is a floating aquatic plant whose alternate long petioled leaves arise from creeping rhizomes. Ovate leaves form a mat on the surface of the water; their petioles are attached to the centres of the leaf undersides. Leaves are smooth-edged, hairless, and 2 to 10 centimetres in diameter. They resemble miniature water-lily leaves. All underwater parts are covered in a thick clear mucilage.

Solitary flowers are axillary on long stems that extend a few centimetres above the water's surface. Flowers have 12 to 18 stamens, four to 18 styles, three or four sepals, and three or four petals; dull purple-pink sepals and petals look alike. Flowers last two days. On the first day, flowers extend above the water's surface and are functionally female. That night, flowers recede below the surface and emerge the second day as a functionally male flower, releasing their pollen to the wind. The flower then recedes below the surface again, where seeds develop.

VITAL STATISTICS

Maximum height: n/a
Flowering season: June to September

Wetlands

Top: The solitary flowers arise just above the water's surface. Bottom: The round leaves float on the water's surface.

315

Lily family / Liliaceae

Eastern rose twisted-stalk

Streptopus lanceolatus (formerly *S. roseus*)

Rose twisted-stalk, rose mandarin

Native Species

VITAL STATISTICS

Maximum height: 50 centimetres
Flowering season: Late May to June

HABITAT: Eastern rose twisted-stalk grows in acidic coniferous and mixed forests throughout Nova Scotia.

CHARACTERISTICS: Eastern rose twisted-stalk has a stout stem with forking sparsely hairy branches. The 5- to 10-centimetre-long alternate leaves are sessile and elliptical to lanceolate. Leaves are corrugated with distinct parallel veins and smooth but ciliate-haired edges.

One-centimetre-long flowers are solitary and hang from the upper leaf axils on thin hairy stems. Each flower has six pink tepals with darker purple streaks and spots and slightly recurved tips. The stigma has a three-cleft tip. Flowers become bright red globular berries.

Top: The nodding solitary flowers have pink lily-like flowers with darker markings on the inside.
Middle: Flowers are solitary from each leaf axil.
Bottom: The elliptical leaves are ribbed and sessile; flowers develop into red berries later in summer.

Gentian family / Gentianaceae

Plymouth gentian

Sabatia kennedyana
Plymouth rose gentian

HABITAT: Plymouth gentian is a wetland plant that either grows along the shores of sandy-peaty ponds or is partly submerged in shallow water. In Nova Scotia it is restricted to Yarmouth County; it is an Atlantic Coastal Plain species and is rare throughout its range.

CHARACTERISTICS: Plymouth gentian is a clump-forming plant with several upright non-branching stems arising from a stoloniferous rootstock. Basal leaves are lance-shaped and up to 8 centimetres long. Stem leaves are opposite, lanceolate, up to 5 centimetres long, and sessile or partially clasping the stem. All leaves are smooth-edged and hairless.

Up to 25 long-stemmed lightly fragrant flowers are produced in a loose panicle. Individual flowers reach 5 centimetres in diameter, with five to 12 stamens, a two-cleft style, and nine to 11 pink petals surrounding a yellow centre which is outlined in red. Sepals are narrow and green.

VITAL STATISTICS

Maximum height: 75 centimetres
Flowering season: August

Wetlands

Top: Each flower has nine to 11 petals and a central yellow centre outlined in red. Bottom: The basal leaves are lance-shaped, smooth-edged, and hairless.

Aster family / Asteraceae

Pink tickseed

Coreopsis rosea
Pink coreopsis

 Native Species

VITAL STATISTICS

Maximum height: 60 centimetres
Flowering season: Late July to
August

HABITAT: Pink tickseed is found along damp sandy, gravelly, or peaty shorelines. It is restricted to the extreme southwestern area of the province. It is an Atlantic Coastal Plain species.

CHARACTERISTICS: Pink tickseed is a slender upright plant which forms colonies as plants increase by subterranean rhizomes. Linear almost threadlike leaves are opposite, often with tufts of leaves in the leaf axils. Some leaves are either bi- or tripinnate. The entire plant is hairless.

Flowers are produced in a loose corymb. Long-stemmed individual flowers are about 2.5 centimetres wide with eight pink, rarely white, ray florets, each of which has three notches at its end. Each flower has several yellow disc florets at its centre.

Top: Each flower head has eight ray florets with three terminal teeth surrounding a central cluster of yellow disc florets. Bottom: Leaves are linear and threadlike.

Wetlands

Native Species

Philadelphia fleabane

Erigeron philadelphicus

Common fleabane, Philadelphia daisy

HABITAT: Philadelphia fleabane is found in old moist meadows and on damp slopes. It is uncommon and widely scattered in the province.

CHARACTERISTICS: Philadelphia fleabane is an upright clumping plant with few branches, except near the top. Plants produce several evergreen overwintering rosettes of oblong to spatulate leaves. Up to 10-centimetre-long stem leaves are alternate and oblong to lanceolate and clasp the stems. Leaf edges have small widely spaced teeth. Leaves are usually hairless but may have fine hairs along their edges; stems have scattered white hairs.

Flowers, produced in a loose corymb, are nodding in bud but become erect upon opening. Individual flowers are about 2 centimetres wide and composed of 100 or more threadlike ray florets which surround a mass of yellow disc florets. Ray florets vary from white to pale pink to purple-pink. Little hairs on seeds allow them to be blown on the wind.

VITAL STATISTICS

Maximum height: 50 centimetres
Flowering season: June to August

Top: Each flower head has numerous threadlike ray florets surrounding a central cluster of yellow disc florets. Bottom: The narrow leaves clasp the stem.

Disturbed

319

Violet family / Violaceae

Blue violet

Viola species

Native Species

VITAL STATISTICS
Maximum height: 20 centimetres
Flowering season: May to July

HABITAT: Five species of tufted blue violets with short thick rhizomes occur in damp to wet meadows and pastures, swamps, marshes, stream and pond shorelines, and moist open woodlands in Nova Scotia.

CHARACTERISTICS: These blue violets are tufted plants with basal leaves arising from a small but stout rhizome. Leaves are generally long petioled, with ovate to heart-shaped blades and generally rounded teeth; they are pubescent or hairless.

Flowers often overtop the leaves. Two-centimetre-wide solitary flowers have five violet-blue petals, which often have white bases. Darker veins are usually evident at the base of the petals. The upper two petals often arch backward; the lower three arch forward; the two lateral side petals often have beards; and the lower petal has a short spur. Non-petalled flowers are produced later in the season.

The following key may help in species identification:

1a. Lateral petals hairless: *V. selkirkii*

1b. Lateral petals bearded: move to step 2

2a. "Beard" hairs have swollen tips: *V. cucullata*

2b. "Beard" hairs have tapering tips: move to step 3

Top: The base of marsh blue violet's lateral petals is bearded. Middle: Marsh blue violet has heart-shaped leaves. Bottom: Northern bog violet has heart-shaped leaves with rounded teeth; it is best identified by its preference for limestone.

3a. Edges of sepals hairless; leaves usually hairless: *V. nephrophylla*

3b. Edges of sepals with ciliate hairs: move to step 4

4a. Leaf blade 1.5 to 3 times longer than wide, arrow-shaped; lower leaves pubescent; teeth on leaf edge pointed: *V. sagittata*

4b. Leaf blade as wide as or wider than long; lower leaves pubescent; teeth rounded: *V. sororia* (includes *V. septentrionalis*)

Specific locations and habitats of each species:

V. cucullata, marsh blue violet: various wetlands throughout the province; common. This species is the provincial floral emblem for New Brunswick.

V. nephrophylla, northern bog violet: calcareous wetlands and wet woodlands; localized and widely scattered.

V. sagittata, arrow-leaved violet: drier open sites; common in Annapolis Valley.

V. selkirkii, great spurred violet: moist, often calcareous slopes and brooksides; localized mainly in northern regions.

V. sororia (includes *V. septentrionalis*), woolly blue violet: moist, but not wet, open sites; common.

Top: Great spurred violet is distinguished by its beardless lateral petals. Middle: Woolly blue violet has long hairs on its beard and soft hairs on its leaves and flower stems. Bottom: Arrow-leaved violet is easily distinguished by its narrow leaves.

Violet family / Violaceae

Labrador violet

Native Species

Viola labradorica (formerly *Viola conspersa*)
Northern blue violet, alpine violet, American dog violet

VITAL STATISTICS	
Maximum height: 20 centimetres	
Flowering season: May to June	

HABITAT: Labrador violet is locally common in moist pastures and swamps and less common in open woodlands. It is found mainly in the northern half of the province.

CHARACTERISTICS: Labrador violet is a tufted plant with trailing leafy stems, a feature that separates it from the previous group of blue violets. Alternate leaves, which are up to 6 centimetres in length, are ovate to heart-shaped, with rounded teeth. Stems and leaves are generally hairless; the top leaf surface may have a few hairs.

Two-centimetre-wide flowers, produced from the leaf axils, are solitary atop stems that are up to 8 centimetres long. Flowers have five pale violet to violet-blue petals. The two lower lateral petals have beards; the lowermost petal has a spur which is about 0.6 centimetres long. Plants produce non-petalled flowers later in the season.

Early blue violet, *V. adunca,* uncommon in Nova Scotia, is found primarily along North Mountain and northward through Cape Breton, where it grows along brooksides and wet slopes and in cold woods. It is similar to Labrador violet but smaller and more tufted. Leaves are covered in fine hairs; leaf edges are rolled back. Petioles have winged edges.

Top: Labrador violet often has paler violet-blue flowers than other blue violets. Middle: Labrador violet has leafy trailing stems and a tufted habit. Bottom: Early blue violet has a tighter, more tufted habit than Labrador violet.

322

Robbin's milk-vetch

Astragalus robbinsii

Common fleabane, Philadelphia daisy

Native Species

HABITAT: Robbin's milk-vetch, a rare calciphile of limestone gravels and ledges, is restricted to Cape D'Or and West Advocate, both in Cumberland County.

CHARACTERISTICS: Robbin's milk-vetch is a low clumping to matted plant. Arching upright stems may reach 40 centimetres, but plants are generally less than 20 centimetres in height. Alternate pinnate leaves have four to seven pairs of 0.8- to 2.2-centimetre-long oblong leaflets. Leaf undersides have scattered stiff hairs; upper surfaces are generally hairless.

Flowers are usually produced on one-sided racemes. The 1.5-centimetre-long pea-like flowers are pale violet with a darker keel; sepals and developing seed pods have scattered black or white hairs.

VITAL STATISTICS

Maximum height: 40 centimetres
Flowering season: June

Top: Flowers are produced on a one-sided raceme; blossoms are pale violet with a darker keel. Middle: The alternate leaves are pinnately compound with oblong leaflets. Bottom: Seed pods have scattered short black hairs.

Barrens

Pea family / Fabaceae

Beach pea

Lathyrus japonicus
Sea pea, sea vetchling

Native Species

VITAL STATISTICS

Maximum height: 150 centimetres
Flowering season: July to September

HABITAT: Beach pea grows just above the upper tide zone in gravelly to sandy beaches around the coast.

CHARACTERISTICS: Beach pea is a clumping tangled plant whose tendrils twine around themselves. Leaves are blue- to grey-green, alternate, and pinnately compound with four to 10 ovate to elliptical leaflets. Smooth or pubescent 2.5- to 5-centimetre-long leaflets are opposite or alternate. Leaves end in a branching tendril. The base of each leaf has a pair of leafy ovate stipules which are as large as the leaflets.

Tight racemes of six to 10 pea-like flowers are produced from the upper leaf axils. The flower stem is generally shorter than the petiole of the accompanying leaf. Individual flowers are 1.5 to 2 centimetres long; standards vary from purple to violet-blue while the wings are paler. The 3- to 7-centimetre-long seed pod is like a miniature pea pod.

Marsh vetchling, *L. palustris*, is a slender upright plant found in wet coastal marshes or damp meadows. Its pinnate leaves have two to five pairs of opposite elliptical leaflets and a terminal tendril. Plants are smooth or pubescent. Its purple-pink to violet-blue flowers are not as crowded as those of beach pea; marsh vetchling is also distinguished by its winged stem, arrowhead-like stipules, and its flower stem, which is longer than the petiole of the accompanying leaf.

Top: A beach pea flower often has a two-toned effect: its banner and wings are usually slightly different colours. Middle: Beach pea flowers are on compact one-sided racemes; its pinnate leaves have rounded leaflets. Bottom: Marsh vetchling has fewer and more widely spaced flowers on its raceme than beach pea; leaflets are narrow.

Pea family / Fabaceae

Large-leaved lupine

Lupinus polyphyllus
Garden lupine

Introduced Species

HABITAT: Large-leaved lupine grows in dry disturbed areas such as roadsides, embankments, and waste places. This western North American introduction has been firmly naturalized.

CHARACTERISTICS: A stout clumping plant with many non-branching stems arising from a thick rootstock, large-leaved lupine has both basal and alternate stem leaves. Long petioled basal leaves are palmately compound with nine to 18 6- to 13-centimetre-long lanceolate to elliptical leaflets. Leaflets have white hairs below and ciliate hairs along their edges. Stems and upper leaf surfaces are generally hairless. Stem leaves are smaller than basal leaves, and have shorter petioles.

Stems terminate in a raceme, which is up to 70 centimetres long, of pea-like flowers. Individual 1.5-centimetres-long flowers are usually blue-purple but may be white to shades of blue-purple or pink, often with contrasting white or yellow patches on their standards. Flowers develop pea-like seed pods up to 8 centimetres long and covered in velvety white hairs. Pods turn brown-black when ripe.

Nootka lupine, *L. nootkatensis*, is occasionally encountered in Yarmouth County. It may reach 70 centimetres in length; the raceme an additional 30 centimetres. Stems and leaves are covered in silky white hairs. Flowers are blue-purple with a contrasting white patch on their standards. Plants bloom two to three weeks earlier than large-leaved lupine.

VITAL STATISTICS
Maximum height: 120 centimetres
Flowering season: Late June to early August

Top: Large-leaved lupine flowers are held on a dense cylindrical raceme; blue flowers are most common but may occasionally be pink. Bottom: Nootka lupine always has two-toned blue and white flowers.

Disturbed

325

Pea family / Fabaceae

Alfalfa

Medicago sativa

Introduced Species

VITAL STATISTICS
Maximum height: 100 centimetres
Flowering season: June to August

HABITAT: Alfalfa, a central Asian species introduced to Atlantic Canada as a fodder crop, is naturalized along dry roadsides and in old meadows and waste places throughout much of the province, although it is scattered on Cape Breton Island.

CHARACTERISTICS: Alfalfa is an upright bushy plant with multiple branching stems from a stout taproot. Alternate leaves are trifoliate, each leaflet oblanceolate to oblong and sharply toothed along its outer half. Each leaflet may reach 2.5 centimetres in length. The terminal leaflet has a distinct stem. The leaflet's top surface is hairless; the underside is lightly pubescent. Petioles are finely pubescent. A pair of triangular stipules is present at the base of each leaf.

Flowers are produced in axillary globular to cone-shaped racemes. Pea-like flowers, each 0.7 to 1.2 centimetres long, are blue-violet to purple, rarely white. Seed pods are coiled.

Top: The globular to cone-shaped racemes are among the upper leaf axils. Middle: Less commonly, flowers are white. Bottom: The terminal leaflet of the trifoliate leaves has a distinct stem; the other leaflets are sessile.

**Native
Species**

Saint John River locoweed

Oxytropis campestris var. johannensis
Newfoundland oxytrope

HABITAT: Saint John River locoweed is a calci-phile restricted to the limestone gravels and cliffs of northern Inverness County and Cape D'Or, Cumberland County.

CHARACTERISTICS: Saint John River locoweed is a tufted to mat-forming plant with prostrate stems radiating from a central taproot. Leaves are alternate and pinnately compound with 15 to 31 linear to lanceolate leaflets, which may be alternate or paired along the length of the leaf. Stems and leaves are covered in white pubescent hairs. At the base of each leaf is a pair of stipules.

Flowers are produced in dense round terminal racemes. Individual purple to violet-blue flowers are 0.5 to 0.7 centimetres in length. The standard has a large purple-striped white patch. Sepals and seed pods are covered in pubescent hairs.

VITAL STATISTICS

Maximum height: 30 centimetres
Flowering season: June to August

Barrens

Top: Flowers are in rounded racemes. Bottom: The matted plants have pinnate leaves with many small narrow leaflets.

Pea family / Fabaceae

Tufted vetch

Vicia cracca
Cow vetch, bird vetch, Canada pea

Introduced Species

VITAL STATISTICS

Maximum height: 2 metres
Flowering season: Late June to
August

HABITAT: Tufted vetch, a European species naturalized throughout Nova Scotia, grows in disturbed habitats.

CHARACTERISTICS: Tufted vetch is a delicate climbing vine that clings to neighbouring vegetation. Stems are ridged along their length. Alternate 6- to 12-centimetre-long leaves are pinnately compound with eight to 12 pairs of oblong to linear leaflets. Leaves end in a forking tendril and have a pair of small narrow stipules at their bases. Leaflets may be smooth or finely pubescent.

One-sided axillary racemes have 10 to 30 reflexed blossoms. Individual pea-like flowers are blue-violet to purple and 1 to 1.3 centimetres long. Pea pods reach 2 to 3 centimetres in length and contain up to eight seeds.

Common vetch, *V. sativa*, is an annual with paired axillary, nearly sessile, showy 1.5- to 3-centimetre-long flowers. Standards are purple; wings are violet-red to magenta. Narrow pea pods may reach 8 centimetres in length. It is found mainly in central Nova Scotia.

Scattered in waste places, four-seed vetch, *V. tetrasperma*, is a slender annual which reaches 40 centimetres in length. Pinnate leaves have three to five pairs of narrow leaflets. Axillary 0.8-centimetre-long flowers are solitary or in groups of two or three. Flowers are pale lilac-blue with dark purple-blue veins on the standard and a dark-tipped keel. The seed pod reaches 1.3 centimetres.

Top: Tufted vetch flowers are held in one-sided racemes. Middle: Common vetch's purple banner and violet-red wings create a two-toned blossom. Bottom: Four-seed vetch flowers, held in small groups, are pale lilac-blue with dark purple-blue veins on its banners.

Introduced Species

Borage family / Boraginaceae

Common viper's bugloss

Echium vulgare

Bluedevil, blueweed

HABITAT: Common viper's bugloss, a European introduction, is naturalized but localized along roadsides and in old meadows and other dry waste places throughout Nova Scotia.

CHARACTERISTICS: Common viper's bugloss is a slender biennial. In the first season, plants produce a flat rosette of elongate lanceolate leaves which are up to 15 centimetres long. Leaves often have raised white spots; leaf edges are smooth but may be undulating. In the second year, plants produce several upright stems. Stem leaves are also narrow and lanceolate but sessile and smaller than the basal leaves. The entire plant, including the five narrow sepals, is covered in stiff white hairs.

Early in the flowering season, blooms appear in wand-like spikes. Close examination reveals that flowers are produced in axillary one-sided cymes, many of which are produced along the upper stems. Each cyme has a small narrow leaf or bract at its base. As the season progresses, the cymes elongate to become side-branches, giving plants a bushier appearance. Funnel-shaped flowers, composed of five fused petals, are 0.9 to 1.2 centimetres in diameter and open as pink buds but quickly turn vivid blue. The five stamens extend beyond the petals; they have blue pollen and contrasting red filaments. A single threadlike style has a pair of stigmas.

VITAL STATISTICS	
Maximum height: 80 centimetres	
Flowering season: June to September	

Top: The stamens extend beyond the funnel-shaped blue flowers. Middle: Each side-branch of the wand-like flower cluster is created by a one-sided scorpioid cyme. Bottom: First-season plants produce a basal rosette of long narrow leaves.

Disturbed

Mint family / Lamiaceae

Ground ivy

Glechoma hederacea

Creeping Charlie, gill-over-the-ground, run-away-robin

Introduced Species

VITAL STATISTICS

Maximum height: 30 centimetres
Flowering season: May to October

HABITAT: Ground ivy is a European introduction found in damp and shaded waste areas throughout much of Nova Scotia.

CHARACTERISTICS: Ground ivy is a trailing matted plant. Stems, square in cross-section, trail along the ground and usually root at their nodes. Opposite long petioled leaves are round or fan-shaped with rounded teeth; they are 2 to 3 centimetres in diameter. Upright flowering stems also have opposite rounded leaves, which may be smooth or have scattered stiff hairs. Leaves and stems are usually purple-tinted. Plants emit a minty fragrance when bruised.

Violet-blue flowers are sessile, usually in two groups of two to three flowers among the upper leaf axils. Individual tubular flowers, each about 2 centimetres long, have five petals arranged in a two-lipped fashion. Two petals fuse to form a two-lobed upper lip; the other three, a three-lobed lower lip. The middle lower lobe is the largest and is often two-lobed. This lower lobe and the throat of the flower are mottled with dark veins. The inside of the throat is hairy.

Top: Each flower is tubular; the middle lobe of the three-lobed lower lip is the largest. Bottom: The fan-shaped leaves are in pairs and the flowers axillary.

Disturbed

 **Native Species**

American pennyroyal

Hedeoma pulegioides

American false pennyroyal, pudding-grass

HABITAT: American pennyroyal, a European introduction, is found in waste areas and rocky pastures, and, less commonly, along seashores. It is common in the Annapolis Valley but scattered in the central-northern regions.

CHARACTERISTICS: American pennyroyal is a branched or unbranched annual. Stems are square in cross-section and pubescent. Opposite small leaves, each reaching 2.5 centimetres in length, are elliptical to oblong with a few hairs. Short petioled leaves have smooth edges or scattered obscure teeth. The plant emits a mint-like fragrance when bruised.

Flowers are produced in small axillary clusters of two to four flowers. Individual flowers are about 0.5 centimetres long. Tubular flowers have a two-lipped appearance with two fused petals forming an upper lip and three a lower lip. The lowermost petal is often notched. Flowers are pale violet-blue with a darker blue throat.

VITAL STATISTICS	
Maximum height:	30 centimetres
Flowering season:	August to September

Top: The axillary two-lipped flowers are pale blue with a darker throat. Bottom: The small elliptical leaves are opposite and covered in fine hairs.

Coastal

Disturbed

Mint family / Lamiaceae

Field mint

Mentha arvensis

Wild mint, common mint, Canada mint, corn mint

Native Species

VITAL STATISTICS

Maximum height: 60 centimetres
Flowering season: July to September

HABITAT: Field mint is found in open damp meadows and along roadsides and shorelines throughout Nova Scotia.

CHARACTERISTICS: Field mint is a bushy plant with upright or ascending stems from a creeping rhizome. Stems, square in cross-section, have downward-facing pubescent hairs and are often tinted red. Opposite, sharply toothed leaves are ovate, elliptical, or lanceolate with short petioles. Leaves, covered in long pubescent hairs, especially on the undersides, vary from 2 to 8 centimetres in length. All parts of the plant emit a minty fragrance when bruised.

Sessile flowers are produced in dense clusters among the upper leaf axils. The 0.4-centimetre-long funnel-shaped lilac-pink to purple flowers have a two-lipped appearance. The upper lip is shallowly lobed and wider than the lower lip's three lobes. Four stamens and single style with a two-forked stigma extend beyond the petals. The throat of the flower is hairy.

Red mint, *M. X gentilis*, prefers wet sites and is distinguished by its almost hairless leaves and often purple-tinted stems. Spearmint, *M. spicata*, is also found in wet sites. Its flowers are in narrow terminal spikes and its leaves appear rugose. Peppermint, *M. X peperita*, also inhabits wet places and is distinguished by its short terminal spikes.

Top: Field mint has sessile flowers in the leaf axils of the upper leaves. Middle: Spearmint has narrow terminal spikes of lilac-pink flowers. Bottom: Peppermint has short terminal spikes.

Wetlands

Disturbed

332

Common self-heal

 **Native Species**

Prunella vulgaris
Heal-all, self-heal

HABITAT: Common self-heal occurs in waste places as well as on pastures and lawns and along roadsides throughout Nova Scotia.

CHARACTERISTICS: Common self-heal is a tufted plant with loosely ascending stems. Prostrate rhizomes, often purple-tinted, root at the nodes. Stems, square in cross-section, are hairy when young but often hairless as they mature. Opposite toothed leaves are lanceolate and oblong or ovate and may reach a length of 9 centimetres. Leaves may be hairless or have scattered hairs and often appear crinkled.

Flowers are produced in club- or cone-like clusters. Each cluster has a pair of leaves at its base. The base of each flower has a small scale-like bract. Sepals are white, hairy, and often purple-tinted. Tubular 0.8- to 1.5-centimetre-long flowers have five fused petals that give them a two-lipped appearance. The upper two petals fuse to form a hood; the lower three petals, a three-lobed lip. The lowest lobe is the largest; it is shallowly notched with a fringed edge. Flowers are violet-blue to lavender with four stamens and a single style hidden within the tube.

VITAL STATISTICS
Maximum height: 30 centimetres
Flowering season: June to September

Top: Individual flowers appear two-lipped; the upper petals form a hood, the lower is three-lobed.
Bottom: The base of each flower has a scale-like bract; flowers are in terminal cone-shaped racemes.

Disturbed

333

Mint family / Lamiaceae

Marsh skullcap

Scutellaria galericulata

Common skullcap

VITAL STATISTICS

Maximum height: 100 centimetres
Flowering season: Mid-July to August

Wetlands

HABITAT: Marsh skullcap grows along rocky shorelines and streamsides throughout Nova Scotia.

CHARACTERISTICS: Marsh skullcap is a clumping plant with narrow, usually unbranched, stems arising from creeping rhizomes. Stems are square in cross-section with hairs along their corners. Opposite leaves, each up to 8 centimetres in length, are lance-shaped to oblong with rounded teeth and a rounded base. Leaves are rugose and glossy on the upper surfaces but have finely hairy undersides; they have short petioles or are sessile.

Tubular two-lipped flowers are trumpet-shaped and 1.5 to 2 centimetres long. They are produced in nearly sessile one-sided pairs from the axils of the upper leaves. The fused petals are blue to violet and covered in fine hairs. Upper petals form a narrow hood over the wider lower lip. The throat of the flower is white with darker blue spots; the sepals are often purple-tinted.

Mad-dog or blue skullcap, *S. lateriflora*, is bushier than marsh skullcap, although it occurs in similar habitats and blooms at the same time. It has ovate, usually hairless, leaves, which are up to 10 centimetres long. Leaves have rounded bases, coarse teeth, and distinct petioles. Flowers are produced in axillary or terminal one-sided racemes, which are up to 15 centimetres long. Each flower is 0.8 centimetres long with a small broad bract at its base.

Top: The paired tubular flowers appear two-lipped; the flower's throat is white with darker blue spots. Middle: Marsh skullcap's paired leaves are sessile and its stems square. Bottom: Blue skullcap produces flowers in one-sided axillary racemes; its leaves have petioles.

334

Canada toadflax

 Native Species

Nuttallanthus canadensis (formerly *Linaria canadensis*)
Old field toadflax, blue toadflax

HABITAT: Canada toadflax occurs in waste places and along roadsides, especially sandy sites. It is scattered, primarily in the southern half of the province.

CHARACTERISTICS: Canada toadflax is a slender annual or biennial. Overwintering plants have several flat rosettes, which arise in spring as non-branching stems. Four-centimetre-long stem leaves are linear, opposite on the lower stem and alternate on the upper stem. The stem is often purple-tinted; stems and leaves are hairless.

Light blue to blue-violet flowers are produced in a loose narrow terminal raceme. Individual 1-centimetre-wide flowers are snapdragon-like: two petals are fused to form a two-lobed upper lip; three petals form a larger three-lobed lower lip. The throat of the flower is white with two raised ridges. A thin curving 0.2- to 0.6-centimetre-long spur is located behind the lower lip. Five fused sepals form a pubescent tube behind the flower.

Dwarf snapdragon, *Chaenorrhinum minus*, is an introduced multiple branching annual scattered in waste places from Halifax northward. Plants reach 40 centimetres in height. Linear to oblong leaves are generally alternate but occasionally opposite. Leaves, stems, and flowers are covered in glandular hairs. Flowers are solitary among the upper axils and form leafy racemes. Individual lilac-coloured snapdragon-like flowers are 0.5 to 0.8 centimetres wide with a paler lilac throat. Flowers have short stout spurs.

VITAL STATISTICS
Maximum height: 80 centimetres
Flowering season: May to September

Top: Canada toadflax's snapdragon-like flowers are blue-violet with a paler throat and in racemes.
Bottom: Dwarf snapdragon has solitary flowers in the upper leaf axils; the plant is covered in fine sticky hairs.

Disturbed

335

Plantain family / Plantaginaceae

American speedwell

Veronica americana
American brooklime

VITAL STATISTICS

Maximum height: 60 centimetres
Flowering season: June to September

Wetlands

HABITAT: American speedwell occurs in wet habitats such as streamsides, shorelines, thickets, and ditches. Although widespread, this plant is rare or absent from the Atlantic coast.

CHARACTERISTICS: American speedwell is a trailing matted plant whose stem tips are often ascending. Stems often root at their nodes. Opposite leaves are lanceolate, elliptical to ovate, shallowly toothed, and petioled on the lower part of the stem, but sessile and clasping closer to the flowers. Leaves may reach 7 centimetres in length. Stems and leaves are hairless.

Flowers are produced in axillary racemes from the upper leaves. These racemes may reach 15 centimetres in length. Flowers, each about 0.5 centimetres wide, are composed of four pale violet-blue petals, the uppermost of which is the widest. The petal base has dark blue-violet veins. Each flower has two exerted stamens and a single style.

Marsh speedwell, *V. scutellata*, is a thinner, weaker plant than American speedwell and has long stolons. Stems may reach 75 centimetres in length. Sessile opposite leaves are linear to lanceolate, with smooth edges or fine teeth. Widely spaced white or lilac to lavender-blue flowers are produced in axillary racemes on a zigzag stem. The upper stem and new leaves are often red or purple-tinted. It blooms mid-June to September. It is scattered province-wide but common in the northern and central regions.

Top: American speedwell flowers are pale blue with darker veins and in racemes. Middle: American speedwell has trailing stems; its opposite leaves are hairless. Bottom: Marsh speedwell often has white flowers with pale blue veins.

Long-leaved speedwell

Veronica longifolia
Garden speedwell

**Introduced
Species**

HABITAT: Long-leaved speedwell, a European species originally grown in Nova Scotia as a garden ornamental, is naturalized along roadsides, primarily in the southern part of the province.

CHARACTERISTICS: Long-leaved speedwell is a slender clumping plant with unbranched lower stems and a few upper flowering branches. Stems and leaves may be hairless or have a fine, pale pubescence. Opposite or whorled leaves are lanceolate, short petioled, and sharply toothed.

Stems end in long narrow racemes, which may occupy nearly one-third of the plant's height. Individual deep violet-blue flowers are 0.6 to 0.8 centimetres wide and have four petals: a single upper and three wide-spreading lower petals. Flowers also have two exerted stamens and a single style that give a bottle-brush look to the racemes.

VITAL STATISTICS
Maximum height: 100 centimetres
Flowering season: July to August

Top: Flowers are in many narrow racemes.
Bottom: The flowers have a bottlebrush appearance; its opposite leaves are narrow and sharply toothed.

Plantain family / Plantaginaceae
Common speedwell

Veronica officinalis
Common gypsyweed

VITAL STATISTICS

Maximum height: 20 centimetres
Flowering season: July to August

HABITAT: Common speedwell, a European species found in disturbed places such as roadsides, old pasturelands, woodland trails, and lawns, is especially fond of shady rich soils.

CHARACTERISTICS: A trailing mat-forming plant, common speedwell's opposite leaves reach 5 centimetres in length; they vary from ovate, oblong, to elliptical and have short petioles and fine teeth. The entire plant is covered in soft hairs.

Ten- to 20-centimetre-high erect flower stems are produced from leaf axils near the ends of the stems. Flowers are produced in a dense raceme. Individual flowers are about 0.8 centimetres wide with four petals. The lower petal is narrower than the other three; all are lilac to lavender-blue with dark veins. Flowers have two stamens and a single style. The throat of the flower is hairy. The developing seed capsules have a heart-like shape.

Germander speedwell, *V. chamaedrys*, occurs in similar habitats to common speedwell, but it is less common and widely scattered. Although trailing, it produces more erect stems than common speedwell, to 40 centimetres tall; round leaves are essentially sessile with larger, rounder teeth. It blooms from May to July; the bright blue flowers in axillary racemes have dark blue veins. Individual flowers are up to 1.2 centimetres wide.

Top: The lavender-blue flowers are in narrow racemes; the lowermost petal is narrower than the other petals. Middle: Common speedwell stems are trailing with opposite oval leaves. Bottom: Germander speedwell has rounder leaves with larger rounded teeth than common speedwell; its axillary flowers are bright blue.

Plantain family / Plantaginaceae

 Introduced Species

Thyme-leaved speedwell

Veronica serpyllifolia

HABITAT: A European species, thyme-leaved speedwell is found in damp disturbed areas throughout the province.

CHARACTERISTICS: Thyme-leaved speedwell is an evergreen mat-forming plant. Stems are trailing and often root at their nodes. Opposite leaves, up to 1.5 centimetres in length, are sessile and ovate, with obscure rounded teeth. Leaves and stems are usually hairless.

Flowers are produced on upright terminal racemes. Each has a leafy bract at its base. Individual flowers are 0.6 to 0.8 centimetres wide with four pale blue petals veined in a darker blue. The lower petal is narrower than the other three. Flowers have two stamens and a single style. The developing seed capsules are heart-shaped.

Corn speedwell, *V. arvensis*, is a narrow annual that grows to a height of 30 centimetres with small opposite toothed leaves. Lower stem leaves are round and short-stalked; the upper, sessile. Stems and leaves have long hairs. Sessile 0.2- to 0.3-centimetre-wide violet-blue flowers are produced on narrow racemes, each with a narrow leafy bract at their base.

Bird's-eye speedwell, *V. persica*, is another long-haired annual but its 0.8- to 1.2-centimetre-wide violet-blue flowers with white centres are solitary in the leaf axils and held on thin stems. Petioled leaves are ovate to round with coarsely toothed edges. Both corn and bird's-eye speedwells are European species widely scattered in disturbed habitats and bloom from June to September.

Top: Thyme-leaved speedwell has upright racemes of pale blue flowers with darker veins, especially on the uppermost petal; leaves are round and almost smooth along their edges. Middle: Corn speedwell's sessile flowers are partly hidden among the many narrow hairy bracts. Bottom: Bird's-eye speedwell has solitary flowers among the upper leaf axils; the violet-blue flowers have white centres.

Disturbed

False pimpernel family / Linderniaceae

Yellow-seed false pimpernel

Lindernia dubia

Slender false pimpernel, moist-bank pimpernel

Native Species

VITAL STATISTICS

Maximum height: 30 centimetres

Flowering season: Late June to October

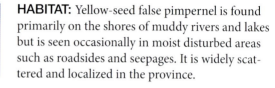

HABITAT: Yellow-seed false pimpernel is found primarily on the shores of muddy rivers and lakes but is seen occasionally in moist disturbed areas such as roadsides and seepages. It is widely scattered and localized in the province.

CHARACTERISTICS: Yellow-seed false pimpernel is a low bushy, but open, annual with arching stems. Stems are square in cross-section and often tinted red. Opposite leaves are up to 3.5 centimetres long, elliptical to ovate, with smooth or slightly toothed edges. They are either sessile or nearly sessile. The entire plant is hairless.

Flowers, which are 0.5 to 1 centimetres long, are solitary in the upper leaf axils. Produced at the ends of 2.5-centimetre-long slender pedicles, the pale violet-blue flowers are tubular with a two-lipped appearance: the upper lip is two-lobed and hoodlike, the lower, three-lobed and wide-spreading. Inside the floral tube are four stamens and a single style.

Top: The solitary pale violet blue flowers appear two-lipped; the lower lip has three wide-spreading lobes. Bottom: The hairless leaves are opposite, sessile, and only slightly toothed.

340

Native
Species

Square-stemmed monkeyflower

Mimulus ringens

Blue monkeyflower, Allegheny monkeyflower

HABITAT: Square-stemmed monkeyflower grows in wet marshes and along shorelines and streams. It is found primarily in the western half of Nova Scotia; it is rare or absent in the southwest Atlantic coast region and eastern Cape Breton.

CHARACTERISTICS: Square-stemmed monkeyflower is a slender clumping plant with stems arising from stoloniferous rhizomes. Stems are square in cross-section. Opposite leaves, which are up to 10 centimetres in length, are lanceolate to elliptical, sessile or clasping, with toothed edges. Leaves and stems are hairless.

Long petioled flowers are solitary among the upper leaf axils. The 2.5-centimetre-long pale blue-violet flowers have a two-lipped snapdragon-like appearance. The upper two petals are fused into an erect two-lobed lip; the lower three petals form a wide-spreading three-lobed lower lip. The base of the lowermost petal has two yellow ridges that lead into the hairy throat. The outside surface of the petals is covered in fine glandular hairs; inside the throat are four stamens and a two-lobed stigma. Fused sepals form a five-ridged tube with five pointed teeth at its end.

VITAL STATISTICS
Maximum height: 120 centimetres
Flowering season: July to August

Wetlands

Top: The flowers appear two-lipped; the base of the lower lip has two yellow ridges. Bottom: The narrow opposite leaves are sessile with toothed edges and the flowers axillary.

Bladderwort family / Lentibulariaceae

Common butterwort

Pinguicula vulgaris
Slender false pimpernel, moist-bank pimpernel

Native
Species

VITAL STATISTICS

Maximum height: 12 centimetres
Flowering season: June to early
August

HABITAT: Common butterwort prefers wet calcareous gravels, open seepages, and wet shorelines. It is rare in Nova Scotia and restricted to the northern end of Cape Breton in Inverness County.

CHARACTERISTICS: Common butterwort is a small rosetted plant. Basal spatulate to elliptical leaves are fleshy and yellow-green and have smooth upward-curling edges. Insects adhere to its sticky and greasy upper leaf surface. Leaves may reach 5 centimetres in length.

Purple funnel-shaped flowers are solitary and arise on leafless glandular stems, which reach 12 centimetres in length. Each rosette produces up to nine flowers. Individual flowers are up to 1.5 centimetres wide and have a two-lipped appearance: the upper lip is two-lobed; the lower, three-lobed. A narrow downward-curving spur extends behind the lower lip. The inside of the throat has long white hairs. The five sepals are often dark purple-tinted and covered in glandular pubescence. Inside the throat are two stamens and a single disc-shaped stigma.

Top: The funnel-shaped flowers appear two-lipped; the inside of the flower has long white hairs. Middle: Plants produce a low rosette of yellow-green leaves with smooth upward-curling edges. Bottom: Solitary flowers arise on leafless stems.

Native
Species

Water lobelia

Lobelia dortmanna
Water gladiole

HABITAT: Water lobelia grows in gravelly or rocky-bottomed ponds and slow-moving streams throughout Nova Scotia. It is usually restricted to water less than 150 centimetres in depth.

CHARACTERISTICS: Water lobelia is an aquatic plant with a tuft of evergreen linear leaves. Its hollow leaves are fleshy, curving, and 2.5 to 7.5 centimetres long.

One to 11 widely spaced flowers are produced in a raceme at the end of a leafless hairless stem that arises up to 30 centimetres above the water's surface. Each flower has a narrow 1- to 2-centi-metre-long floral tube and five petals. The flower opening has a two-lipped appearance. The upper lip has two narrow lobes that curve backward; the lower lip has three larger wide-spreading lobes. Petals are pale blue or almost white. Inside the floral tube are five stamens and a single style.

Kalm's or bog lobelia, *L. kalmia*, is found in damp calcareous wetlands. It has slender 15- to 30-centimetre-high stems, spatulate to obovate and slightly toothed basal leaves, alternate linear stem leaves, and a loose one-sided raceme of 0.7- to 1.6-centimetre-long flowers. Flowers have five petals: two small narrow backward-curving petals form an upper lip; three larger, broader petals, a three-lobed lower lip. Flowers are blue with a conspicuous white eye on the lower lip. It is rare and confined to Cape Breton.

VITAL STATISTICS
Maximum height: 30 centimetres
Flowering season: August

Wetlands

Top: Petal bases are fused into a tube; the pale blue flowers appear two-lipped. Middle: Water lobelia flowers are on narrow leafless racemes that arise directly from the water. Bottom: Kalm's lobelia flowers are blue with conspicuous white eyes.

343

Bellflower family / Campanulaceae

Indian tobacco

Lobelia inflata

Wild tobacco

Native Species

VITAL STATISTICS

Maximum height: 100 centimetres
Flowering season: July to August

HABITAT: Indian tobacco grows along roadsides or in open woodlands and waste places throughout the province, except northern Cape Breton.

CHARACTERISTICS: Indian tobacco is a tall leafy annual or biennial. Overwintering plants have a basal rosette of ovate leaves. Flowering plants have alternate elliptical to ovate sessile leaves with toothed edges. Leaves may reach 8 centimetres in length. The stem and leaf undersides are hairy.

Pale violet flowers are produced in terminal and axillary racemes among the upper leaves. Individual 0.7- to 1-centimetre-long flowers have a two-lipped appearance created by the fusing of five petals. The upper lip has two narrow erect lobes; the lower, three larger wide-spreading lobes. The base of the lower lip has a pale yellow patch with white hairs. Each flower has a stalk and a small leaf or leafy bract at its base. This plant is toxic if ingested.

Pale spike lobelia, *L. spicata*, is uncommon in the rich dry meadows of Kings, Colchester, and Cumberland counties. Its unbranched stems may reach 100 centimetres in height. Leaves are lanceolate, toothed, sessile or short petioled, and hairless. The lower portion of the main stem is pubescent; the upper, smooth. Flowers are about 1 centimetre long, light blue, and sessile; they are produced in a dense terminal narrow raceme reaching up to 30 centimetres in length.

Top: The pale violet flowers appear two-lipped, with two narrow upper lobes and three wide-spreading wider lobes. Middle: Indian tobacco flowers are in racemes that are both terminal and from the upper leaf axils. Bottom: Pale spike lobelia has stemless flowers in dense terminal spikes.

Native
Species

Pickerelweed

Pontederia cordata
Water gladiole

HABITAT: Pickerelweed is found in shallow water or along muddy shores. It is abundant in the southwest of the province but scarce on Cape Breton Island.

CHARACTERISTICS: Pickerelweed is a stout clumping plant that forms large colonies as plants spread via thick rhizomes. The waxy leaves are basal, arising directly from the rhizome, and held on hollow petioles which reach 60 centimetres in length. Leaf bases are often submersed. Leaf blades, which are up to 18 centimetres in length, vary from ovate, oblong, to lanceolate, with smooth edges and a heart-shaped base. Leaves and petioles are hairless.

Thick flower stems have one stem leaf. Above this leaf is a spathe from which a dense spike of flowers, which is up to 12 centimetres long, emerges. The stem above the spathe, as well as the sepals, is covered in glandular hairs. Individual flowers are 1.5 to 2 centimetres wide. Flowers have six blue-violet tepals, three arched upward and three arched downward, imparting a two-lipped effect. The uppermost tepal has a distinct yellow spot at its base. Flowers have six anthers of varying lengths, usually three long and three short, and a single style.

VITAL STATISTICS
Maximum height: 50 centimetres
Flowering season: June to September

Wetlands

Top: Each flower has three long and three short stamens; the uppermost petal has a central yellow blotch.
Bottom: Flowers are in dense racemes; the smooth leaves are commonly heart-shaped.

Iris family / Iridaceae

Blue flag

Iris versicolor
Harlequin blue flag, northern blue flag

Native Species

VITAL STATISTICS

Maximum height: 80 centimetres
Flowering season: June to July

HABITAT: Blue flag occurs in wet to damp habitats throughout Nova Scotia.

CHARACTERISTICS: Blue flag is a clumping grass-like plant. Leaves are basal, strap- or sword-like, hairless, and smooth-edged. Their bases are often purple-tinted.

Flowers are produced on stout leafless stems. Stems may be single or have two to three branches, each producing one to three flowers. Deep blue or blue-violet flowers are showy, each about 10 centimetres wide; they have three downward-arching broad sepals (the falls) and three erect narrower petals (the standards). The base of the sepals is white to yellow with blue-violet veins. Both sepals and petals may have darker veins. The standards are about half as long as the sepals. The thick cylindroid seed capsule is three-angled and has a nipple-like beak at its terminus.

Slender blue flag, *I. prismatica*, is rare and found only in Inverness, Annapolis, and Guysborough counties. It has slender leaves, flowers which are more slender than those of blue flag, and sharply three-angled seed capsules.

Beach-head iris, *I. hookeri*, is confined to peaty shores, headlands, and salt marshes near the coast. It is only half the size of blue flag, reaching a maximum height of 50 centimetres. Its flowers have tiny narrow standards, rounded falls and more globular seed capsules without a terminal beak. It blooms slightly earlier than blue flag.

Top: Each blue flag flower has three large falls, the base of which is often yellow with dark veins, and three smaller standards. Middle: Blue flag produces large grass-like clumps with broad sword-shaped leaves. Bottom: Beach-head iris flowers have three rounded falls and three minute standards.

Wetlands

346

 **Native Species**

Spurred gentian

Halenia deflexa

HABITAT: Rare in Nova Scotia, spurred gentian is restricted primarily to Cape Breton, where it grows on peaty coastal headlands.

CHARACTERISTICS: Spurred gentian is a tufted leafy annual or biennial. Its leaves are opposite, sessile, smooth-edged, fleshy, and spoon- to lance-shaped. Leaves, often purple-tinted, have three distinct veins. The entire plant is hairless. The stem is square in cross-section.

Flowers are in crowded, both terminal and axillary, cymes. Flowers vary in length from 0.8 to 1.5 centimetres; individual flowers have four narrow green sepals and four pointed petals, which vary from purple to bronze to yellow-green. Each petal has a perpendicular spur at its base. Flowers rarely open fully.

VITAL STATISTICS

Maximum height: 30 centimetres
Flowering season: July to September

Top: Each flower, which never opens fully, has four petals with perpendicular spurs; shown here are two colour extremes. Bottom: Shown here is the usual spurred gentian flower colour; flowers are clustered at the tip and among the upper leaf axils.

Coastal

347

Madder family / Rubiaceae

Azure bluets

Houstonia caerulea
Mountain bluets, Quaker-ladies

 Native Species

VITAL STATISTICS
Maximum height: 20 centimetres
Flowering season: Mid-May to mid-June

HABITAT: Azure bluets are encountered in damp meadows, lawns, and open hillsides throughout most of Nova Scotia.

CHARACTERISTICS: Azure bluets is a small tufted annual or short-lived perennial with both basal and stem leaves. The former are spatulate to elliptical and up to 1.5 centimetres in length. Stem leaves are opposite, lance-shaped to linear, and smaller than the basal leaves. They are hairless or may have fine hairs. Unbranched stems are thin and threadlike.

Flowers are solitary on the ends of thin wiry stems. Individual flowers are about 1 centimetre wide with four pale blue petals set at the end of a narrow tube. Each flower has a yellow eye, four stamens, and a single style with a bifid stigma. Some flowers have long stamens and a short style; others, short stamens and a long style. This is known as dimorphism or dimorphous flowers.

Top: Each flower is solitary with four pale blue petals, and each centre has a yellow eye. Bottom: Plants are low and tufted, often with small oval leaves.

Buttercup family / Ranunculaceae

European columbine

Aquilegia vulgaris
Garden columbine

Introduced
Species

HABITAT: European columbine, a garden escape originally introduced as a garden ornamental, is found along roadsides and trails and in waste areas near settlements throughout the province.

CHARACTERISTICS: European columbine is a tufted plant. The long petioled leaves are basal and biternately compound. Leaflets are lobed with rounded teeth. The lower stem leaves, which are alternately arranged, are similar, with shorter petioles than the basal leaves; upper stem leaves are trifoliate and sessile. Upper leaf surfaces are smooth and waxy; undersides are finely hairy.

Nodding flowers, produced in loose clusters, are up to 5.5 centimetres wide. Flowers have five petals, each with a hooked spur at the basal end, five petal-like sepals, numerous stamens, and five styles. Flowers are usually violet-blue but may also be pale blue, wine-red, pink, or white. Petals may be white or paler at their tips, imparting a bi-coloured effect to blossoms. Each flower develops five pointy-tipped narrow tubelike capsules that are joined at the base.

VITAL STATISTICS

Maximum height: 120 centimetres
Flowering season: Late May to June

Top: Each flower has five petal-like sepals and five petals with hooked spurs at their basal end.
Middle: Flowers, which are nodding, vary from blue to wine-red (shown here) to pink to white. Bottom: Leaves are mostly basal and biternately compound; leaflets are lobed with rounded teeth.

Disturbed

349

Plumbago family / Plumabaginaceae

Sea-lavender

Limonium carolinianum

Marsh rosemary

Native Species

VITAL STATISTICS

Maximum height: 60 centimetres
Flowering season: Mid-July to
September

HABITAT: Sea-lavender occurs in salt marshes and peaty seashores. It is common along the Fundy coast, scattered elsewhere, and uncommon along the Atlantic coast.

CHARACTERISTICS: Sea-lavender is a leafy tufted plant arising from a thick rootstock. Hairless smooth-edged leaves are oblong and spatulate to elliptical. Leaves are basal and commonly 20 to 30 centimetres in length with long petioles, and they have a leathery texture.

Numerous flowers are produced in airy spraylike panicles of one-sided racemes atop relatively stout leafless stems. Sepals are finely pubescent at their base; flowers are about 0.3 centimetres wide with five lavender petals. Inside the flower are five stamens and five styles.

Top: The tiny flowers are in open panicles, each blossom has five small lavender-blue petals.
Bottom: The elliptical leaves are basal, creating a tufted habit.

Coastal

 Introduced Species

Meadow geranium
Geranium pratense
Meadow cranesbill

HABITAT: Meadow geranium, a European plant introduced as a garden ornamental, is occasionally found in waste areas and along trails and roadsides near settlements throughout Nova Scotia.

CHARACTERISTICS: Meadow geranium is a clumping plant with multiple unbranched stems arising from a thickened rhizome. Basal leaves have long petioles. Leaves are palmately lobed with seven to nine divisions; each division is subsequently deeply lobed and each lobe has large rounded teeth. Stem leaves are opposite and short-stalked or sessile. Leaves and stems are pubescent. Upper stems and flower stalks are often purple-tinted.

Flowers are produced in loose branching corymbs. Buds are nodding before they open. Flower stems and pedicles are slightly sticky with glandular hairs. Three- to 4-centimetre-wide flowers are saucer-shaped; they have five violet-blue petals with pale veins, five pointed finely hairy green sepals, 10 stamens, and a single style with a five-parted thin starlike stigma. Seeds are produced at the bottom of a bill-like structure. When seeds are ripe, part of the bill curls back, catapulting the seeds.

VITAL STATISTICS

Maximum height: 70 centimetres
Flowering season: June to August

Top: Unopened flowers typically nod; open outward-facing flowers have five violet-blue petals with pale veins. Middle: White-flowered plants are less common. Bottom: Leaves are palmately lobed with seven to nine divisions, each of which is lobed and toothed.

Disturbed

Dogbane family / Apocynaceae
Lesser periwinkle

Introduced Species

Vinca minor
Running myrtle, common periwinkle

VITAL STATISTICS

Maximum height: 30 centimetres
Flowering season: May and June

HABITAT: Lesser periwinkle is a European species that was introduced to Nova Scotia as a garden plant. It is now found occasionally along roadsides, trails, and the edges of deciduous and mixed forests near larger communities throughout the province.

CHARACTERISTICS: Lesser periwinkle is an evergreen groundcover with 1.5- to 3-centimetre-long opposite leaves that are glossy, hairless, and smooth-edged. Plants produce upright flowering stems with three to five pairs of leaves, as well as elongate non-flowering creeping stems that often root along their length.

Flowers are solitary from each pair of leaves along the upright stems. Each flower is 1.5 to 3 centimetres wide with five blue-violet petals that are fused at their base into a tube.

Top: Flowers are solitary; the five blue-violet petals are fused at their base. Bottom: The glossy leaves are paired and hairless with smooth edges; plants form evergreen groundcovers.

Oysterleaf

Mertensia maritima
Sea lungwort

Introduced Species

HABITAT: Oysterleaf is common on sandy or gravelly shorelines around the entire coastline of Nova Scotia.

CHARACTERISTICS: Early in the season, oysterleaf has tufted basal leaves; later, plants become trailing and mat-like. Their leaves are waxy, fleshy, and blue-grey to grey-green. Basal leaves are petioled and ovate to spatulate; stem leaves are alternate, short-petioled to sessile, and ovate to elliptical. All leaves are hairless and smooth-edged. The upper-outer portion of all leaves often has small bumps on its surface.

Flowers are produced in terminal leafy cymes. Individual flowers, which are up to 0.9 centimetres long, are bell-like with five lobes. Flowers are pink when they open but quickly turn bright blue. Within the bell are five stamens and a single style.

VITAL STATISTICS
Maximum height: 20 centimetres
Flowering season: Mid-June to August

Top: Blue bell-shaped flowers open from pink flower buds. Middle: Trailing flowering stems end in leafy cymes. Bottom: Young plants and early-in-the-season plants have tufted basal leaves; leaves are typically blue-tinted.

Coastal

353

Borage family / Boraginaceae

Small forget-me-not

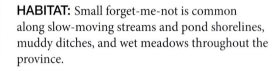

Myosotis laxa

Small-flowered forget-me-not, bay forget-me-not, tufted forget-me-not

VITAL STATISTICS

Maximum height: 40 centimetres
Flowering season: June to September

HABITAT: Small forget-me-not is common along slow-moving streams and pond shorelines, muddy ditches, and wet meadows throughout the province.

CHARACTERISTICS: Small forget-me-not is a matted semi-aquatic plant with weak rounded trailing stems. Alternate lanceolate leaves, which are up to 10 centimetres in length, are nearly sessile with smooth edges. The upper leaf surface has short bristly hairs. Trailing stems do not root at their nodes; plants do not produce stolons.

Flowers are produced at the ends of branches on one-sided cymes. As they mature, cymes become more raceme-like and the flowers are widely spaced. Unopened flowers are held in a tight coil. Each five-petalled flower is 0.2- to 0.5-centimetre wide and bright blue with a yellow eye. The bases of the petals form a floral tube which is shorter than or equal to the length of each petal.

European or large forget-me-not, *M. scorpioides*, has stolons and squared stems that root at the nodes. Leaves are oblong and wider and shorter (to 5 centimetres) than those of small forget-me-not. Flowers are up to 0.5 to 1 centimetre wide, and the length of the floral tube is greater than that of an individual petal. Flowers are closer together than those of small forget-me-not. It is locally common.

Top: Small forget-me-not leaves are smooth-edged and sessile; flowers are on one-sided cymes.
Bottom: European forget-me-not has larger flowers and broader leaves than small forget-me-not.

Borage family / Boraginaceae

Woodland forget-me-not

Myosotis sylvatica
Garden forget-me-not

Introduced
Species

HABITAT: Woodland forget-me-not, introduced from Europe as a garden ornamental, is occasionally naturalized in waste areas near settlements in the province.

CHARACTERISTICS: Woodland forget-me-not is a tufted biennial or short-lived perennial plant. Basal leaves are oblong to elliptical with smooth edges and winged petioles. Stem leaves are alternate and sessile. Stems, leaves, and sepals are covered in short soft hairs. The stems may be purple-tinted.

Flowers, which are 0.6 to 0.8 centimetres wide, are produced on one-sided cymes that elongate to become more raceme-like. Individual flowers have five clear blue, rarely pink or white, petals which are fused at their base to produce a floral tube. Flowers have a central yellow eye, five stamens, and a single style.

Rough forget-me-not, *M. arvensis*, is similar to woodland forget-me-not but only reaches 40 centimetres in height; flowers are just 0.3 to 0.4 centimetres wide. It blooms mid-May through September. Plants are covered in hairs. Common in the Annapolis Valley, rough forget-me-not is scattered to rare farther north.

Stickseed, *Lappula squarrosa*, is a related annual with forget-me-not-like flowers produced in elongate racemes on plants up to 60 centimetres tall. Their flowers are commonly more cupped than those of true forget-me-not. The entire plant is rough-haired; seeds have hooked bristles that stick to fur and clothing. It is widely scattered.

Top: Woodland forget-me-not is a bushy tufted plant with sessile elliptical leaves; stems may be purple-tinted. Middle: Rough forget-me-not has hairy sepals. Bottom: Stickseed has long white-haired sepals and cup-shaped flowers.

VITAL STATISTICS
Maximum height: 50 centimetres
Flowering season: June to July

Disturbed

Borage family / Boraginaceae

Prickly comfrey

Symphytum asperum

Introduced Species

VITAL STATISTICS

Maximum height: 150 centimetres
Flowering season: Mid-June to July

HABITAT: Prickly comfrey, a European species likely introduced in Atlantic Canada as a garden ornamental, and not widely scattered in Nova Scotia, is found in waste areas, especially near settlements.

CHARACTERISTICS: Prickly comfrey is a robust leafy plant that forms large clumps. Stems and leaves are covered in rough prickly hairs. Alternate leaves are elliptical and petioled, with smooth but often undulating edges. They are rugose with distinct veins. The lowermost leaves may reach 20 centimetres in length.

Nodding flowers are produced in one-sided cymes, both terminally and axillary from the upper leaf axils. Five fused petals produce a tubular flower, which is up to 1.5 centimetres long, with a bell-like end. Flowers are pink when they open but rapidly turn blue; they also have five stamens hidden within the floral tube and a single thread-like style that extends beyond the petals.

Common comfrey, *S. officinale*, occurs in similar habitats as prickly comfrey but mostly in Kings and Pictou counties. Hairs are not as stiff as those on prickly comfrey and the upper leaves have winged petioles. Flower colours include dirty white, pale straw yellow, or dull purple.

Top: Prickly comfrey's pink buds open into blue bell-like flowers; leaves are rugose with undulating smooth edges. Bottom: Common comfrey's nodding flowers are commonly dirty white to straw yellow.

Native Species

Blue vervain

Verbena hastata

American blue vervain, false vervain, swamp verbena, simpler's-joy

HABITAT: Blue vervain is seen along river bottoms, shore- and streamsides, and wet meadows. It is scattered in Nova Scotia, most likely to be seen from Kings County to Cumberland County.

CHARACTERISTICS: Blue vervain is a tall clumping plant. Stems are square in cross-section, slightly hairy, and often purple-tinted. Opposite leaves, which up to 15 centimetres long, are narrow and lanceolate with coarsely toothed edges, a veiny appearance, and a short petiole. Lowermost leaves may have a pair of short lobes at their base.

Flowers are produced in a panicle of numerous dense narrow racemes up to 12 centimetres in length. Individual flowers are about 0.6 centimetres wide with five violet-blue petals that are fused at the base to form a short tube.

VITAL STATISTICS

Maximum height: 150 centimetres
Flowering season: August to September

Top: Flowers are in dense racemes. Middle: The paired narrow leaves are coarsely toothed and petioled. Bottom: Many narrow racemes combine to form a panicle of flowers.

Wetlands

357

Bellflower family / Campanulaceae

Common harebell

Campanula rotundifolia
Common bluebell, Scottish bluebell

Native Species

VITAL STATISTICS

Maximum height: 40 centimetres
Flowering season: Mid-June to
September

HABITAT: Common harebell grows along coastal headlands, coastal meadows, rocky roadsides, and gravelly streamsides throughout Nova Scotia.

CHARACTERISTICS: Common harebell forms colonies by thin subterranean rhizomes. Usually less than 15 centimetres tall, this tufted, creeping plant occasionally reaches 40 centimetres. Round to heart-shaped toothed basal leaves have narrow petioles and develop in late summer, overwinter, and shrivel before flowering commences. Leaves on the upright non-branching stems are alternate, linear, often smooth-edged, and primarily sessile. The entire plant is hairless.

Nodding bell-shaped flowers are solitary or, more commonly, in loose racemes. The 1.5-centimetre-long flowers have five pointed violet-blue, rarely white, lobes; five threadlike sepals; five stamens; and one style with a three-lobed stigma.

Marsh bellflower, *C. aparinoides*, grows from Cumberland and Hants counties east to Antigonish. Slender, branching plants reach 100 centimetres in length; linear sessile leaves have hairy undersides and hairy widely toothed edges. Solitary, often nodding, bell-like 1- to 1.5-centimetre-long flowers have five white or pale blue pointed lobes.

Creeping bellflower, *C. rapunculoides*, has unbranched stems up to 100 centimetres long. Narrow heart-shaped leaves are coarsely toothed. Nodding 2.5-centimetre-long, violet-blue bell-like flowers bloom on one-sided racemes in July and August.

Top: Common harebell has linear stem leaves and loose racemes of nodding bell-shaped flowers.
Middle: Marsh bellflower's weak stems have a few pale blue bell-like flowers. Bottom: Creeping bellflower has nearly sessile flowers on dense one-sided racemes.

Barrens

Coastal

Disturbed

358

Native Species   Introduced Species

Wild chives

Allium schoenoprassum
Chives

HABITAT: Chives has both native and European varieties; within Nova Scotia, only native chives is encountered in the wild, restricted to coastal lowlands, particularly calcareous areas. It is rare and widely scattered along the Fundy coast and Cape Breton.

CHARACTERISTICS: Chives is a clumping, grass-like plant arising from a cluster of small bulbs. All leaves are basal, linear, terete, and hollow with a distinctive onion smell when bruised. All parts of the plant is hairless.

Flower stems are leafless, stiffer, and taller than the leaves. Before the flowers open, they are encased in a thin purple or pink-tinted sheath, which splits to reveal a hemispherical umbel of flowers 2.5 to 4 centimetres in diameter. Individual 1- to 1.4-centimetre-long flowers have six narrow purple tepals. The European form usually has leaves which are longer than the flower stems.

Wild leek, *A. tricoccum*, is rarely found in rich deciduous woodlands in western areas of the province. From a cluster of bulbs arise 10- to 30-centimetre-long, elliptical to lanceolate, smooth, fleshy leaves. These are shrivelled by the time flowering commences. Atop 15- to 40-centimetre-high leafless flower stems is produced a hemispherical cluster of white six-tepaled flowers. Plants emit a strong onion smell when bruised. Wild leek blooms in June.

Top: Flowers are in dense hemispherical umbels; note the papery remains of the "skin" that protected the unopened buds. Middle: Wild chives has leafless flower stems that arise above its grass-like leaves. Bottom: Wild leek produces a hemispherical umbel of white flowers with six tepals, six stamens, and a single style.

VITAL STATISTICS

Maximum height: 50 centimetres
Flowering season: Late June to July

Wetlands

Coastal

Disturbed

359

Iris family / Iridaceae

Strict blue-eyed grass

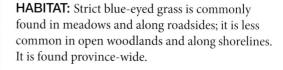

Native Species

Sisyrinchium montanum (formerly *S. angustifolium*)
Common blue-eyed grass, mountain blue-eyed grass

VITAL STATISTICS
Maximum height: 35 centimetres
Flowering season: Late May to July

HABITAT: Strict blue-eyed grass is commonly found in meadows and along roadsides; it is less common in open woodlands and along shorelines. It is found province-wide.

CHARACTERISTICS: Strict blue-eyed grass is a tufted grass-like plant. Leaves are basal, linear, flattened, grass-like, and smooth-edged.

Flowers stems, which are taller than the leaves, are stiff, winged, and non-branching and have two leaf-like bracts, one below the flowers and the other overtopping the flowers. Flowers are produced in an umbel of two to five flowers. Individual flowers are 1.5 to 2.5 centimetres wide with six deep violet-blue, bristle-tipped tepals. Each flower has a central yellow eye. Flowers have six stamens and a single style. Flowers later develop into 0.4- to 0.7-centimetre-diameter globular seed capsules which turn dark brown when seeds are ripe.

Eastern blue-eyed grass, *S. atlanticum*, an Atlantic Coastal Plain species found primarily in southern Nova Scotia, differs from strict blue-eyed grass in that these plants are taller, reaching 50 centimetres in height, flower stems are zigzagged and usually branching, and the two bracts adjacent to the flowers are nearly equal in length.

Top: Each flower has six deep violet-blue bristle-tipped petals and a central yellow eye. Middle: Strict blue-eyed grass produces clumps of grass-like foliage and straight flower stems. Bottom: Eastern blue-eyed grass has zigzagged flower stems.

Buttercup family / Ranunculaceae

Round-lobed hepatica

 Native Species

Anemone americana (formerly *Hepatica americana*)

Round-leaved hepatica

HABITAT: Round-lobed hepatica is seen occasionally in dry, deciduous, or mixed woodlands of central Nova Scotia.

CHARACTERISTICS: Round-lobed hepatica is a tufted woodland plant. Leaves, each about 7.5 centimetres wide, are wider than they are long; they are basal, tri-lobed, leathery, and evergreen and turn purple-brown through the winter months. The petiole is 10 to 15 centimetres long and covered in long soft hairs. The top sides of leaves are hairless; the undersides have long hairs, which are often lost as the season progresses. The leaf edges are smooth with fine hairs. New leaves, which may be mottled purple-brown, appear after the plant flowers.

Flowers are solitary at the ends of hairy purple-tinted stems. Flowers usually have six or seven (but up to 12) sepals which are petaloid and lavender-blue, pink, or white. Flowers are 1.5 to 2.5 centimetres wide and have numerous stamens and pistils at their centres. Flowers close, and often nod at night or on cloudy days. Each flower has three purple-green sepal-like bracts below their colourful sepals.

VITAL STATISTICS

Maximum height: 15 centimetres
Flowering season: May

Mixed Forest

Deciduous Forest

Top: Plants often produce solitary flowers with seven or more petaloid sepals. Middle: Flowers are often pink; the flower stems have long hairs. Bottom: Leaves are tri-lobed and often mottled when they unfurl.

361

Aster family / Asteraceae

Wild chicory

Cichorium intybus

Chicory, wild chicory

Introduced Species

VITAL STATISTICS

Maximum height: 100 centimetres
Flowering season: July to September

HABITAT: Wild chicory is a European plant found in disturbed habitats such as roadsides and waste places throughout Nova Scotia. It is common in the Annapolis Valley.

CHARACTERISTICS: Wild chicory is a slender biennial or short-lived perennial arising from a taproot. Early in the season, first-year plants form a flat rosette of lanceolate, sharply toothed, sharply lobed, or pinnatifid leaves, similar to those of dandelion. Alternate stem leaves are similar but have smaller, widely spaced teeth and are sessile or partly clasp the stem. Hairs grow along the lower central vein of each leaf. The stem is grooved, green or purple-tinted, hairy on the lower portion but often hairless above. All parts of the plant ooze a milky sap when cut.

Flowering stems appear spike-like or as an open branching panicle. The widely spaced flowers are produced in clusters of two to three along mostly leafless stems. Individual flower heads are 2.5 to 3.5 centimetres wide with 10 to 20 bright blue ray florets. Each ray floret ends in five teeth and is finely hairy on the outside. Flower heads have no disc florets; the base of each ray floret has a tubular blue stamen and a single style with a bifid, curled stigma. Flowers close during sunny after-noons. Seed tips have a tuft of hairs.

Top: Each flower has several blue ray but no disc florets; each floret ends in five teeth. Bottom: Leaves are deeply lobed and sharply toothed, appearing like those of dandelion.

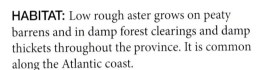 **Native Species**

Aster family / Asteraceae

Low rough aster

Eurybia radula (formerly *Aster radula*)

Rough aster, rough wood aster

HABITAT: Low rough aster grows on peaty barrens and in damp forest clearings and damp thickets throughout the province. It is common along the Atlantic coast.

CHARACTERISTICS: Low rough aster is a slender plant with non-branching stems arising from cord-like subterranean rhizomes. Alternate sessile leaves, up to 8 centimetres long, are lance-olate to elliptical with sharp teeth. Leaf surfaces are covered in short stiff hairs; leaves appear veined.

Flowers are produced in a loose corymb but, in exposed locations, may be solitary. Each 2.5- to 3.5-centimetre-wide flower head is composed of 20 to 30 pale violet-blue ray florets and a similar number of yellow disc florets that turn red with age. Seeds have a tuft of tawny hairs at their tips.

Large-leaved aster, *E. macrophylla*, is found in dry open woods and clearings in south-central Nova Scotia. Growing to 100 centimetres in height and blooming from July to September, this plant forms leafy clumps. The lowermost leaves are heart-shaped, long petioled, and up to 20 centi-metres long; upper leaves are smaller and become sessile. All leaves are alternate, sharp-toothed, and rough textured. Flowers are produced in a loose corymb. Individual flower heads are 2 to 2.5 centimetres wide with nine to 16 narrow pale violet-blue ray florets. Flower stems have glandu-lar-tipped hairs.

VITAL STATISTICS
Maximum height: 90 centimetres
Flowering season: July to September

Top: Each flower has about 20 lavender-blue ray florets surrounding a central cluster of yellow disc florets. Middle: Stems of low rough aster are generally unbranched and the narrow sessile leaves have sharp teeth. Bottom: Large-leaved aster's heart-shaped lower leaves have petioles; its flowers are in open corymbs.

Aster family / Asteraceae

Tall blue lettuce

Lactuca biennis

Wild blue lettuce, biennial lettuce, blue wood lettuce

VITAL STATISTICS

Maximum height: 200 centimetres
Flowering season: July to September

HABITAT: Tall blue lettuce, which is found in disturbed areas such as roadsides and waste places, is scattered throughout the province.

CHARACTERISTICS: Tall blue lettuce is a slender but coarse biennial plant. In the first season, plants produce a flat rosette of nearly elliptical leaves, which are up to 30 centimetres in length. These leaves are pinnatifid, deeply divided into several wide coarsely toothed lobes with pointed tips and have distinct winged petioles. Alternate stem leaves are smaller than those in the rosette, less divided, and sessile. Stems and leaf undersides are slightly hairy. The stem is non-branching except near its top. All parts of the plant exude a milky sap when cut.

Flowers are densely packed into multiple branched panicles. Individual flower heads are 0.6 to 0.7 centimetres wide with 15 to 30 pale blue ray florets. The base of each floret has a tubular blue stamen and a single style with a curled bifid stigma. The phyllaries often have purple-tinted tips. Flower heads develop into small dandelion-like seed heads. Each seed has a tuft of white hairs at its top.

Top: Each flower has 15 or more blue ray florets but no disc florets; phyllaries often have purple-tinted tips. Bottom: Stem leaves are sessile and pinnatifid with deeply cut lobes.

Aster family / Asteraceae

Bog aster

Oclemena nemoralis (formerly *Aster nemoralis*)

Leafy bog aster

Native Species

HABITAT: Bog aster grows in wetland habitats and on peaty barrens throughout Nova Scotia, especially along the Atlantic coast.

CHARACTERISTICS: A slender plant with non-branching thin stems, bog aster forms loose colonies via subterranean rhizomes. Its numerous closely spaced alternate leaves are linear to narrow lanceolate. Up to 6 centimetres long, leaves are sessile with revolute slightly toothed edges, and a rugose appearance. Leaves and stems are slightly hairy.

Flower heads are solitary or in loose corymbs with fewer than 10 flower heads. Each 2.5- to 4-centimetre-diameter flower head has 15 to 25 lilac-purple ray florets and a similar number of yellow disc florets that turn red with age. Each flower stem has three to eight narrow bracts. Seed tips have tufts of golden hairs.

Whorled wood aster, *O. acuminata*, a woodland species found province-wide, grows to a height of 50 centimetres and blooms in August and September. Its upper leaves are larger than the lower; alternate upper leaves are closely spaced and appear to be whorled. Leaves are lance-shaped to elliptical and sessile with sharply toothed edges, and they have scattered hairs along the lower midvein. Plants produce a globular corymb of flower heads. Each 2.5- to 4-centimetre-diameter flower head has 10 to 18 narrow partially twisted white or pale lilac ray florets. Disc florets change from yellow to red as they age.

VITAL STATISTICS

Maximum height: 70 centimetres

Flowering season: August to September

Top: Bog aster flowers may be solitary. Middle: Bog aster has numerous closely spaced linear leaves. Bottom: Whorled wood aster produces its elliptical leaves in a whorl-like cluster.

Aster family / Asteraceae

Heart-leaved aster

Native Species

Symphyotrichum cordifolium (formerly *Aster cordifolius*)
Common blue wood aster

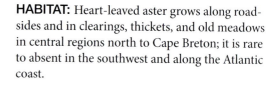

VITAL STATISTICS

Maximum height: 90 centimetres
Flowering season: August to October

HABITAT: Heart-leaved aster grows along road-sides and in clearings, thickets, and old meadows in central regions north to Cape Breton; it is rare to absent in the southwest and along the Atlantic coast.

CHARACTERISTICS: Heart-leaved aster is a clump-forming plant. Stems are non-branching, except near the flowers, and often tinted red. The stem is usually smooth; rarely it may have a few fine hairs. The basal and lower alternate stem leaves may reach 12 centimetres in length; they are heart-shaped and sharply toothed with scattered hairs and relatively long petioles.

Flowers are produced in a many-flowered, dense panicle. Individual flower heads are 1.5 to 2 centimetres wide with 10 to 16 pale violet-blue ray florets and a similar number of creamy yellow disc florets that become red with age. Each flower head stem has a few small narrow bracts. Seeds have a tuft of white to pink-tinted hairs at their ends.

Lindley's aster, *S. ciliolatum*, is found in habitats similar to those of heart-leaved aster; it is distinguished by its winged petioles and hairy leaf edges. Although lower and basal leaves are heart-shaped, the upper leaves are lanceolate. Lindley's aster produces 2.5- to 3.5-centimetre-wide flowers, which are often on narrower panicles than those of heart-leaved aster. Lindley's aster is uncommon and scattered in central and north Nova Scotia.

Top: Leaves are heart-shaped with fine teeth and relatively long petioles; flowers are in dense panicles. Bottom: Lindley's aster flowers are often in more narrow panicles than those of heart-leaved aster.

Aster family / Asteraceae

New York aster

Symphyotrichum novi-belgii (formerly *Aster novi-belgii*)

Michaelmas daisy

HABITAT: New York aster is common along coastal areas, such as shorelines, headlands, and salt marshes. It is also found along roadsides and in old meadows and thickets.

CHARACTERISTICS: New York aster is a clumping plant that may be slender in sheltered sites or dense in exposed habitats. Stout stems are usually hairless and often tinted red or purple. Basal leaves have winged petioles; alternate stem leaves are sessile and partly clasp the stem. Leaves, which are up to 20 centimetres long, are narrow lanceolate to elliptical, generally hairless, with smooth or slightly toothed edges. Basal leaves have generally withered by the time flowering commences. In sheltered sites, plants reach 100 centimetres in height, but in their more usual exposed habitats near the coast, plants are less than 30 centimetres tall.

Flowers are produced in open or dense panicles at the ends of upper branching stems. Individual flower heads, which are 2.5 to 4 centimetres in diameter, have 15 to 35 violet-blue ray florets and about twice as many yellow disc florets that become reddish-brown with age. Seeds have a tuft of yellow-brown hairs attached to their tops. This species is perhaps the most common blue aster in Nova Scotia.

Top: Each flower has many narrow violet-blue ray florets that surround a central cluster of disc florets; disc florets redden as they age. Middle: The narrow leaves are hairless and plant stems often tinted red or purple. Bottom: Flowers are in a loose panicle.

Wetlands

Barrens

Coastal

Disturbed

367

Aster family / Asteraceae

Purple-stemmed aster

Symphyotrichum puniceum (formerly *Aster puniceus*)
Red-stemmed aster, swamp aster, rough aster

VITAL STATISTICS

Maximum height: 200 centimetres
Flowering season: Late July to September

HABITAT: Purple-stemmed aster is found along streamsides, roadside ditches, and swamps throughout Nova Scotia.

CHARACTERISTICS: Purple-stemmed aster is a coarse tall clumping plant. It is the tallest of the blue-violet asters in the province. Stems are stout, distinctly purple or red-purple, and variably hairy. Basal and alternate stem leaves are lanceolate, stiff-haired, and up to 20 centimetres long. Lower, larger leaves have widely spaced teeth along their edges; upper, smaller leaves may be smooth-edged. All stem leaves clasp the stem. Basal leaves, which have petioles, shrivel by the time flowering commences.

Flowers are produced in open panicles at the ends of wide-spreading branches. Individual flower heads are 2.5 to 3.5 centimetres in diameter with 20 to 50 violet-blue ray florets and a similar number of yellow disc florets that age to red-purple. Seeds have a tuft of white hairs at their ends.

New England aster, *S. novae-angliae*, naturalized in the Halifax, Antigonish, and Sydney areas, is as tall as or taller than purple-stemmed aster, but it prefers drier sites. Crowded lanceolate leaves are smooth-edged and hairy and clasp the stem. The main stem is also finely hairy. Flowers are produced in dense corymbs. Individual flower heads have 40 to 50 violet-purple ray florets surrounding yellow disc florets that age to red-purple. Its phyllaries curl back, a feature that distinguishes it from purple-stemmed aster, whose phyllaries are straight.

Top: The upper narrow leaves are mostly smooth-edged and clasp the stem. Middle: Flowers are in open panicles and the stems often purple-tinted. Bottom: New England aster has crowded narrow leaves that clasp the stem; its flowers are in a dense corymb.

GLOSSARY

alternate (leaves): leaves borne one at a time along the length of a stem

annual: living for only one year

anther: the tip of the stamen; anthers produce pollen

auricle: a small ear-like appendage

axil: the angle created by (and between) two leaves

axillary: located in the axil (of leaves)

beard: a cluster of long or stiff hairs

biennial: living for two years; generally flowering and fruiting in the second year

bipinnate (leaf): a pinnate leaf whose leaflets are also pinnate

biternate (leaf): a ternate (trifoliate) leaf whose leaflets are also ternate, resulting in each leaf being composed of nine leaflets

bract: a leaf (often modified) located immediately under a flower

bracteole: a small bract

branchlet: a smaller side-branch that grows out of a larger branch

bristle: a stiff hair

burr: a seed or fruit with short stiff bristles or hooks

calcareous: containing lime

calciphile: a plant that thrives on lime-rich soil

calyx: the combined sepals of a flower, which often protects the flower in the bud stage

clasping: embracing or surrounding, usually refers to a leaf base around a stem

colonial: describes plants that form colonies (groups) via underground stems (rhizomes)

compound leaf: a leaf composed of two or more leaflets

compound umbel: a flower cluster in which each stalk of the umbel produces a smaller umbel of flowers; this type of inflorescence is typical of members of the parsley family (Apiaceae)

cordate: heart-shaped

corolla: combined flower petals; often the coloured portion of a flower

corymb: a flat-topped flower cluster in which individual flower stalks grow upward from various points on the main stem to approximately the same height

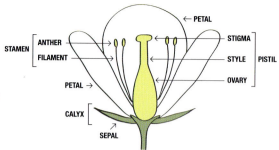

crenate: having rounded teeth along the leaf edge

cyme: a flower cluster in which the main axis and each branch end in a flower that opens before the flowers below or to the side of it

deltoid: triangular in outline

dioecious: unisexual plants in which male and female flowers are on separate plants

dimorphic (flowers): have flowers of two forms

disc floret: any of the small tubular flowers at the centre of a flower head in members of the aster family (Asteraceae)

disjunct: a plant whose population is far removed from the main population of that plant

division (of a leaf): a sub-unit of a leaf such as a leaflet or deep lobe

elliptical: in the shape of an ellipse, broadest in the middle and tapering at each end

elongate(d): long or lengthened

endemic: plant populations that are confined to a single and relatively small geographic area

ephemeral: appearing for a short period of time

escape: a non-native species that has become naturalized

exerted: protruding or projecting

farina: a powder-like substance

felted: densely covered in fine hairs

filament: the stalk of a stamen, to which the anther is attached

flower head (daisy): an aster family (Asteraceae) flower head that is composed of many separate unstalked flowers packed closely together; the outer flowers have one conspicuous large petal (ray floret) and the central disk is formed of flowers with smaller petals (disc floret)

flower head (non-daisy): a dense cluster of sessile or nearly sessile flowers

glandular: having glands that excrete a substance that makes stems or leaves sticky

glandular-tipped: having glands, at the tips of hairs, that excrete a substance that makes stems or leaves sticky

globular: rounded

hemiparasitic: a plant that obtains some nourishment from its host but is also capable of photosynthesis

herbaceous: plants with stems that die back in the winter

inflorescence: the flowering part of a plant

intervale: a tract of low-lying land along a river

lanceolate: lance-shaped

leaflet: a small leaf; one of the segments of a compound leaf

linear: long and narrow with parallel edges

lobe: a rounded division of a leaf

localized: confined to a small area

midrib: the central or main rib of a leaf, which runs from stem to tip

monoecious: species in which male and female flowers grow on the same plant

nectar spur: part of a sepal or petal that develops into an elongated hollow spike extending behind the flower and contains nectar

net veins: distinct veins that form a net-like pattern

nodding: an upright stem or structure that droops at the tip

non-stoloniferous: not bearing stolons

nutlet: a small nut

oblanceolate: lance-shaped with the widest part of the leaf at the tip (farthest from the stem)

oblong: two to three times longer than broad, with parallel sides

obovate: inverted egg-shaped: narrowest at the base, widest at the terminal end

old meadows: areas once cultivated but left fallow for many years

opposite (leaves): leaves that are borne two at a time (paired) along the length of a stem

orbicular: circular

ornamental: species that are planted to beautify gardens

ovate: egg-shaped

palmate: a lobed leaf with a hand-like silhouette

panicle: a branched raceme, with each branch having a smaller raceme of flowers; the terminal bud of each branch continues to grow, producing more side shoots and more flowers, resulting in a cluster of flowers

pedicle: the stem of an individual flower

pendant: hanging downward from a stem

petal: a division of the corolla

petaloid: coloured and resembling a petal

petiole: the stalk of a leaf

← PHYLLARIES

phyllaries: modified bracts located at the base of a flower head of flowers of the aster family

pinnate (leaf): a leaf composed of many smaller leaflets arranged on either side of the main axis

pinnatifid (leaf): a dissected leaf that is pinnately deeply cleft; appears pinnately compound but does not have separate leaflets.

pistil: the entire female portion of a flower, composed of an ovary (where seeds are produced), a style (stalk), and a stigma (pollen-receptive tip)

plumose: feather-like

prickle: a sharp slender outgrowth from bark that is thinner than a thorn and not anchored as deeply in the branch

prostrate: growing flat along the ground

pubescent: covered in short downy hairs (not as dense as "felted")

raceme: a flower spike; the flowers have stalks of equal lengths, and the tip of the stem continues to grow and produce more flowers

ray floret: any of the small strap-shaped ("petalled") flowers in the flower head of certain flowers of the aster family (Asteraceae)

recurved: curving downward

reflexed: curled back toward the stem

reniform: kidney-shaped

reticulated: covered with veins that interconnect in a net-like pattern

revolute: rolled under (usually referring to the leaf edge)

rhizome: a prostrate or underground stem

rhombic: square-shaped

rosette (leaves): a cluster of leaves at the base of a plant

rugose: wrinkled

seed head: a dense cluster of seeds

sepal: a division of the calyx; a small leaf under the flower

sessile: lacking flower stems or leaf stems

SESSILE
(STALKLESS)

silique: a two-chambered seed capsule which is longer than wide; it is confined to the mustard family (Brassicaceae)

spadix: a flowering spike with a fleshy stem, indicative of the arum family

spathe: a large bract enclosing an inflorescence

spatulate: spatula or narrow spoon-shaped

spike: a group of sessile flowers arising from the main stem

stamen: the male portion of a flower, composed of a filament (stalk) and an anther

standard: the uppermost petal on flowers of the pea family (Fabaceae)

stigma: the pollen-receptive tip of the pistil (the female part of a flower)

stipule: a small leaf-like appendage at the base of a regular leaf

stolon: a runner or low-lying branch that tends to root itself

stoloniferous: bearing stolons

style: the narrow elongate portion of the pistil (the female part of a flower)

STIPULE

sub-opposite: almost opposite

substrate: a plant's growing medium

suckering: producing vegetative shoots from underground roots and rhizomes

swale: a low, moist tract of land

taproot: a plant's main or primary root

tendril: a threadlike structure used by climbing plants to wrap around or hook a support

tepal: the name for a "petal" on flowers (such as tulips) in which petals (corolla) and sepals (calyx) look alike

TENDRIL

terminal: located at the end

ternate: composed of three parts, such as a leaf with three leaflets

thorn: a sharp woody outgrowth from a stem that is anchored more deeply—and is often thicker—than a prickle

trifoliate: a leaf composed of three leaflets

triternate (leaf): a biternate leaf whose divisions are ternate, resulting in a triangular-shaped leaf with approximately 27 leaflets

tuber: a swollen root-like stem located below the ground

twining: twisting

umbel: a flower cluster in which all flower stalks are of the same length, so that the flower head is rounded like an umbrella

umbellet: a smaller, secondary umbel

undulated: with a wavy edge

villous: having long silky hairs

wide-spreading: held horizontal, like outspread arms

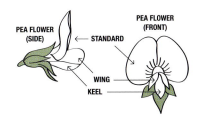

PEA FLOWER (SIDE)   PEA FLOWER (FRONT)
← STANDARD
WING
KEEL

wing: one of the two side petals on flowers of the pea family (Fabaceae)

whorled (leaves): having three or more leaves originating from the same point on a stem

NOVA SCOTIA WILDFLOWERS BY FAMILY

This section lists the Nova Scotia wildflowers (native and introduced) described in this field guide, grouped by family.

Acoraceae
Acorus americanus

Sweetflag family
American sweetflag

Alismataceae
Alisma triviale
Sagittaria cuneata
Sagittaria graminea
Sagittaria latifolia

Water-plantain family
northern water-plantain
northern arrowhead
grass-leaved arrowhead
broad-leaved arrowhead

Alliaceae
Allium schoenoprassum
Allium tricoccum

Onion family
Wild chives
Wild leek

Amaranthaceae
Amaranthus albus
Amaranthus albus
Amaranthus retroflexus
Atriplex glabriuscula
Atriplex patula
Chenopodium album
Chenopodium glaucum
Salicornia depressa
Salicornia maritima
Salsola kali
Suaeda maritima

Amaranth family
white amaranth
tumbleweed
redroot amaranth
glabrous saltbush
common orach
common lamb's-quarters
oak-leaved goosefoot
Virginia glasswort
sea glasswort
saltwort
sea-blite

Apiaceae
Aegopodium podagraria
Angelica atropurpurea
Angelica sylvestris
Anthriscus sylvestris
Carum carvi
Cicuta bulbifera

Parsley family
goutweed
purple-stemmed angelica
woodland angelica
wild chervil
wild caraway
bulbous water-hemlock

Cicuta maculata	spotted water-hemlock
Conioselinum chinense	hemlock-parsley
Daucus carota	Queen Anne's lace
Heracleum mantegazzianum	giant hogweed
Heracleum maximum	American cow parsnip
Heracleum sphondylium	common hogweed
Hydrocotyle americana	American water pennywort
Hydrocotyle umbellata	water pennywort
Ligusticum scoticum	Scotch lovage
Osmorhiza berteroi	mountain sweet cicely
Osmorhiza claytonii	hairy sweet cicely
Osmorhiza longistylis	smooth sweet cicely
Pastinaca sativa	wild parsnip
Pimpinella saxifraga	burnet saxifrage
Sanicula marilandica	black snakeroot
Sanicula odorata	yellow snakeroot
Sium suave	common water-parsnip
Zizia aurea	golden alexanders

Apocynaceae — Dogbane family
Apocynum androsaemifolium	spreading dogbane
Apocynum cannabinum	Indian hemp
Vinca minor	lesser periwinkle

Araceae — Arum family
Arisaema triphyllum	Jack-in-the-pulpit
Calla palustris	wild calla
Symplocarpus foetidus	eastern skunk cabbage

Araliaceae — Ginseng family
Aralia hispida	bristly sarsaparilla
Aralia nudicaulis	wild sarsaparilla
Aralia racemosa	American spikenard
Panax trifolius	dwarf ginseng

Asclepiaceae — Milkweed family
Asclepias incarnata	swamp milkweed
Asclepias syriaca	common milkweed

Asparagaceae — Asparagus family
Maianthemum canadense	wild lily-of-the-valley
Maianthemum racemosum	large false Solomon's-seal
Maianthemum stellatum	star-flowered false Solomon's-seal
Maianthemum trifolium	three-leaved false Solomon's-seal
Medeola virginiana	Indian cucumber-root
Polygonatum pubescens	hairy Solomon's-seal

Asteraceae	Aster family
Achillea millefolium	common yarrow
Achillea millefolium var. *lanulosa*	woolly yarrow
Achillea ptarmica	sneezeweed
Ageratina altissima	white snakeroot
Ambrosia artemisiifolia	common ragweed
Ambrosia trifida	giant ragweed
Anaphalis margaritacea	pearly everlasting
Antennaria howellii subsp. *neodioica*	northern pussytoes
Antennaria parlinii	Parlin's pussytoes
Anthemis cotula	stinking chamomile
Arctium minus	common burdock
Arnica lonchophylla	long-leaved arnica
Artemisia biennis	biennial wormwood
Artemisia stelleriana	beach wormwood
Artemisia vulgaris	common wormwood
Aster puniceum	purple-stemmed aster
Bidens beckii	water beggarticks
Bidens cernua	nodding beggarticks
Bidens connata	purple-stemmed beggarticks
Bidens frondosa	devil's beggarticks
Bidens vulgata	tall beggarticks
Centaurea nigra	black knapweed
Cichorium intybus	wild chicory
Cirsium arvense	Canada thistle
Cirsium muticum	swamp thistle
Cirsium palustre	marsh thistle
Cirsium vulgare	bull thistle
Conyza canadensis	horseweed
Coreopsis rosea	pink tickseed
Doellingeria umbellata	flat-top white aster
Erechtites hieraciifolia	eastern burnweed
Erigeron annuus	annual fleabane
Erigeron hyssopifolius	hyssop-leaved fleabane
Erigeron philadelphicus	Philadelphia fleabane
Erigeron strigosus	rough fleabane
Eupatorium dubium	coastal plain Joe-Pye weed
Eupatorium perfoliatum	common boneset
Eurybia macrophylla	large-leaved aster
Eurybia radula	low rough aster
Euthamia caroliniana	slender-leaved goldenrod
Euthamia graminifolia	grass-leaved goldenrod
Eutrochium maculatum	spotted Joe-Pye weed
Galinsoga quadriradiata	hairy galinsoga
Gnaphalium uliginosum	low cudweed

Helianthus tuberosus	Jerusalem artichoke
Hieracium murorum	wall hawkweed
Hieracium scabrum	rough hawkweed
Hieracium umbellatum	narrow-leaved hawkweed
Hieracium vulgatum	common hawkweed
Hypochaeris radicata	hairy cat's-ear
Inula helenium	elecampane
Jacobaea vulgaris	tansy ragwort
Lactuca biennis	tall blue lettuce
Lactuca canadensis	Canada lettuce
Lactuca hirsuta	hairy lettuce
Lactuca serriola	prickly lettuce
Lapsana communis	common nipplewort
Leontodon autumnalis	fall dandelion
Leucanthemum vulgare	oxeye daisy
Matricaria discoidea	pineappleweed
Oclemena acuminata	whorled wood aster
Oclemena nemoralis	bog aster
Omalotheca sylvatica	woodland cudweed
Packera aurea	golden groundsel
Packera paupercula	balsam groundsel
Packera schweinitziana	swamp ragwort
Petasites frigidus	Arctic sweet coltsfoot
Pilosella aurantiaca	orange hawkweed
Pilosella caespitosa	meadow hawkweed
Pilosella flagellaris	whiplash hawkweed
Pilosella floribunda	pale hawkweed
Pilosella officinarum	mouse-ear hawkweed
Pilosella piloselloides	tall hawkweed
Prenanthes altissima	tall rattlesnakeroot
Prenanthes racemosa	purple rattlesnakeroot
Prenanthes trifoliolata	three-leaved rattlesnakeroot
Pseudognaphalium obtusifolium	rabbit tobacco
Rudbeckia hirta	black-eyed Susan
Rudbeckia laciniata	cut-leaved coneflower
Senecio pseudoarnica	seaside ragwort
Senecio sylvaticus	woodland ragwort
Senecio viscosus	sticky ragwort
Senecio vulgaris	common ragwort
Solidago bicolor	white goldenrod
Solidago canadensis	Canada goldenrod
Solidago flexicaulis	zigzag goldenrod
Solidago gigantea	giant goldenrod
Solidago hispida	hairy goldenrod
Solidago juncea	early goldenrod
Solidago latissimifolia	Elliot's goldenrod

Solidago macrophylla	large-leaved goldenrod
Solidago multiradiata	multi-rayed goldenrod
Solidago nemoralis	grey-stemmed goldenrod
Solidago puberula	downy goldenrod
Solidago rugosa	rough-stemmed goldenrod
Solidago sempervirens	seaside goldenrod
Solidago uliginosa	bog goldenrod
Sonchus arvensis	field sow-thistle
Sonchus asper	prickly sow-thistle
Sonchus oleraceus	common sow-thistle
Symphyotrichum boreale	rush aster
Symphyotrichum ciliolatum	Lindley's aster
Symphyotrichum cordifolium	heart-leaved aster
Symphyotrichum lanceolatum	white panicled aster
Symphyotrichum lateriflorum	calico aster
Symphyotrichum novae-angliae	New England aster
Symphyotrichum novi-belgii	New York aster
Symphyotrichum puniceum	purple-stemmed aster
Symphyotrichum tradescanti	Tradescant's aster
Tanacetum parthenium	feverfew
Tanacetum vulgare	common tansy
Taraxacum officinale	common dandelion
Tragopogon pratensis	meadow goatsbeard
Tripleurospermum inodorum	scentless chamomile
Tussilago farfara	coltsfoot
Xanthium strumarium	rough cockleburr

Balsamaceae	Balsam family
Impatiens capensis	spotted jewelweed
Impatiens glandulifera	purple jewelweed
Impatiens pallida	pale jewelweed

Berberidaceae	Barberry family
Caulophyllum thalictroides	blue cohosh

Boraginaceae	Borage family
Echium vulgare	common viper's bugloss
Lappula squarrosa	stickseed
Mertensia maritima	oysterleaf
Myosotis arvensis	rough forget-me-not
Myosotis laxa	small forget-me-not
Myosotis scorpioides	European forget-me-not
Myosotis sylvatica	woodland forget-me-not
Symphytum asperum	prickly comfrey
Symphytum officinale	common comfrey

Brassicaceae	Mustard family
Barbarea vulgaris	bitter wintercress
Boechera stricta	Drummond's rockcress
Brassica juncea	Chinese mustard
Brassica nigra	black mustard
Brassica rapa	field mustard
Cakile edentula	American sea rocket
Capsella bursa-pastoris	shepherd's-purse
Cardamine dentata	toothed bittercress
Cardamine diphylla	two-leaved toothwort
Cardamine pensylvanica	Pennsylvania bittercress
Cardamine pratensis	meadow bittercress
Descurainia sophia	flixweed
Draba arabisans	rock draba
Draba glabella	smooth draba
Draba norvegica	Norway draba
Erucastrum gallicum	common dog mustard
Erysimum cheiranthoides	wormseed mustard
Hesperis matronalis	dame's rocket
Lepidium campestre	field peppergrass
Lepidium densiflorun	common peppergrass
Nasturtium officinale	watercress
Raphanus raphanastrum	wild radish
Rorippa palustris	marsh yellowcress
Rorippa sylvestris	creeping yellowcress
Sisymbrium altissimum	tall tumble mustard
Sisymbrium officinale	common tumble mustard
Thlaspi arvense	field penny-cress
Cabombaceae	Cabomba family
Brasenia schreberi	watershield
Callitrichaceae	Water-starwort family
Callitriche heterophylla	large water-starwort
Callitriche palustris	spring water-starwort
Campanulaceae	Bellflower family
Campanula aparinoides	marsh bellflower
Campanula rapunculoides	creeping bellflower
Campanula rotundifolia	common harebell
Lobelia dortmanna	water lobelia
Lobelia inflata	Indian tobacco
Lobelia kalmia	Kalm's lobelia
Lobelia spicata	pale spike lobelia

Cannabaceae	Hemp family
Humulus var. *lupuloides*	American hops
Humulus lupulus	hops
Caprifoliaceae	Honeysuckle family
Linnaea borealis	twinflower
Caryophyllaceae	Pink family
Cerastium arvense	field chickweed
Cerastium fontanum subsp. *vulgare*	common mouse-ear chickweed
Cerastium semidecandrum	five-stamen mouse-ear chickweed
Cerastium tomentosum	snow-in-summer
Dianthus armeria	Deptford pink
Honckenya peploides	seabeach sandwort
Minuartia groenlandica	Greenland stitchwort
Moehringia lateriflora	grove sandwort
Sagina nodosa	knotty pearlwort
Sagina procumbens	procumbent pearlwort
Saponaria officinalis	bouncing-bet
Silene dioica	red campion
Silene flos-cuculi	ragged robin
Silene latifolia	white campion
Silene noctiflora	night-flowering catchfly
Silene vulgaris	bladder campion
Spergula arvensis	corn spurrey
Spergularia canadensis	Canada sand-spurrey
Spergularia rubra	red sand-spurrey
Spergularia salina	saltmarsh sand-spurrey
Stellaria graminea	grass-leaved starwort
Stellaria media	common chickweed
Celastraceae	Bittersweet family
Parnassia parviflora	small-flowered grass-of-Parnassus
Cistaceae	Rockrose family
Lechea intermedia	large-pod pinwheel
Colchicaceae	Autumn-crocus family
Uvularia sessilifolia	sessile-leaved bellwort
Convallariaceae	Lily-of-the-valley family
Convallaria majalis	European lily-of-the-valley
Convolvulaceae	Morning-glory family
Calystegia sepium	hedge bindweed
Convolvulus arvensis	field bindweed

Cuscuta cephalanthi	buttonbush dodder
Cuscuta gronovii	swamp dodder
Cornaceae	Dogwood family
Cornus canadensis	bunchberry
Cornus suecica	Swedish bunchberry
Crassulaceae	Orpine family
Hylotelephium telephium	garden stonecrop
Rhodiola rosea	roseroot
Cucurbitaceae	Gourd family
Echinocystis lobata	wild cucumber
Droseraceae	Sundew family
Drosera filiformis	thread-leaved sundew
Drosera intermedia	spoon-leaved sundew
Drosera rotundifolia	round-leaved sundew
Ericaceae	Heath family
Chimaphila umbellata	common pipsissewa
Epigaea repens	trailing arbutus
Gaultheria hispidula	creeping snowberry
Hypopitys monotropa	pinesap
Moneses uniflora	one-flowered wintergreen
Monotropa uniflora	Indian pipe
Orthilia secunda	one-sided wintergreen
Pyrola americana	round-leaved pyrola
Pyrola asarifolia	pink pyrola
Pyrola chlorantha	green-flowered pyrola
Pyrola elliptica	shinleaf
Pyrola minor	lesser pyrola
Eriocaulaceae	Pipewort family
Eriocaulon aquaticum	seven-angled pipewort
Euphorbiacae	Spurge family
Euphorbia maculata	spotted spurge
Euphorbia polygonifolia	seaside spurge
Euphorbia vermiculata	wormseed spurge
Fabaceae	Pea family
Amphicarpaea bracteata	American hog-peanut
Apios americana	American groundnut
Astragalus robbinsii	Robbin's milk-vetch
Desmodium canadense	Canada tick-trefoil

Desmodium glutinosum	large tick-trefoil
Lathyrus japonicus	beach pea
Lathyrus palustris	marsh vetchling
Lathyrus pratensis	meadow pea
Lotus corniculatus	bird's-foot trefoil
Lupinus nootkatensis	Nootka lupine
Lupinus polyphyllus	large-leaved lupine
Medicago lupulina	black medick
Medicago sativa	alfalfa
Meliolotus albus	white sweet-clover
Meliolotus altissimus	tall yellow sweet-clover
Meliolotus officinalis	white sweet-clover
Oxytropis campestris var. *johannensis*	Saint John River locoweed
Securigera varia	crown vetch
Trifolium arvense	rabbit's-foot clover
Trifolium aureum	yellow clover
Trifolium campestre	low hop clover
Trifolium dubium	small hop clover
Trifolium hybridum	alsike clover
Trifolium pratense	red clover
Trifolium repens	white clover
Vicia cracca	tufted vetch
Vicia sativa	common vetch
Vicia tetrasperma	four-seed vetch

Gentianaceae — Gentian family
Bartonia paniculata	branched bartonia
Bartonia virginica	yellow bartonia
Halenia deflexa	spurred gentian
Sabatia kennedyana	Plymouth gentian

Geraniaceae — Geranium family
Erodium cicutarium	common storksbill
Geranium bicknelii	Bicknell's geranium
Geranium pratense	meadow geranium
Geranium robertianum	herb-Robert

Hippuridaceae — Mare's-tail family
| *Hippuris vulgaris* | common mare's-tail |

Hypericaceae — St. John's-wort family
Hypericum canadense	Canada St. John's-wort
Hypericum ellipticum	pale St. John's-wort
Hypericum fraseri	Fraser's St. John's-wort
Hypericum mutilum	dwarf St. John's-wort
Hypericum perforatum	common St. John's-wort

Hypericum punctatum	spotted St. John's-wort
Hypericum virginicum	Virginia marsh St. John's-wort

Iridaceae — Iris family
  Iris hookeri — beach-head iris
  Iris prismatica — slender blue flag
  Iris pseudacorus — yellow iris
  Iris versicolor — blue flag
  Sisyrinchium atlanticum — eastern blue-eyed grass
  Sisyrinchium montanum — strict blue-eyed grass

Juncaginaceae — Arrowgrass family
  Triglochin maritime — seaside arrowgrass
  Triglochin palustris — marsh arrowgrass

Lamiaceae — Mint family
  Clinopodium vulgare — wild basil
  Galeopsis bifida — bifid hemp-nettle
  Galeopsis tetrahit — common hemp-nettle
  Glechoma hederacea — ground ivy
  Hedeoma pulegioides — American pennyroyal
  Lamium amplexicaule — common dead-nettle
  Lamium purpureum — purple dead-nettle
  Lycopus americanus — American water-horehound
  Lycopus uniflorus — northern water-horehound
  Mentha arvensis — field mint
  Mentha spicata — spearmint
  Mentha X gentilis — red mint
  Mentha X piperita — peppermint
  Prunella vulgaris — common self-heal
  Scutellaria galericulata — marsh skullcap
  Scutellaria lateriflora — mad-dog skullcap
  Stachys palustris — marsh hedge-nettle
  Teucrium canadense — Canada germander
  Thymus pulegioides — lemon thyme

Lentibulariaceae — Bladderwort family
  Pinguicula vulgaris — common butterwort

Liliaceae — Lily family
  Clintonia borealis — corn lily
  Erythronium americanum — yellow trout lily
  Lilium canadense — Canada lily
  Streptopus amplexifolius — clasping-leaved twisted-stalk
  Streptopus lanceolatus — eastern rose twisted-stalk

Linaceae	Flax family
Linum catharticum	fairy flax
Linderniaceae	False pimpernel family
Lindernia dubia	yellow-seed false pimpernel
Lythraceae	Lythrum family
Decodon verticillatus	swamp loosestrife
Lythrum salicaria	purple loosestrife
Malvaceae	Mallow family
Malva alcea	vervain mallow
Malva moschata	musk mallow
Malva neglecta	dwarf mallow
Malva pusilla	round-leaved mallow
Melanthiaceae	Bunchflower family
Trillium cernuum	nodding trillium
Trillium erectum	red trillium
Trillium grandiflorum	white trillium
Trillium undulatum	painted trillium
Melastomataceae	Melanstome family
Rhexia virginica	Virginia meadow beauty
Menyanthaceae	Bog buckbean family
Menyanthes trifoliata	bog buckbean
Nymphoides cordata	little floatingheart
Molluginaceae	Carpetweed family
Mollugo verticillata	green carpetweed
Myrsinaceae	Myrsine family
Lysimachia ciliata	fringed yellow loosestrife
Lysimachia maritima	sea milkwort
Lysimachia terrestris	swamp yellow loosestrife
Lysimachia thyrsiflora	tufted yellow loosestrife
Trientalis borealis	northern starflower
Nymphaceae	Waterlily family
Nuphar microphylla	small yellow pond-lily
Nuphar odorata	white water-lily
Nuphar variegata	yellow pond-lily
Nymphaea odorata	fragrant water-lily

384

Onagraceae	Evening primrose family
Chamerion angustifolium	fireweed
Circaea alpina	small enchanter's-nightshade
Circaea canadensis	broad-leaved enchanter's-nightshade
Epilobium ciliatum	northern willowherb
Epilobium leptophyllum	bog willowherb
Epilobium palustre	marsh willowherb
Ludwigia palustris	marsh seedbox
Oenothera biennis	common evening primrose
Oenothera parviflora	small-flowered evening primrose
Oenothera perennis	perennial evening primrose

Orchidaceae	Orchid family
Arethusa bulbosa	dragon's-mouth
Calopogon tuberosus	grass pink
Coeloglossum viride	frog orchid
Corallorhiza maculata	spotted coralroot
Corallorhiza trifida	early coralroot
Cypripedium acaule	pink lady's-slipper
Cypripedium arietinum	ram's-head lady's-slipper
Cypripedium parviflorum	yellow lady's-slipper
Cypripedium reginae	showy lady's-slipper
Epipactis helleborine	broad-leaved helleborine
Goodyera oblongifolia	Menzie's rattlesnake-plantain
Goodyera pubescens	downy rattlesnake-plantain
Goodyera repens	dwarf rattlesnake-plantain
Goodyera tesselata	checkered rattlesnake-plantain
Liparis loeselii	Loesel's twayblade
Listera australis	southern twayblade
Listera convallarioides	broad-leaved twayblade
Listera cordata	heart-leaved twayblade
Malaxis monophyllos var. *brachypoda*	white adder's-mouth orchid
Malaxis unifolia	green adder's-mouth orchid
Platanthera aquilonis	tall northern green orchid
Platanthera blephariglottis	white fringed orchid
Platanthera clavellata	club-spur orchid
Platanthera dilatata	tall white bog orchid
Platanthera flava	tubercled orchid
Platanthera grandiflora	large purple-fringed orchid
Platanthera hookeri	Hooker's orchid
Platanthera huronensis	Lake Huron orchid
Platanthera huronensis	fragrant green orchid
Platanthera lacera	ragged-fringed orchid
Platanthera macrophylla	large round-leaved orchid
Platanthera obtusata	blunt-leaved orchid
Platanthera orbiculata	lesser round-leaved orchid

Platanthera psycodes	small purple-fringed orchid
Pogonia ophioglossoides	rose pogonia
Spiranthes casei	Case's ladies'-tresses
Spiranthes cernua	nodding ladies'-tresses
Spiranthes lacera	northern slender ladies'-tresses
Spiranthes lucida	shining ladies'-tresses
Spiranthes ochroleuca	yellow ladies'-tresses
Spiranthes romanzoffiana	hooded ladies'-tresses

Orobanchaceae — Broomrape family
    Conopholis americana — American cankerroot
    Epifagus virginiana — beechdrops
    Euphrasia nemorosa — common eyebright
    Euphrasia randii — Rand's eyebright
    Melampyrum lineare — American cow-wheat
    Odontites vulgaris — red bartsia
    Orobanche uniflora — one-flowered broomrape
    Pedicularis palustris — marsh lousewort
    Rhinanthus minor — little yellow rattle

Oxalidaceae — Shamrock family
    Oxalis corniculata — creeping wood-sorrel
    Oxalis montana — common wood-sorrel
    Oxalis stricta — European wood-sorrel

Papaveraceae — Poppy family
    Capnoides sempervirens — pink corydalis
    Chelidonium majus — greater celandine
    Dicentra cucullaria — Dutchman's breeches
    Fumaria officinalis — common fumitory
    Sanguinaria canadensis — bloodroot

Phrymaceae — Lopseed family
    Erythranthe moschata — musk monkeyflower
    Mimulus ringens — square-stemmed monkeyflower

Plantaginaceae — Plantain family
    Chaenorrhinum minus — dwarf snapdragon
    Chelone glabra — white turtlehead
    Gratiola aurea — golden hedge-hyssop
    Gratiola neglecta — clammy hedge-hyssop
    Linaria dalmatica — Dalmatian toadflax
    Linaria vulgaris — butter and eggs
    Nuttallanthus canadensis — Canada toadflax
    Plantago lanceolata — narrow-leaved plantain
    Plantago major — common plantain

Plantago maritima	seaside plantain
Verbascum thapsus	common mullein
Veronica americana	American speedwell
Veronica arvensis	corn speedwell
Veronica chamaedrys	germander speedwell
Veronica longifolia	long-leaved speedwell
Veronica officinalis	common speedwell
Veronica persica	bird's-eye speedwell
Veronica scutellata	marsh speedwell
Veronica serpyllifolia	thyme-leaved speedwell
Plumabaginaceae	Plumbago family
Limonium carolinianum	sea-lavender
Polygalaceae	Milkwort family
Polygala polygama	racemed milkwort
Polygala sanguinea	blood milkwort
Polygonaceae	Buckwheat family
Fallopia cilinodis	fringed black bindweed
Fallopia convolvulus	Eurasian black bindweed
Fallopia japonica	Japanese knotweed
Fallopia sachalinensis	giant knotweed
Fallopia scandens	climbing false buckwheat
Persicaria amphibia	water smartweed
Persicaria arifolia	halberd-leaved smartweed
Persicaria hydropiper	marshpepper
Persicaria hydropiperoides	false waterpepper
Persicaria lapthifolia	pale smartweed
Persicaria maculosa	spotted lady's-thumb
Persicaria pensylvanica	Pennsylvanian smartweed
Persicaria punctata	dotted knotweed
Persicaria sagittata	arrow-leaved smartweed
Polygonum aviculare	common knotweed
Polygonum fowleri	Fowler's knotweed
Rumex acetosa	garden sorrel
Rumex acetosella	sheep sorrel
Rumex brittanica	greater water dock
Rumex crispus	curled dock
Rumex obtusifolius	blunt-leaved dock
Rumex pallidus	seabeach dock
Rumex triangulivalvis	willow-leaved dock
Pontederiaceae	Pickerelweed family
Pontederia cordata	pickerelweed

Portulacaceae	Purslane family
Claytonia caroliniana	Carolina spring beauty
Portulaca oleracea	common purslane
Potamogetonaceae	Pondweed family
Potamogeton species	pondweed
Primulaceae	Primrose family
Primula laurentiana	Laurentian primrose
Primula mistassinica	Mistassini primrose
Ranunculaceae	Buttercup family
Actaea pachypoda	doll's-eyes
Actaea rubra	red baneberry
Anemone americana	round-lobed hepatica
Anemone canadensis	Canada anemone
Anemone multifida	cut-leaved anemone
Anemone parviflora	small-flowered anemone
Anemone quinquefolia	woodland anemone
Anemone riparia	Virginia anemone
Anemone virginiana	Virginia anemone
Aquilegia vulgaris	European columbine
Caltha palustris	marsh marigold
Coptis trifolia	goldthread
Halerpestes cymbalaria	seaside buttercup
Ranunculus abortivus	kidney-leaved buttercup
Ranunculus acris	tall buttercup
Ranunculus aquatilis	white water buttercup
Ranunculus flammula	lesser spearwort
Ranunculus gmelinii	small yellow water buttercup
Ranunculus recurvatus	hooked buttercup
Ranunculus repens	creeping buttercup
Thalictrum pubescens	tall meadow-rue
Rosaceae	Rose family
Agrimonia gryposepala	hooked agrimony
Agrimonia striata	woodland agrimony
Alchemilla filicaulis	thin-stemmed lady's mantle
Alchemilla monticola	hairy lady's mantle
Alchemilla venosa	veined lady's mantle
Alchemilla xanthochloa	intermediate lady's mantle
Comarum palustre	marsh cinquefoil
Filipendula rubra	queen-of-the-prairie
Filipendula ulmaria	queen-of-the-meadow
Fragaria vesca	woodland strawberry
Fragaria virginiana	wild strawberry

388

Geum aleppicum	yellow avens
Geum canadense	white avens
Geum laciniatum	rough avens
Geum macrophyllum	large-leaved avens
Geum peckii	eastern mountain avens
Geum rivale	water avens
Potentilla anglica	English cinquefoil
Potentilla anserina	common silverweed
Potentilla argentea	silvery cinquefoil
Potentilla intermedia	downy cinquefoil
Potentilla norvegica	rough cinquefoil
Potentilla recta	sulphur cinquefoil
Potentilla simplex	old field cinquefoil
Rubus chamaemorus	cloudberry
Rubus pubescens	dewberry
Rubus repens	dewdrop
Sanguisorba canadensis	Canada burnet
Sibbaldiopsis tridentata	three-toothed cinquefoil

Rubiaceae — Madder family
Galium asprellum	rough bedstraw
Galium mollugo	smooth bedstraw
Galium palustre	marsh bedstraw
Galium tinctorium	Dyer's bedstraw
Galium trifidum	three-petalled bedstraw
Galium triflorum	three-flowered bedstraw
Houstonia caerulea	azure bluets
Mitchella repens	partridgeberry

Santalaceae — Sandalwood family
Comandra umbellata	bastard toadflax
Geocaulon lividum	northern comandra

Sarraceniaceae — Pitcher plant family
Sarracenia purpurea	northern pitcher plant

Saxifragaceae — Saxifrage family
Chrysosplenium americanum	American golden saxifrage
Mitella nuda	naked mitrewort
Saxifraga aizoides	yellow mountain saxifrage
Saxifraga paniculata	white mountain saxifrage
Tiarella cordifolia	heart-leaved foamflower

Solancaeae — Nightshade family
Solanum nigrum	European black nightshade
Solanum physalifolium	ground-cherry nightshade

Solanum ptycanthum   eastern black nightshade

Urticaceae   Nettle family
    Laportea canadensis   Canada wood nettle
    Urtica dioica   stinging nettle

Utriculariaceae   Bladderwort family
    Utricularia cornuta   horned bladderwort
    Utricularia minor   lesser bladderwort

Valerianaceae   Valerian family
    Valeriana officinalis   common valerian

Verbeniaceae   Verbena family
    Verbena hastata   blue vervain

Violaceae   Violet family
    Viola adunca   early blue violet
    Viola arvensis   European field pansy
    Viola blanda   sweet white violet
    Viola cucullata   marsh blue violet
    Viola labradorica   Labrador violet
    Viola lanceolata   lance-leaved violet
    Viola macloskeyi   small white violet
    Viola nephrophylla   northern bog violet
    Viola pubescens   downy yellow violet
    Viola renifolia   kidney-leaved violet
    Viola sagittata   arrow-leaved violet
    Viola selkirkii   great spurred violet
    Viola sororia   woolly blue-violet
    Viola tricolor   Johnny-jump-up

INDEX / PLANTS BY LATIN NAME

Species listed are included in this book with a full-page description or are mentioned in the description of another species. Former (but still familiar) Latin names are indented.

INDEX / PLANTS BY COMMON NAME

Species listed are included in this book with a full-page description or are mentioned in the description of another species.

PHOTO CREDITS

Patricia Henschen: little floatingheart (1, 2)

Gene Hertzberg: round-leaved sundew (1), small round-leaved orchid (2), naked mitrewort (3), large round-leaved orchid

Charlie Hickey: Indian tobacco (2), whiplash hawkweed

Sonnia Hill: Pennsylvanian smartweed (2), racemed milkwort

Jason Hollinger: blue cohosh (1), dwarf rattlesnake-plantain, heart-leaved twayblade (2), common wood-sorrel (2)

William Hull: wild cucumber (2)

Neill Kenmuir: common hogweed

Cindy Kilpatrick: kidney-leaved violet

Olivia Kwong: hairy sweet cicely

Louis M. Landry: American spikenard, bulbous water-hemlock, swamp dodder (1), bog willowherb, tall blue lettuce (2), Canada lettuce (2), Indian tobacco, arrow-leaved smartweed (1, 2), downy goldenrod, corn spurrey (2), Canada sand-spurrey, calico aster, heart-leaved foamflower (2), Fraser's St. John's-wort (2), nodding trillium (1, 3), European field pansy, rough hawkweed (1, 2)

Matt Lavin: square-stemmed monkeyflower (2)

Uli Lorimer: swamp loosestrife (1), trailing arbutus (3), whorled wood aster, tall rattlesnakeroot, golden hedge-hyssop (1), two-leaved toothwort (2), large tick-trefoil

Alain Maire: biennial wormwood, trailing arbutus (2), pale St. John's-wort, shinleaf, zigzag goldenrod, shining ladies'-tresses

Betsy McCully: slender-leaved goldenrod

Bill McLaughlin: Plymouth gentian (1)

Susan Meades: marsh bellflower, creeping snowberry (1), large-leaved aster, Lindley's aster

Jason S. Morris: common pipsissewa (1, 2)

Walter Muma: early goldenrod

Brian O'Brien: tubercled orchid (2), yellow snakeroot

410

Douglas Alden Peterson: white panicled aster

Tom Potterfield: American hog-peanut

Homer Edward Price: white snakeroot (2, 3), spreading dogbane (1, 2), wild sarsaparilla (3), wild chicory (2), Philadelphia fleabane (2), night-flowering catchfly, painted trillium (3)

Corey Raimond: branched bartonia, pink corydalis, Pennsylvania bittercress, northern comandra (1), American water pennywort (1), heart-leaved twayblade (1), smooth sweet cicely, clammy hedge-hyssop, spearmint

Jay Ross: water beggarticks

Andree Reno Sanborn: dewdrop (1, 2), calico aster (2)

Jennifer Schlick: two-leaved toothwort, American golden saxifrage (1), Carolina spring beauty (2), kidney-leaved buttercup, broad-leaved arrowhead (1), heart-leaved foamflower (1)

Melanie Schori: hooked buttercup

Forest and Kim Starr: black mustard, woodland ragwort

Will Stuart: white goldenrod (2)

Superior National Forest: Bicknell's geranium

Robert Svvenson: prickly comfrey

Arieh Tal: large-pod pinwheel (1, 2)

Mike Turner: halberd-leaved smartweed

Giles Watson: American sweetflag (1)

Doug Waylett: early coralroot, common dog mustard, naked mitrewort (1, 2), green-flowered pyrola, lesser pyrola

Wayne Webber: tall tumble mustard

Western New Mexico University Department of Natural Sciences: Indian hemp, spotted water-hemlock, wild basil (2), flixweed (1, 2), wormseed spurge, common dead-nettle, dwarf mallow (2), field mint, peppermint, green carpetweed (1, 2), dotted knotweed, common purslane (1, 2), cut-leaved coneflower, European black nightshade (1), field penny-cress (2), blue vervain (3), American speedwell

Mary Winter: small yellow water buttercup

Kerry M. Woods: Fraser's St. John's-wort (1)

Andrey Zharkikh: seaside buttercup, dalmatian toadflax, drummond's rockcress (2), willow-leaved dock

ABOUT THE AUTHOR

Todd Boland is the author of *Trees & Shrubs of Newfoundland and Labrador, Trees & Shrubs of the Maritimes*, and *Wildflowers of Fogo Island and Change Islands*. He is the Research Horticulturalist at the Memorial University of Newfoundland Botanical Garden.

Boland has written about and lectured on various aspects of horticulture and native plants internationally. He is a founding member of the Newfoundland and Labrador Wildflower Society (1990) and an active website volunteer with the North American Rock Garden Society.

Born and raised in St. John's, Newfoundland and Labrador, Boland graduated from Memorial University of Newfoundland with an M.Sc. in Biology and a specialization in Plant Ecology. Alpine plants are his longstanding outdoor gardening passion; indoors, he maintains an ever-increasing orchid collection. Photography and bird watching occupy any non-gardening downtime.

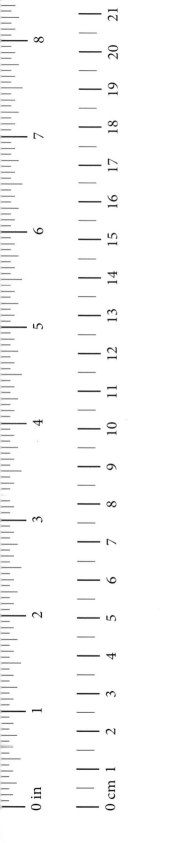